Decision by default

Decision by default

Peacetime conscription and
British defence 1919–39

Peter Dennis

Duke University Press
Durham, N.C. 1972

Printed in Great Britain by
Ebenezer Baylis and Son Limited
The Trinity Press,
Worcester, and London
and set in Monotype Plantin

Library of Congress Catalog Card No. 72–190372

I.S.B.N. 0–8223–0272–1

To my Father and Mother

Contents

Acknowledgments

Generous financial support from Duke University and the Australian-American Educational Foundation enabled me to spend several happy years at Duke, the outcome of which is this study. Professor Theodore Ropp aroused my interest in the subject and has guided my efforts. Professor William E. Scott assisted me with detailed suggestions on the diplomatic aspects. I am deeply indebted to them both, as I am to Professor Richard A. Preston for his continued interest in my work.

Sir Basil and Lady Liddell Hart welcomed me many times to States House, where I enjoyed access to Sir Basil's private papers and his unrivalled knowledge of the military history of the period. The sad news of Sir Basil's death reached me as I was working on the first draft of this study.

Lord Boothby, K.B.E., and several other public figures who have asked to remain anonymous, kindly granted me valuable interviews.

The officials and staffs of the Public Record Office, King's College (London), especially Mr Antony Grant, Cambridge University Library, and the Royal United Service Institution were unfailingly helpful. Quotations from Crown copyright records in the Public Record Office appear by permission of the Controller of H.M. Stationery Office.

My colleagues at the Royal Military College of Canada, Barry Hunt, Adrian Preston, and Anthony Wyand, have afforded me constant encouragement and stimulation.

I thank Mrs Iris Walkland for her discerning eye in reading the proofs.

Finally I wish to thank William K. Stuart, Richard W. Reifsnyder J. Frederick Wolfe, Henry E. Seaton III, and Gordon F. Grant. Their contribution is greater than they realize.

I alone am responsible for any errors of fact or interpretation.

Kingston, Ontario   P.D.

Abbreviations

The following abbreviations have been used in reference to material in the Public Record Office (London):

Air   Air Ministry Papers
Cab. Cabinet Office Papers
F.O.   Foreign Office Papers
W.O. War Office Papers

Other abbreviations used in the notes are explained at first use.

Introduction

The introduction of peacetime conscription in Britain in April 1939 has generally been ignored in studies of the pre-war period, or given short shrift as an inevitable step in the intensification of defence preparations. Yet the fact alone that this was the first time in Britain that there had been compulsory military service in peacetime would indicate that something more than a passing mention was in order. After all conscription was closely linked to the concept of a large-scale continental commitment, which, in turn, emerged in the late 1930s as a fundamental issue in the debate over British foreign and defence policy.

The reaction against the horrifying casualties of the Great War persuaded a large segment of public and political opinion in Britain that continental ventures, which were a departure, it was said, from Britain's 'traditional strategy', were counter-productive: they tied Britain to French strategy, and dangerously overstretched British resources, which had to maintain a large Navy, defend an Empire, and now support an Air Force. These arguments for a policy of 'limited liability' were reinforced by technological advances, particularly the development of air power and mechanized land forces, which indicated that speed, and hence time, would be of the essence in a future war. Since, in all probability, Britain could not rely upon having sufficient time to mobilize large land forces and disembark them on the Continent, the proponents of limited liability argued that Britain should be prepared to make her contribution on the sea and in the air, and through her industrial and financial capacity. Thus the greater part of the burden of military operations would fall to Britain's continental allies.

Peacetime conscription seemed to be firmly ruled out in 1936, when Stanley Baldwin pledged that it would not be introduced by his government. Within a year, his successor as Prime Minister, Neville Chamberlain, had persuaded the Cabinet to adopt a policy of 'limited liability' on land, and to concentrate Britain's resources on the provision of naval and air support for her continental allies, together with the maintenance of imperial security

1

and British financial stability. Labour fears that the unemployment problem might be tackled by introducing compulsory military service, and widespread distrust of conscription in peacetime as the forerunner of continental military ventures, were thereby largely allayed. The fear was not of conscription itself: that, in a wartime situation, seemed the natural way of ensuring that everyone would 'do their bit'; but peacetime conscription to build up a huge army smacked of commitment to a continental strategy. Memories of the western front in the Great War were still strong.

The Government's military advisers, however, with support from individuals in the Cabinet and the Foreign Office, argued that there were compelling military and political reasons why Britain should make a significant contribution on land. Without the assurance, definite or implied, of such a contribution, French morale would be weakened: her foreign policy would seek an accommodation with Germany and Italy, if necessary on terms unfavourable to herself, and, if war did break out, her Army would be disheartened by the belief that Britain would 'fight to the last French soldier'. The danger was, therefore, that if Britain adopted a policy of limited liability, she would risk alienating her one continental ally.

It was not until after the crisis of September 1938 that conscription became a political issue, in the sense that it was debated in Parliament and discussed critically in the press. But an even more lively topic of public interest at that time was the anti-aircraft defence of Great Britain, which the crisis had shown to be less than adequate to meet a possible aerial attack. This concern over anti-aircraft defence coincided with an increase in pressure from the French, who looked to Britain to replace the divisions that had been lost with the dismemberment of Czechoslovakia. In early 1939 conscription became, directly and indirectly, the leading issue in the debate on British defence policy. By then the French were looking desperately for a sign that Britain would enter into a firm continental commitment.

Thus Chamberlain was brought to take the very step he had pledged his government against—to introduce conscription in peacetime, as a political gesture to French and allied opinion, and to public and parliamentary opinion in Britain. The political arguments of the military ultimately prevailed over the military objections of the politicians.

1 Readjustment and realignment 1919–28

The end of the Great War in 1918 and the signing of the Treaty of Versailles in 1919 marked the collapse of the old order in Europe. Set against the hopes of the twenties, which in retrospect seem not a little extravagant, were the pressing problems of readjustment both in a reconstructed Europe and the wider world. The creation of new states in Europe, based—so their creators and supporters claimed—on the principle of self-determination and the recognition of the rights of nationalities; the establishment of a communist state in Russia, with all the threats that a revolutionary ideology seemed to pose to her European neighbours; the French demand for security against a rise of German militarism; the emergence of Japan as major power in the Far East: these were but some of the difficulties facing statesmen as they sought to secure the peace that had been so painfully won.

In Britain, as elsewhere, these problems and their solution were exacerbated by internal developments. The Labour party became increasingly strong, challenging the Conservative and Liberal control of government, and their solutions to the problems posed by necessary readjustment to the post-war situation. A class-conscious working class, channelling its political power through the Labour party and its industrial power through the Trades Union Congress, was a force in public life that no government could henceforth ignore. The Liberal party dropped into permanent decline, as the issues upon which it had risen to power and from which it had drawn its strength were either solved or displaced by ones of greater immediacy.

The first fifteen years in Britain after the end of the Great War were marked by an intense pacifism and an overriding preoccupation with solving the problems of economic dislocation and depression.[1] Both of these had particular importance for the armed forces.

---

[1] For general surveys of the inter-war period in Britain see Charles Loch Mowat, *Britain between the Wars, 1918-1940* (London: Methuen, 1955) and A.J.P. Taylor, *English History 1914–1945* (Oxford: Clarendon Press, 1965).

Four years of fighting almost naturally produced some degree of pacifist reaction, but it was the character of the military conflict that was of special significance. The seemingly senseless struggles on the western front, where indecisive offensives resulted in huge casualties, became indelibly associated with war. Haig, Passchendaele, the Somme: these names conjured up visions of irresponsible generalship, recklessly committing millions of men to battles they could never win. In his memoirs,[1] Lloyd George set the tone for much of the criticism:

It is the story . . . of the two or three individuals who would rather the million perish than that they as leaders should own—even to themselves—that they were blunderers. Hence the immortal renown and the ghastly notoriety of the Verdun, Somme and Passchendaele battlefields . . . the notoriety attained by a narrow and stubborn egotism, unsurpassed among the records of disaster wrought by human complacency.

While the military establishment never lacked supporters, both in public and private life, who were only too ready to spring loudly to its defence, it was not difficult for critics, whatever their particular axe happened to be, to bring into disrepute the senior ranks of the Army.

The Royal Air Force was too young to be drawn into this sort of argument over its role in the war; it had to face criticism on other counts. In naval circles, the Jutland controversy provoked heated dispute, but, in general, neither the senior nor the junior of the services suffered such a loss of public confidence as that borne by the Army.

The battles of the western front seemed to sum up all that was wrong with Britain's military policy. Committed to a continental strategy in secret talks with the French in 1906,[2] Britain was tied to French strategic thinking, which looked to huge offensives to break through the German lines. By 1916–17 the French had exhausted their Army, and their generals were discredited. The

---

[1] David Lloyd George, *The War Memoirs of David Lloyd George* (6 vols. London: Nicholson & Watson, 1933–6), IV, 2110–11.
[2] See George W. Monger, *The End of Isolation: British Foreign Policy 1900–1907* (London: Nelson, 1963), chap. 9. In 1905–6, during the first Moroccan crisis, British proposals for military assistance, provisional and non-committal, had grown into an obligation of honour, at least in the eyes of the French.

burden then fell to the British, and mutinies in the French forces forced Haig to undertake an offensive in the Ypres area to divert German pressure from the French front. This, at any rate, was Haig's story.[1] The British could not escape from the continental campaign to which a pre-war decision had apparently committed them. This was the first general conclusion which critics drew from the war.

Secondly, the tactics used by the generals were heavily criticized. Given that Britain was committed to a continental strategy, and putting aside the possibility of an 'indirect approach'[2] such as the Gallipoli plan, the generals were accused of failing to face up to the realities of the battlefield, of living in the military past, of fighting the battles of the last war but one.[3] Specifically they were charged with a fixation with the role of the cavalry and unprotected infantry, which was required to advance under the dubious cover of artillery fire that usually proved more of a hindrance than a help by destroying the key element of surprise and churning up the ground over which the troops had to walk, run, or stumble. When a new weapon, such as the tank, did appear, critics said that its potential was ridiculed, denigrated, and misused by a conservative, prejudiced command that was unwilling to look beyond the traditional methods, even though these had been conspicuously unsuccessful.

Thus, at the end of the war, although the Army was 'victorious', it was accused of serious, even criminal, mistakes. It had embarked on a continental strategy and, once committed, had recklessly engaged in offensives using out-of-date tactics that resulted in unprecedented blood-letting. The decision to send forces to the Continent was ultimately a political one, but it was put down—rightly, in fact—to pressure from the Army.[4] The pacifism that

[1] See Robert Blake (ed.), *The Private Papers of Douglas Haig* (London: Eyre & Spottiswoode, 1952), p. 232.
[2] Liddell Hart was not the first military writer to point to the possibilities of the 'indirect approach', but, as Jay Luvaas writes, 'he did organize and blend these lessons gleaned from past wars into an elevated doctrine adaptable to mechanized war.' *The Education of an Army: British Military Thought, 1815–1940* (Chicago: University of Chicago Press, 1964), p. 398. See also Liddell Hart, *Thoughts on War* (London: Faber, 1944), pp. 231, 238, 241.
[3] Liddell Hart wrote: 'And now, in the year of grace 1932, we began in our training to apply the experience of the Boer War, selecting the positive lessons that our unconventional foes then taught us.' *When Britain Goes to War: Adaptability and Mobility* (London: Faber, 1932), pp. 235–6.
[4] See Monger, *The End of Isolation*, chap. 9.

was so strong in the inter-war period was therefore directed particularly against the Army, which was held largely responsible for the destruction of a generation of British youth.

Many of those who rejected pacifism, and who were interested in defence matters—and they were a small minority—demanded that Britain return to what they called her 'traditional strategy', namely, of relying on the military efforts on land of continental allies, while using her superiority at sea to blockade the enemy and mount small offensives on its flank.[1] Defenders of the Army command rejected this interpretation, and the subject became the centre of an acrimonious debate during the 1920s and 1930s. Yet those who attacked the western-front concept ignored the fact that there was no alternative front open to Britain that could have produced victory. While insisting that Britain's naval superiority gave her the strategic mobility to launch indirect attacks, proponents of the 'traditional strategy' tended to overlook the first part of their definition of that strategy—the reliance on allies for the major effort on land. Arguments that Britain should have switched her land efforts from the western front to such theatres as the Dardanelles ignored the influence of the French, Britain's continental ally, and the role and condition, especially from the end of 1916 on, of the French Army. Here it is important to note that the concept of a continental commitment was attacked from two sides: by the pacifists, who were opposed to all war, and by the supporters of the 'traditional strategy' theory, who denied the need for a major continental role for the British Army.

Political leaders during the 1920s and 1930s were prone to forget, in their anxiety to avoid a repetition of 1914–18, that an alliance with a major continental power had always been an integral part of British strategy. During the Versailles negotiations, the French insisted on measures that would preserve the integrity of France against further German aggression. From the beginning the French, especially the military, pressed for the detachment from Germany and permanent French occupation of the Rhineland, which would give France a strong frontier against Germany for

---

[1] See, for example, the lecture given by Liddell Hart in January 1931 at the Royal United Service Institution: 'Economic Pressure or Continental Victories'. *Journal of the Royal United Service Institution [JRUSI]*, LXXVI (August 1931, no. 503), 486–510; and Liddell Hart, *The British Way in Warfare* (London: Faber, 1932).

the first time since Napoleon. The British and Americans opposed this claim, though not the principle—French security—upon which it rested. President Wilson argued that it was contrary to the concept of self-determination, that it would chronically inflame Franco-German tension, and that the separation would be economically ruinous to Germany. Lloyd George felt that, in addition to these considerations, the annexation of the Rhineland by France would create too great an imbalance on the Continent, to Britain's disadvantage. To satisfy the French demand for security against Germany, Wilson and Lloyd George offered military guarantees of France's eastern frontier on the condition that the French drop their proposals to detach the Rhineland from Germany. Eventually the French agreed that the Rhineland should be occupied for fifteen years, with progressive troop withdrawals every five years, depending on the German compliance with the terms of the treaty.

The French were shocked to find, shortly afterwards, that they had lost everything. The United States Senate refused to ratify the treaty between France and the United States, which Wilson had put forward in place of a tripartite Anglo-French-American guarantee. Lloyd George had stipulated that the Anglo-French treaty would only come into effect when the American-French treaty had been ratified and, with the Senate's refusal, the British contracted out of their treaty. The French were left with nothing. They had given up their demands for a Rhine frontier on the express understanding that Britain and the United States would guarantee the integrity of their frontier with Germany. Now they were abandoned by their former allies, and—to make their position even worse—the United States did not enter the League of Nations, which might have provided a substitute watchdog against German ambitions.[1]

France therefore looked to her own devices to secure her position against Germany. Lacking the support of an alliance with her former allies, she concluded a series of mutual defensive pacts with smaller powers in Europe: with Belgium in 1920, Poland in 1921, Czechoslovakia in 1925, Rumania in 1926, and Yugoslavia in 1927. Thus France involved herself in the problems

[1] See Paul Birdsall, *Versailles Twenty Years After* (London: Allen & Unwin, 1941), pp. 195-223; Seth P. Tillman, *Anglo-American Relations at the Paris Peace Conference of 1919* (Princeton: Princeton University Press, 1961), pp. 189-93.

of central and eastern Europe, the very areas where the peace settlement had planted the seeds of potential conflict over the redrawing of frontiers and the establishment of so-called 'national' states (which were, in reality, polyglot unions with sizeable minorities). Secondly, the French were convinced that their only chance of ensuring their security was to apply the letter of the Treaty of Versailles against Germany. When the German authorities in the Ruhr defaulted on reparation deliveries in December 1922, and again in January 1923, Raymond Poincaré, the French Premier, took the tough line, and, on 11 January, French and Belgian troops entered Essen. The American troops were immediately withdrawn, and although the British troops remained stationed around Cologne, they did nothing to stop the French occupation. Politically, British action was confined to protests against French policy, which proceeded to seal off the Ruhr and set up a French administration to run the Ruhr's industries in the face of a German campaign of passive resistance and noncooperation, and demanded total surrender by the German authorities before they would begin to negotiate. The disastrous inflation of German currency ruined the middle class and enabled German industry to recapitalize and rebuild. By refusing to give France the guarantees they had promised, Britain and America forced her into extreme, hard-line measures against Germany, upon which her former allies could exert no moderating influence, with the result that the difficult problems of post-war reconstruction and readjustment to the new power balance in Europe were exacerbated.

Although the occupation of the Ruhr forced a complete surrender on the part of the German government, it brought the French no closer to the security they sought. Despite the collapse of the Anglo-American guarantees, and a setback to the hopes built around the League occasioned by the American decision not to join, efforts to settle tensions in Europe continued. Two abortive attempts were made during 1923–5. The Draft Treaty of Mutual Assistance (1923) proposed that all members of the League assist any member who was the victim of a war of aggression, the military obligation being limited to those powers on the Continent where the aggression took place. The Council of the League was to decide the exact duties of each member, and it was on this point that the supporters of the Draft Treaty encountered difficulties. The British government objected to the burdens the Treaty would impose on the British Navy and to the restrictions that it would place on the military role of the Empire. In particular it opposed the giving of authority over British military forces to an extra-British body, and feared that acceptance of the Treaty would herald a return to the pre-war alliance systems. Consequently, Ramsay MacDonald's Labour government rejected the Draft Treaty on 18 July 1924.

Labour's decision obliged them to seek another solution, since they had insisted that, when in power, they would put some teeth into the League. The Geneva Protocol, an Anglo-French proposal of 6 September 1924, laid down that international legal disputes should be submitted to the Permanent Court of International Justice for a binding decision, while non-legal disputes were to go to the Council of the League. Furthermore, there were provisions for the submission to international arbitration of disputes normally within the jurisdiction of domestic authorities. The Dominions were anxious lest this expose them to unacceptable decisions regarding immigration policies, and the British Foreign Office strongly opposed the encroachment of international authority upon the making of national policy. The Labour government was out of office in November, and the Conservative government decided against ratification.

Within a year the Locarno Treaty was signed in London, and Europe seemed to have settled down to a period of peace and relaxed tension. Austen Chamberlain, British Foreign Minister, recognized that France had a right to some degree of security on her eastern frontier, and, in March 1925, he reacted favourably to German proposals for negotiations. The following month the French government fell, and was replaced by a government in which Aristide Briand was Foreign Minister. Briand was anxious to promote a Franco-German reconciliation within the framework of adequate French security, and he therefore welcomed the German initiative. Negotiations between representatives of France, Britain, Germany, Italy, and Belgium began in London in September, and on 16 October, at Locarno, the various instruments of the Locarno Pact were signed. The most important annex, the Rhineland Pact, involved the recognition by the German government of the Franco-German frontier established by the Treaty of Versailles, and the guarantee, collectively and severally, of that frontier by France, Germany, Britain, Belgium, and Italy. No such undertaking was made in respect of Germany's eastern frontiers. The 'spirit of Locarno' set a high-water mark of goodwill in Europe. A year later, 8 September 1926, Germany joined the League, where Briand's welcoming speech epitomized the new hopes of European peace.[1] The splendid generalities of Locarno were not, however, translated into concrete measures. They could not be. Although Britain had guaranteed the Franco-German border against aggression both ways, it was doubtful if she ever seriously entertained the possibility of having to assist Germany against France. Conversely, the spirit of Locarno could not conceal the fact that Germany would eventually rebuild its strength and challenge French power in Europe. Staff talks between the French and British (or between Britain and any other Locarno signatory) were ruled out by the terms of the Pact, which was directed against general aggression over the Franco-German frontier. Britain avoided translating the guarantees of Locarno into specific military measures; in fact, the impossibility of assuming commitments under the Locarno system was, in British eyes, one of its advantages.

The settlement of the Franco-German frontier under the Locarno Pact, and Britain's effectual withdrawal from European problems, with the negative military implications of that settlement, meshed neatly with fiscal policy. During the 1920s, the Conservative, Labour, and Liberal parties were on common ground in opposing heavy expenditure on the armed forces. While each was vitally concerned with economic stability and recovery, they offered different solutions. The Conservatives proposed a stringent policy of cutting public expenditure and balancing the budget, whereas Labour sought to maintain living standards, wage levels, and national assistance for the unemployed. In either case, however, large expenditure on the armed forces was not envisaged.

Restrictions on spending were imposed shortly after the armistice. On 15 August 1919, the War Cabinet, consisting of David Lloyd George, Lord Curzon, Andrew Bonar Law, and Sir Eric Geddes, decided that for the purpose of framing estimates, the armed forces should act on the assumption that 'the British Empire will not be engaged in any great war during the next ten

[1] See W. N. Medlicott, *British Foreign Policy Since Versailles, 1919-1963* (London: Methuen, 2nd rev. ed., 1968), pp. 58-63, 69-74; René Albrecht-Carrié, *A Diplomatic History of Europe since the Congress of Vienna* (New York and Evanston: Harper & Row, 1958), pp. 406-22.

years, and that no Expeditionary Force[1] is required for this purpose'. Defence expenditure was to be limited to £120 million annually, £75 million of which was to be divided between the War Office and the Air Ministry. Furthermore, they laid down that the Admiralty should not, without Cabinet authority, make any alteration in the pre-war standard that determined the size of the Navy.[2] These decisions were made on the basis of very limited evidence. Arthur Balfour, Secretary of State for Foreign Affairs, was not present at the meeting either of the Finance Committee which made the original recommendation or the War Cabinet which adopted it.[3] The situation in Europe was still fluid, and no one could predict what measures might be necessary before international order was restored. The Finance Committee, however, had decided that a reduction in defence expenditure was needed, regardless of the consequences. The decision, therefore, was purely an empirical one. The Chief of the Imperial General Staff, Sir Henry Wilson, submitted a formal protest against the imposition of arbitrary financial limitations, but to no avail.[4]

This was the origin of the 'ten-year rule', which persisted in various forms until 1932, when the 'no war' period was modified to five years. It meant that when drawing up estimates to submit to the Treasury, the armed forces could not countenance war within ten years, a restriction which put them in an impossible position when it came to strategic planning. Furthermore, this was not calculated to infuse a forward-looking spirit into the senior commanders. When, for all intents and purposes, war was

[1] The term 'Expeditionary Force' was used during the 1920s and early 1930s, when it generally gave way, for the latter half of the 1930s, to the term 'Field Force'. In late 1938 and 1939 both terms were frequently used. For the purpose of clarity in this study, 'Expeditionary Force' has been used throughout.

[2] Cab. 23/15. 616A. Minutes of War Cabinet meeting, 15 Aug. 1919. The naval standard as set forth by Winston Churchill, First Lord of the Admiralty, on 18 March 1912, was based on a 16:10 (i.e. a 60 per cent superiority) ratio of British to German 'Dreadnought' type ships. Great Britain, *Parliamentary Debates (House of Commons)*, Fifth Series, XXXV, 1555–6. All quotations from *Parliamentary Debates* are from the House of Commons, Fifth Series, hereafter cited as 5 *Parl. Debs.* See also Arthur J. Marder, *From the Dreadnought to Scapa Flow: The Royal Navy in the Fisher Era, 1904–1919*, Vol. 1, *The Road to War, 1904–1914* (London: Oxford University Press, 1961), pp. 283–4.

[3] Hankey, 'Imperial Defence Preparations: The Basis of Service Estimates', 2 July 1928. C.P. 232(28), Cab. 24/196.

[4] (Major-General Sir) Charles E. Callwell, *Field-Marshal Sir Henry Wilson, His Life and Diaries* (2 vols. London: Cassell, 1927), II, 208.

not to be envisaged within ten years, it was placed in the realm of hypothetical considerations, which discouraged progressive thinking spurred on by a sense of urgency. When this was allied with financial stringency, it was natural that the Army should limit itself to variations on the traditional methods, rather than spend large amounts out of limited funds on expensive new weapons. Military conservatism and financial limitations combined with political dictates to stifle, at least at the top level of the military establishment, military rethinking and experimentation.[1]

As the post-war recession worsened, the Government came under strong pressure to economize. A manifesto to this effect was signed by 170 M.P.s, and the financiers of the City of London demanded extreme deflationary measures. The Government therefore appointed a committee, headed by a former member of the War Cabinet and Minister of Transport, Sir Eric Geddes, to find further economies that could be made in the estimates for 1922–3. The 'Geddes axe' fell on 10 February 1922, and of the recommended cuts of £75 million, £46.5 million came from the armed forces estimates. The Committee proposed that Army expenditure for 1922–3 be reduced from £75.198 million to £55 million, with more extensive cuts in future years, and that the establishment of the Army be reduced by 50,000 officers and men, out of an establishment in 1922 of 217,500 (exclusive of 71,500 British troops serving in India). The Navy was to be reduced by 35,000 officers and men (out of an establishment of 118,500), and its budget cut from £81 million to £60 million in 1922–3 as the preliminary for progressive cuts in future estimates. The Air Force estimates were cut by £5.5 million. Under Admiralty pressure the

[1] A. J. P. Taylor writes that the ten-year rule was 'sound political judgment when it started, and even its prolongation could be justified. There was not much point in maintaining great armaments when no conceivable enemy existed.' Apart from a dubious reading of the situation in Europe, Asia, and the Middle East in the 1920s—as if, for example, Locarno abolished the threat of aggression—this ignores the totally unrealistic position in which the armed forces were placed. Planning that had to be made on the basis of 'no war for ten years' (a period which advanced daily under the reinterpretation of the rule in 1928) could barely be called planning, especially in the light of technological refinements and changes that had to be (or should have been) assimilated into the military machine. Taylor demonstrates his own curious brand of reasoning when he adds: 'Even the final guess of 1932 [no war before 1942] was not all that wrong. Both Hitler and Mussolini fixed on 1943 for the outbreak of the next great war, and the second World War might well have started then if it had not been for a series of accidents and misunderstandings.' *English History*, p. 228.

naval reductions were limited to £10.5 million, but there were, nevertheless, extensive savings, the estimates eventually being a full £139 million below those of 1921, with the 1922 budget being the first of the post-war period to be under £1,000 million.[1]

In the years before the Great War, when there were only two services, the division of responsibility between them tended, for the most part, to be a fairly uncontroversial matter. With the introduction of air power, however, inter-service rivalries were sharpened. Two main issues caused intense fighting and bickering: the division of control, which raised the question of an independent Air Force, and the division of money. In an effort to get some degree of co-ordination of policy, the Chiefs of Staff were formed as a sub-committee of the Committee of Imperial Defence (C.I.D.) in 1923. This had the effect of moving these rivalries to the top level, where seniority of rank had no moderating influence. Lord Ismay, later assistant secretary of the C.I.D. and then secretary, said that the early years of the Chiefs of Staff Sub-Committee 'were signalised by the most blazing rows', and that the mutual hostility was such that meetings were held as infrequently as possible, in some years being as few as four or five.[2] The one interest the services had in common was the desire to squeeze the maximum amount of money out of the Treasury.

[1] Great Britain, *Parliamentary Papers (1922)*, IX, Cmd. 1581. Committee on National Expenditure, 'First Interim Report'. The Geddes Committee noted with disapproval that expenditure on research and experimentation in the armed forces had risen from £702,580 in 1914-15 to £4,217,795 in 1922-3. This activity, the Committee reported, 'carries in its train much indirect increase of expenditure, and also the substitution of new material for old, and of alterations in the engines of war. It inevitably also creates a tendency in the minds of technical advisers to prescribe an accelerated rate of obsolescence in war material.'

Expenditure on the armed forces during the period 1912-23 was as follows (£000s):

	1913-14	1914-15	1919-20	1920-1	1921-2	1922-3
Army	28,346	28,886	395,000	181,000	95,110	45,400
Navy	48,833	51,550	156,528	88,428	80,770	56,200
Air Force	—	—	52,500	23,300	13,560	9,400

Parl. Papers (1924), XXIV, Cmd. 2207. 'Statistical Abstract for the United Kingdom 1908-1922.'

Defence expenditure in 1913 was 3.5 per cent of the national income; in 1933 it was 2.5 per cent. If the decline in money value is taken into account, defence expenditure in the 1920s and early 1930s was less than in the pre-war period.

[2] Lord Ismay, draft of a lecture to the Imperial Defence College, Oct. 1949. Ismay Papers, III/4/12.

13

However, the Treasury tended to put a ceiling on defence expenditure, and then apportion the allotted amount between the services, depending on the annual survey of imperial defence presented by the Chiefs of Staff. It usually happened, therefore, that the reports by the Chiefs of Staff recommended a rounded programme of strengthening defences; 'rounded' because interservice rivalries worked against one service advancing claims to the detriment of the other two.

In their review of imperial defence in 1928, the Chiefs of Staff emphasized the primary imperial role of the Army. Its main commitments were the provision of forces for (1) the defence of ports abroad, particularly Singapore, Malta, Hong Kong, and Gibraltar; (2) the normal garrison of India; (3) adequate local security for the Empire overseas and for areas where Britain had special interests, e.g. Egypt, the Sudan, and China, for which reinforcements had to be readily available; (4) anti-aircraft (A.A.) defence of Britain; (5) garrisons for ports in the United Kingdom; and (6) the maintenance of internal security in Britain. Lastly, from the balance of troops in Britain, both from the Regular Army and the Territorial Army (the part-time volunteers), an expeditionary force was to be formed as Britain's 'initial contribution to meet our commitments in Europe or elsewhere overseas'. This force was the equivalent of five divisions, and it was implicitly accepted that conscription would be necessary to expand it to any appreciable degree.[1]

The Chiefs of Staff noted that the Treaty of Locarno and the provisions of the Treaty of Versailles regarding the demilitarized zone between Germany and France imposed a 'somewhat indefinite liability' on Britain. In view of the limitations of the ten-year rule and the general guarantees of the Locarno Treaty, however, they made no proposals about the defence requirements upon which the fulfilment of that 'indefinite liability' was contingent.[2]

The main danger confronting the British Army, they thought, was war with Russia over the integrity of Afghanistan and ultimately, therefore, of India. They were by no means satisfied that the expeditionary force was ready to be employed in the field, but noted that the financial situation imposed severe restrictions

[1] C.O.S., 'Imperial Defence Policy: A review of Imperial Defence, 1928', 25 June 1928. C.P. 348(28), Cab. 24/198.
[2] C.O.S., C.P. 348(28).

14

on the armed forces, and that the resultant degree of unpreparedness could be accepted only in view of the fact that the nature of
the terrain in Afghanistan and the difficulty of moving troops and
supplies dictated a slower rate of mobilization.[1]

These factors—strict Treasury control, the imperial role of the
Army, and the area in which the expeditionary force was expected
to be used—were central to the protracted argument over the
nature, extent, and pace of modernization of the Army. Mechanization—the combination of mobility and firepower—threatened
to revolutionize the Army and radically alter the traditional
balance between cavalry, artillery, and infantry. The natural
conservatism of the military establishment, a streak of social
and personal prejudice, and the overriding problem of the lack
of money contributed to the reluctance of the senior command to
push ahead with mechanization.

One of the last services performed by Field-Marshal Haig
was to speak in defence of the horse against the claims advanced
by proponents of mechanized warfare:[2]

> I believe that the value of the horse and the opportunity
> for the horse in the future are likely to be as great as
> ever. . . . I am all for using aeroplanes and tanks, but they
> are only accessories to the man and the horse, and I feel
> sure that as time goes on you will find just as much use
> for the horse—the well bred horse—as you have ever done
> in the past.

If others did not claim such universal qualities for the cavalry,
they argued that in the Army's main role as an imperial force,
there were many areas, e.g. India's north-west frontier, where
mechanized vehicles would have a limited value. Hence there
would always be a place for the cavalry and infantry in the British
Army.

Pressure for change and a basic rethinking of tactical and
strategic doctrine came from a few enthusiasts, both within and
outside Army ranks. One of the most influential was Captain
Basil Liddell Hart, perhaps the most prolific writer of the period.
War injuries had restricted Liddell Hart's career, and, after being
invalided out of the Army in 1925, he concentrated on a scientific

---

[1] C.O.S., C.P. 348(28).
[2] Quoted in Liddell Hart, *The Memoirs of Captain Liddell Hart* (2 vols. London:
Cassell, 1965–6), I, 100.

15

study of the military art, based on a sound knowledge of military history. Newspaper correspondent on military affairs (*Daily Telegraph*, 1925–34; *The Times*, 1934–9), lecturer, author of many books and articles, and informal adviser to a host of people interested in and connected with defence matters, he was closely acquainted with the British military and political establishment.

At the suggestion of Lord Thomson, Secretary of State for Air in the Labour government that took office in June 1929, Liddell Hart wrote a paper on 'The Expeditionary Force and Reorganization of the Home Army' for the new Cabinet. He criticized the organization of the expeditionary force which, he said, was both inefficient and uneconomical. It paid only lip-service to 'the truth, universally admitted in the abstract, that fighting power should nowadays be calculated in terms of fire-power, not by man-power.' The Army failed to appreciate the potential impact of mechanized forces, and still thought in terms of large infantry formations and the importance of cavalry. It was clear to Liddell Hart that the limited experiments with armoured forces were hampered by rigid and obsolete concepts of warfare, in which conditions on the battlefield tended to be made to fit theories, rather than theory being adapted to changing circumstances. If financial considerations were paramount, he argued, it was surely better to spend a proportionately greater share on the arm with the most potential, rather than maintain large forces of infantry and cavalry whose effectiveness had been thrown into doubt (to say the least) by the offensives on the western front.[1] The point at issue here was the organization of the expeditionary force, rather than the concept itself. *That* became a cause for argument later.

The War Office did not share these beliefs, and emphasized manpower at the expense of mobile fire-power. In 1922 the Committee of Imperial Defence persuaded the Cabinet to draw on past experience and formulate plans for Britain's role in a future war. Two sub-committees were established, one to study national service, and the other the supply of armaments and munitions, both of which had been vital and controversial issues in the Great War. The first committee submitted its report in July 1922. It decided that in a major war, defined as one in which more than 750,000 recruits would be required by the armed forces, volun-

[1] Liddell Hart Papers, A 2/2.

tary enlistment would not be sufficient, and conscription would have to be introduced.[1]

Following on from this, the C.I.D. appointed in 1923 a Man-Power Sub-Committee, whose members included representatives of the armed forces, the Treasury, Board of Trade, Home Office, and the Ministries of Health, Labour, and Pensions. It drew up a scheme of universal male military service, under which all members of the 'clean cut' group, i.e. those between 18 and 25, would be called up irrespective of occupation, time being allowed for the replacement of individuals considered to be key men in industry.[2] This plan remained the basis of the government's mobilization scheme until 1939.

These reports had a double significance. They showed that the armed forces were still thinking in terms of numbers of men rather than fire-power, and they established wartime conscription as a fundamental principle for the expansion of the services. It was assumed that on the outbreak of war, but not before, the government would introduce legislation to give itself the powers to enforce compulsory military service. The important point was not so much conscription itself, but the timing. Conscription was largely accepted as natural and necessary: it became an issue when its introduction in peacetime was proposed.

A sub-committee appointed by the C.I.D. to consider the cavalry of the line was generally satisfied with the progress made in mechanization, and recommended that the C.I.D. approve the War Office programme of converting cavalry regiments into armoured-car regiments and mechanizing machine-gun equipment and the remaining cavalry brigades, the change to be made 'with due regard to financial considerations'. At the same time it drew particular attention to the 'desirability ... of making the fullest use of the traditions of the Cavalry and of the spirit and special qualities of its personnel in its mechanized substitute.'[3] Another sub-committee stated: 'Cavalry officers, and the class which provides them, are quite ready to look facts in the face, and, with whatever natural regrets, to take no exception to the change from horses to machines.' It added that it was clear that cavalry

[1] Hankey, 'Notes for the Minister' [n.d.], Cab. 21/683.
[2] *Ibid.*
[3] C.I.D. Sub-Committee on the Cavalry of the Line, 'Papers prepared for the use of the Chiefs of Staff in their Third Annual Review of Imperial Defence (1928)', 23 July 1928. C.P. 348(28) attached, Cab. 24/198.

officers would be better qualified than men from any other branch to handle the new mechanized forces.[1] This policy of choosing armoured commanders from branches other than that experienced in handling mechanized forces and familiar with their specialized capabilities was generally followed in the 1920s and 1930s. Despite lip-service to a policy of mechanization, the War Office tended to emphasize manpower—the traditional approach.

Their reluctance to experiment with the new and costly mechanized forces was increased by further financial restrictions in 1928. The Admiralty admitted that its estimates for 1928–9 had been drawn up to bring the Navy to a state of readiness for a major war by 1935. This drew from the Treasury a reminder that the Government had repeatedly endorsed the ten-year rule, which was to be accepted by the services as the basis for framing estimates.[2] As recently as January 1928 the Foreign Secretary, Austen Chamberlain, had advised the C.I.D. that it would be safe to assume that no great war was likely to occur within the next ten years.[3] The Chancellor of the Exchequer, Winston Churchill, was determined to reduce expenditure drastically and, although he had political ties with the Navy and was usually counted one of its most enthusiastic supporters, he wielded an axe no less severe, if not quite as direct, as that of Geddes. He suggested to the Cabinet[4] that

> it should be laid down as a standing assumption that at any given date there will be no major war for ten years from that date; and that this should rule unless or until, on the initiative of the Foreign Office or one of the Fighting Services or otherwise, it is decided to alter it.

This made realistic strategic planning impossible, for military plans had to be related to capability, yet requests for money to maintain or increase armament levels had to be justified on the basis of 'no war for ten years', a ten years that advanced daily. As Sir Maurice Hankey, secretary of the C.I.D. and the Cabinet,

---

[1] 'Report of the Sub-Committee of the C.I.D. on the Strength and Organization of the Cavalry', 3 May 1928. C.P. 178(28), attached, Cab. 24/195.

[2] R. V. Nind (Treasury) to Admiralty, 13 March 1928. C.P. 169(28), Enclosure 1, Cab. 24/195.

[3] Hankey, C.P. 232(28).

[4] Churchill, 'The Basis of Navy Estimates', 15 June 1928. C.P. 169(28), Cab. 24/195.

explained, this put the service chiefs in the position of awakening every morning with the thought, 'Oh God, another ten years has begun!'[1]

The Cabinet asked the C.I.D. to examine in detail the process of drawing up estimates.[2] Churchill pointed out that it was doubtful if the C.I.D. intended that the Admiralty should base its estimates upon the assumption that the Navy should be ready for a major war at the end of the ten-year period.[3] In a paper for the C.I.D., Hankey drew attention to a Cabinet conclusion of 28 July 1927, which laid down that for the purpose of framing estimates, the War Office should rule out the possibility of a European war during the next ten years, and that the 'immediate plans' of the Army should be based upon preparedness for an extra-European war. As far as the Air Force was concerned, the C.I.D. was reminded that the Cabinet had decided in 1925 that the scheme of air expansion for home defence, which it had itself already approved and announced in Parliament, was to be postponed until 1935–6.[4] The C.I.D. recommended that Churchill's ten-year period, advancing daily, should be adopted,[5] and this interpretation was accepted by the Cabinet,[6] remaining in force until 1932.

These were the factors that composed the backdrop against which strategic policy had to be formulated. During the 1920s there appeared to be no immediate threats to European security. Both Communist Russia and Fascist Italy were, for the most part, intent on internal reconstruction, and Germany was crushed by the war and the Treaty of Versailles. French demands for security against a revanchist Germany were directed towards long-term developments, for, while the main provisions of the Versailles Treaty were in effect, Germany was in no position to threaten France seriously—as the total French victory in the Ruhr in 1923 showed. British policy in the 1920s, both before and after Locarno, was based upon minimal commitments, and those only in the most general terms, for there too, internal problems claimed the nation's attention.

---

[1] Hankey, 'Notes for the Minister', Cab. 21/683.
[2] Cab. 23/58, Minutes 34(28)6, 22 June 1928.
[3] Cab. 2/5, Minutes of the 236th meeting of the C.I.D., 5 July 1928.
[4] Hankey, C.P. 232(28).
[5] Cab. 2/5, Minutes of the 236th meeting of the C.I.D., 5 July 1928.
[6] Cab. 23/58, Minutes 39(28)10, 18 July, 1928.

Military questions were given comparatively little consideration, except when disarmament or reductions in expenditure were thought possible or imperative. Hampered by a lack of money, controlled by a conservative command, and overshadowed by the apparently unlimited potential of air power, the Army became the 'Cinderella' of the services. In keeping with the trend of foreign policy in the 1920s, reinforced by a fear of a repetition of the continental involvement of 1914-18, the Army concentrated on an imperial role and, secondarily, the defence of Britain against air attack.

While the European scene was relatively calm, and the 'spirit of Locarno' prevailed, these assumptions, and the policy that developed from them, were generally acceptable. If circumstances changed, however, logically both the assumptions and the policy would have to be reinterpreted in the light of the new situation.

2 The breakdown of Locarno 1929-35

The late 1920s appeared to hold the promise of a final settlement of Europe's problems. The Kellogg–Briand Pact of August 1928 was signed by sixty-five nations who promised to renounce war as an instrument of national policy. In May 1929 the Young Plan was accepted as the basis for the payment of reparations by Germany, and Stresemann persuaded the allies to agree to an accelerated timetable for the withdrawal of occupation troops. The Labour party under Ramsay MacDonald was returned to office in June 1929, having emphasized in its election manifesto, 'Labour and the Nation', that it would make a concerted effort to achieve lasting peace through conciliation, arbitration, disarmament, and general co-operation with the League of Nations.

Within four months, however, there were signs that perhaps solutions would not be found as readily as had been hoped. Stresemann's death on 3 October 1929 removed the one German committed to moderate settlements of Germany's grievances. Three weeks later, on 29 October, the American stock market collapsed, and American capital investment in Europe all but ceased, triggering off a world-wide depression. This had the effect in Germany of strengthening the appeal of the extremist parties which called for drastic political action to restore German prosperity and political influence in Europe. The Social Democrat Chancellor, Hermann Müller, was forced to resign in March 1930, and was succeeded by Heinrich Brüning of the Centre Party. Brüning had openly declared his opposition to the Versailles Treaty, and on being appointed Chancellor, warned that he would rule by decree if the parties in the Reichstag did not co-operate in carrying out his proposals. New elections in September, brought on by a vote of no confidence, saw the National Socialists increase their strength from an insignificant 12 to 107, making them the second largest party in the Reichstag. Henceforth the Nazis could not be dismissed as the lunatic fringe of German political life, especially when, as their electoral support grew,

c

they boasted ever more loudly of the changes they would make when they came to power.

MacDonald's Labour government was caught in the international monetary crisis of 1931, which intensified the economic problems it was already facing from the American collapse, the world-wide agricultural slump, and the shrinking of markets. The Government's fiscal policies, especially its unwillingness to balance the budget by reducing expenditure on unemployment payments, did not inspire confidence from the City financiers, who, through the officials of the Bank of England, pressed the Government to take drastic steps as the price of their co-operation in trying to stabilize the financial situation. This precipitated an internal political crisis, in which the Labour party split, and MacDonald and a few supporters allied themselves with the Conservatives.

The general election of October 1931 resulted in a resounding victory for the new National coalition. The Conservatives won 473 seats, the National Liberals 35, National Labour (MacDonald's breakaway group) 13, while the Labour and Liberal parties retained 52 and 33 respectively. Lloyd George's Liberals were reduced to four, and neither the Communists nor Oswald Mosley's New Party managed to have any of their candidates elected. With such a large majority, the Conservatives naturally dominated the Cabinet, holding eleven out of twenty-two portfolios.

As Prime Minister, Ramsay MacDonald was not up to the task. With a huge Conservative majority as the basis of his government, he would have needed immense energy and strength to give a lead and stamp his own ideas on its policies. But this he lacked: tired and in bad health, he increasingly became a figurehead, presiding over a government he did not control, and retiring as Prime Minister in June 1935. He lingered on in growing isolation as Lord President, until he died at sea in 1937, of little consequence in his government, and reviled by his former Labour colleagues.

As MacDonald's powers began to fail, many of his responsibilities were shouldered by Stanley Baldwin, Lord President of the Council and senior Conservative member of the Cabinet. A shrewd, lazy politician, Baldwin conducted the business of government on the principle of non-interference with individual ministers. His particular interest was domestic affairs, whereas he had a marked aversion to studying foreign policy, which he neither liked nor understood. He was not inclined by temperament, being completely insular in taste and outlook, to acquire a working knowledge of European realities. He much preferred to let things drift, and his ventures into foreign affairs were unavoidable reactions to crises rather than an indication of any initiative on his part. One critic has suggested that Baldwin's career was remarkable for its display of 'the incurable vice of indolence'.[1] Another has recorded that when Baldwin was shown a report on German rearmament by the British military attaché in Berlin, he exclaimed: 'Oh, for God's sake, take that stuff away. If I read it I shan't sleep.'[2]

The Secretary of State for Foreign Affairs in the National government was the leader of the National Liberals, Sir John Simon. A brilliant lawyer and distinguished administrator, Simon had been Home Secretary during the war, but resigned in 1916 in protest against the decision to conscript married men. This was a rare example of firmness on Simon's part, for he usually leant towards conciliation and compromise. He was an able politician, but lacked warmth in his political relationships. Lloyd George once remarked: 'Simon has sat on the fence so long that the iron has entered into his soul.'[3] In the National government he was a firm supporter of disarmament, and later, of appeasement.

Undoubtedly the key figure in the government was the Chancellor of the Exchequer, Stanley Baldwin's successor in the Conservative party, and probably the next Prime Minister. Neville Chamberlain was very different from the rest of the Conservative hierarchy. Educated at Rugby and Mason Science College in Birmingham, he had spent several years as a young man in a sisal-growing project in the Bahamas that was a total failure. Returning to Birmingham, he had a successful business career, and entered local government as a comparative late-comer. He was elected Lord Mayor of Birmingham in 1915, and the

[1] A.L. Rowse, *The Early Churchills, An English Family* (New York: Harper, 1956), p. 333.
[2] Lord Boothby to Ismay, 2 Jan. 1960. Ismay Papers, V/B26/1. The official biography, G.M. Young's *Stanley Baldwin* (London: Hart-Davis, 1952), went awry when Young came to dislike the subject of his book. A. W. Baldwin tried to balance the portrait with *Baldwin My Father: The True Story* (London: Allen & Unwin, 1955). The latest biography, of massive proportions, and unlikely to be superseded for many years, is that by Keith Middlemas and John Barnes, *Stanley Baldwin: A Biography* (London: Weidenfeld & Nicolson, 1969).
[3] Quoted in Taylor, *English History*, p. 54. Simon's memoirs, *Retrospect* (London: Hutchinson, 1952), contain little of interest or value.

following year Lloyd George appointed **him** ...
National Service. He found, however, **that the** ...
authority, and he soon resigned. The **mutual** ...
followed permanently embittered his **relations** ...

It was true that Chamberlain showed **a busi**...
with financial matters, yet as Minister **of** ...
remodelled the health service along **modern** ...
sympathetic realization of the plight **of the** ...
actions during the General Strike of 1926, **whe**...
hard line against the unions, earned **him the** ...
the Labour party. When, in 1937, he **became** ...
could never count on Labour support. **Memo**...
ment-union clash of 1926 were long, **and if** ...
despised and loathed him personally, **he could** ...
conceal his contempt for them.

The contrast in working methods **betwe**...
Chamberlain could not have been **greater.** ...
vised his department closely, and was **a mo**...
industriousness. He had no training **in forei**...
did not deter him from taking an active **intere**...
of foreign policy. He was not a pacifist **in the** ...
hated war as a fearful waste of precious **reso**...
be put to constructive social use. Thus **he co**...
government department in the National **coaliti**...
hard-working, respected by many, but **loved by** ...
with restoring economic prosperity, **incline**...
and soured by experience to avoid the **horrors of** ...
century radical in a key position in **twentieth-c**...

The National government, then, was **nomi**...
Donald, but the real leaders were Bald**win, Sim**...
lain. Baldwin was not interested in **foreign aff**...
left that responsibility to others, inter**fering as** ...
Both Simon and Chamberlain had good **caus**...
entanglements with conscription, which **had b**...
resignation in 1916.

[1] The official biography is that by Keith Feiling, *The Lif*...
Chamberlain (London: Macmillan, 1946). A more **rece**...
Neville Chamberlain (London: Muller, 1961), has **little m**...
study must wait until Chamberlain's papers **are open** ...
the University of Birmingham. Meanwhile, **copies of so**...
letters which do not appear in Feiling's book **can be fo**...
Templewood Papers.

By 1931–2 the relative calm that had apparently settled over the international scene in the latter part of the 1920s began to show signs of breaking up. In eastern Asia, Japanese aggression against China became bolder, and, in September 1931, Japanese troops seized Mukden. By the beginning of 1932 they had occupied most of Manchuria. China appealed to the League of Nations, which thereupon had to face its first real test. The Council of the League twice demanded the withdrawal of Japanese troops, but it lacked— or rather its members were unwilling to give it—the means to force Japanese compliance. If force was to be used, it would basically have to be naval power—British naval power. The other nations with extensive interests in the Far East, Russia and the United States, were not members of the League, and it would thus fall to Britain to bear the brunt of the first League action against an aggressor. Instead, the League produced the Lytton Report, which recognized that while Japan was the aggressor, it had certain legitimate grievances. That was the extent of the League's reponse. Japanese troops continued their operations with marked success, and Japan withdrew from the League in March 1933.

The rise to power of the Nazis in January 1933 strengthened old fears in Europe over the resurgence of Germany. Hitler showed that Nazi Germany would not tolerate second-class treatment by withdrawing from the Disarmament Conference in October 1933, and serving notice of his intention to quit the League in November 1933. The new states in eastern Europe, created partly by the Treaty of Versailles and partly by the military success of nationalist groups operating in the power vacuum that existed after the collapse of the Russian and Austro-Hungarian Empires, distrusted each other, and were in turn hated by the two countries, Germany and Russia, whose defeat had been the occasion of their birth.

The Locarno spirit had not yet vanished, and the Locarno system itself had not been exposed as the toothless symbol it really was, but there was a growing realization in government circles in Britain that international tension was increasing. Concern with economic recovery—and with all the difficult internal political problems that posed—was still the Government's primary preoccupation, and the demands of defence programmes to meet the new situation threatened to upset its plans for the revival of economic prosperity. Financial considerations therefore played a

25

fundamental part in determining the balance between concentration of effort and resources on economic recovery and the growing demands of defence.

The Army of the 1920s and 1930s was still largely tied to the nineteenth-century Cardwell principle of organization, under which it maintained one battalion at home for every battalion serving abroad in the Empire, thus solving the problem of providing reinforcements for imperial garrisons. While the defence of India was Britain's prime military responsibility, the system worked well enough in practice, but as the international tensions shifted and changed, it tended to assume the status of a sacred doctrine, a basic principle that could not be challenged. But international tensions *did* alter, and what had been acceptable for imperial defence in the nineteenth century was not necessarily suited or relevant to the needs of the twentieth century. As long as the Cardwell principle remained in force, however, there could be little flexibility in the organization of the Army: the needs of India and the Empire had first to be satisfied, and then an expeditionary force would be scraped together from the remnants.

Difficulties arose when defence policy required the Army to take into account the possibility of operations in non-imperial theatres, i.e. the Continent. In such a situation, an Army that was basically organized for imperial defence had to readjust to face highly developed continental opponents, while still maintaining imperial garrisons. This basic problem of what role the Army was to adopt, or rather, which role was to be considered primary, was continually debated during the 1930s, and was not finally solved until a few months before the outbreak of war in 1939.

As long as the main threat appeared to rest in central Asia the Chiefs of Staff, and the Army in particular, could accept, albeit uneasily, the poor state of Britain's defences. The War Office made this clear in May 1931, when it emphasized that only the fact that a war in the foreseeable future would be fought in a relatively undeveloped country, where poor communications would make quick mobilization impossible, enabled the services to labour under the restrictions of the ten-year rule. Should the European situation deteriorate, however, the policy would have to be reviewed, for then the question of providing an expeditionary force would become important.

In 1931 the Regular Expeditionary Force consisted of five infantry divisions, one of which was incomplete, and a cavalry division of two cavalry brigades. Imperial commitments absorbed 67 line battalions, leaving 59 line battalions and 10 Guards battalions in the United Kingdom. Of these 69, the expeditionary force required 60, leaving only 9 battalions for the purposes of internal security, reinforcing threatened points overseas, and providing troops to defend lines of communication. The War Office noted that even when the Army accepted a slow rate of mobilization, 'deficiencies in reserves of men and some material constitute a grave problem'. These conditions could not, however,

Table 1. *The strength of the British Army 1913-37.*

I. The strength of the Regular Army (exclusive of troops serving in India)

Year	Cavalry	Artillery	Infantry	Others	Total
1913	19,990	47,533	143,232	36,495	247,250
1922	13,661	37,292	117,628	48,896	217,477
1926	12,579	34,666	120,719	37,794	205,758
1930	11,558	33,506	109,002	34,394	188,460
1934	11,405	32,230	116,698	35,502	195,845
1935	11,382	33,098	114,993	26,674	196,137
1936	10,917	32,441	110,627	38,340	192,325
1937	10,325	31,636	107,758	41,111	190,830

II. The numbers of British troops serving in India

Year	Total
1922	771,357
1926	61,543
1930	59,915
1934	57,665
1935	57,554
1936	57,524
1937	55,259

III. Territorial Army (as reconstituted 1920)

Year	Total
1922	136,600
1926	148,742
1930	137,141
1934	133,735
1935	131,617
1936	141,399
1937	156,765

See: 'Statistical Abstract for the Year 1937', Cmd. 5903. *Parl. Papers* (*1938–1939*), XXV. The Army estimates for the years quoted provide detailed analyses of the Army's establishment.

be accepted as applicable to warfare in Europe, where 'military intervention to fulfil an international obligation, if it were to be effective, would have to be prompt.'[1]

As political unrest in Germany increased, the possibility that the next war would be a European rather than an imperial one became more real. Hankey wrote to Sir Herbert Creedy in the War Office in February 1931 to emphasize that defence policy would have to be reoriented to safeguard against war in Europe:[2]

> The strategic centre of gravity, if it ever really did move eastward, is now starting on a return journey. If there is a danger today it is, in my view, in Europe, and more especially in Eastern Europe, rather than in the Far East or Afghanistan.

The Chiefs of Staff became increasingly dissatisfied with the limitations of the ten-year rule, especially since it tended to force them to assume the greater share of the responsibility for the state of Britain's defence forces, without allowing them to formulate the assumptions upon which policy was based. In June 1931 the Foreign Office circulated a paper examining the assumptions underlying the ten-year rule. It reached the conclusion that the validity of the rule rested on five conditions:[3]

(a) That during the next ten years no two nations will be involved in a dispute about a vital interest which pacific means have failed to solve; or

(b) That of two nations involved in a dispute one will yet be so averse from war as to prefer to abandon its interest rather than fight; or

(c) That of two such nations one will be so weak as to be incapable of fighting with any real hope of success; or

(d) That some organisation exists anxious and able to restrain intending belligerents; or

(e) That a situation does not arise which creates a war psychology.

[1] Army Council, memorandum, 'Distribution and Organization of the Military Forces in Relation to their Commitments and Liabilities, April 1, 1931'. W.O. 32/3488.
[2] Hankey to Creedy, 5 Feb. 1931. W. O. 32/3488.
[3] Quoted in C.O.S., 'Imperial Defence Policy: Annual Review for 1932', 23 Feb. 1932. C.P. 104(32), Cab. 24/229.

By the beginning of 1932, the Army Council could point out that none of the five conditions was being satisfied,[1] and in their annual review of imperial defence, the Chiefs of Staff recommended that the ten-year rule be cancelled. It had, they claimed, produced a 'terrible deficiency in essential requirements' and a 'state of ineffectiveness unequalled in the defensive arrangements of any foreign military power', with a 'consequential inability to fulfil ... major commitments'. In considering the possibility of war against a major power, the Chiefs of Staff drew attention to the rate of mobilization that a potential enemy could achieve. France, Italy, Japan, and Russia had a system of compulsory service, and in Germany 'there seemed to be no sign that there would be antagonism to a return to national compulsory service'. The contrast with Britain did not have to be made explicit. The review bemoaned the fact that the ten-year rule had created a 'complacent optimism in public opinion, and widespread ignorance of the facts of the situation, which increases the difficulty of taking the necessary steps to ameliorate the situation.' In these circumstances the Chiefs of Staff could rightly demand that the rule be cancelled.[2] The Committee of Imperial Defence agreed, and in recommending its abolition to the Cabinet, warned: 'We cannot ignore the writing on the wall.'[3]

The Cabinet accepted the recommendation of the C.I.D., but added a caution that its cancellation should not be interpreted as the justification for increased expenditure 'without regard to the very serious financial and economic situation that still obtains'.[4] This was put in at the insistence of Chamberlain who, several weeks earlier, had said that when the Admiralty had raised the question of the ten-year rule in 1928, the Cabinet had considered that the risk of destroying Britain's financial stability was greater than the degree of unpreparedness resulting from the adoption of the rule. In his opinion the financial position had not sufficiently improved to warrant abandoning the ten-year rule.[5]

Throughout 1932 and 1933 there was mounting pressure on the Government to take serious steps to improve the position of the

[1] Army Council, memorandum, 9 Jan. 1932. C.P. 12(32), Cab. 24/227.
[2] C.O.S., C.P. 104(32).
[3] C.P. 104(32), attached, Cab. 24/229; Cab. 23/70, Minutes 19(32)2, 23 March 1932.
[4] Cab. 23/70, Minutes 19(32)2.
[5] Cab. 23/70, Minutes 12(32)5, 10 Feb. 1932.

29

armed services. The Chief of the Imperial General Staff, Field-Marshal Lord Milne, concluded in a memorandum for the Cabinet that if German policy continued in its present trend, Germany would attack Poland when it was ready, and then turn on France. If the Disarmament Conference concluded a convention, the critical period would come after 1938, but sooner if the Conference broke down. In either case, he said, 'We ought to keep clear of entanglements and make no promises of military support to any group of Powers. An attitude of neutrality, if we remain strong, will increase greatly our weight in the Councils of Europe.'[1]

On two points—alliances and strength—this advice was questionable. It was doubtful if Britain could remain aloof from entanglements, even if she wished. Her strategic position compelled her to defend the Low Countries, which might well be the route chosen for a German invasion of France. A German attack on Poland would, theoretically at least, involve France, and if Germany then decided to take the offensive against France, Britain would be forced to declare war to prevent Germany establishing hegemony over Europe. A direct and unprovoked attack on France would bring the Locarno Treaty powers, of which Britain was one, into the conflict. The Locarno Treaty aside, Britain could not afford to avoid European entanglements; she might not have a formal alliance with France, but it is difficult to see how she could 'keep clear', as Milne suggested. A threat to France or the Low Countries was a threat to Britain, treaty or no treaty. The real question, therefore, was not what obligations Britain would accept, but how she would fulfil them in the interests of her own security.

Secondly, the strength of Britain's armed forces had to be related to potential threats. During the early 1930s, when rearmament was being discussed, war against the United States and France was ruled out from the beginning, and for some years war against Italy was held to be a remote possibility. This meant that in Europe Germany was the only major power with whom war was considered likely. Thus the basic assumption of Britain's defence policy ruled out a neutral position, and this was reinforced by the geographical determinants of strategy. It was true that Britain might try to mediate between the powers, especially where crises in central and eastern Europe threatened to involve France in conflict with Germany, but when it came to the test, Britain would back France. In this context the question of strength

[1] C.I.G.S., memorandum, 28 Oct. 1932. C.P. 362(32), Cab. 24/234.

was important, for the military contribution that Britain could make to a potential alliance largely determined the degree of control she could exert on the pre-war diplomatic front. The danger of entanglements was not so much in the entanglements themselves, as in the inability, through military and hence diplomatic weakness, to influence decisively the policies of the powers involved.

The Chiefs of Staff review of imperial defence for 1933 sounded a gloomy note. The Sino-Japanese war was spreading, and war with Japan in defence of Britain's east Asian possessions was the most immediate threat that Britain had to face. More dangerous, if still in the future, was the possibility of war with Germany. The Foreign Office had advised the Chiefs of Staff that 'the world seems indeed to have gone steadily downhill. The most flagrant case is that of Germany, which is once more manifestly becoming a public menace; the spirit of that country is worse than at any time before 1914'. The Chiefs of Staff warned that Germany was already rearming and, regardless of the outcome of the Disarmament Conference, would continue to do so to the point where she was again a formidable military power. The difference between war in Asia and war in Europe was that in the latter case Britain would become involved, not because of the need to defend any possessions there, but because of commitments entered into under various treaties and because of the need to prevent the Low Countries from being overrun.

In its review of the international situation drawn up for the guidance of the Chiefs of Staff, the Foreign Office said that 'the more the nations of Europe are convinced of our readiness to fulfil our guarantee, the less likelihood will there be that we shall be called upon to do so'. The ten-year rule, however, had rendered Britain unable to do much more than 'to provide for the internal security in the Empire and on mobilization to form an expeditionary force which can only be mobilized gradually for a campaign in undeveloped or partially developed countries in the East'. Now that Britain was facing a possible European war, she was totally unprepared to intervene on the Continent. In her present condition, the most she could do would be to provide a maximum of two divisions, whose equipment would have to be made up partially at the expense of subsequent units of the force. The Chiefs of Staff warned:

To launch so small a force into war on the continent would

be of value from the moral point of view, but most dangerous from every other aspect, since if it became involved in serious fighting we should be unable to reinforce it with adequate units and formations for many months. *One of the great lessons of the last war is that it is impossible to limit the liability once we are committed to any theatre of operations.*[1]

Here was an indication that the Army was thinking in terms of a large-scale continental commitment, for the assumption of the review was that Britain's military contribution would be a land one, with the emphasis on infantry divisions. This raised the problem of reinforcements, but that question was not yet considered in detail.

The concept of a continental strategy was put forward cautiously, since the Army knew that public opinion was completely opposed to anything resembling a repetition of 1914–18, and politicians were only too aware that defence was a difficult political issue. The Disarmament Conference had wide public support, and pacifism attracted many followers. Two instances gave the Government some indication of the strength of the pacifist feeling. On 9 February 1933, the Oxford Union passed a motion 'that this House will in no circumstances fight for its King and Country', by a majority of 275 to 153. The debate would have attracted little attention had not several senior members tried to have it removed from the record.[2] Then it assumed an importance out of all proportion, and was widely interpreted as a sign of Britain's decadence. Churchill sought to put it in perspective:[3]

> One can almost feel the curl of contempt of the manhood of all these peoples [Germany, France, Italy] when they read this message sent out by Oxford University in the name of Young England. Let me assure them it is not the last word.

A more significant indication was the East Fulham by-election of 25 October 1933, when the Conservative candidate, who advocated an increase in the strength of the armed forces, was resoundingly defeated by his Labour opponent: a Conservative

---

[1] C.O.S., 'Imperial Defence Policy: Annual Review for 1933', 12 Oct. 1933. C.P. 264(33), Cab. 24/244, emphasis added.
[2] See Christopher Hollis, *The Oxford Union* (London: Evans Brothers, 1965), p. 185.
[3] *Manchester Guardian*, 18 Feb. 1933.

majority of 14,521 was turned into a Labour majority of 4,840.[1] It has been suggested that the traditional view of the election—that it was a vote for pacifism and a condemnation of increased military expenditure—is wrong, and that the main issues were ones of domestic policies, the means test and unemployment benefits.[2] To Baldwin, however, it appeared to be a clear indication of the popular mood. The election haunted him like a 'nightmare' for the rest of his life,[3] and he later admitted, in November 1936, that the Government, which had not been given an electoral mandate for rearmament, had been forced to balance defence requirements against the education of a public opinion that had not yet awakened to the potential dangers facing Britain.[4]

The public atmosphere, therefore, was not conducive to the favourable reception of an announcement that in a future war Britain would be involved on the basis of unlimited liability. This was echoed in official circles when, in May 1933, the C.I.G.S., Field-Marshal Sir Archibald Montgomery-Massingberd, presiding over the fifth annual Haldane Lecture, said that he disagreed with 'certain critics' who argued that the Army should be organized for another big war in Europe. On the contrary, he stressed, the Army had to face its primary responsibility of 'policing the Empire', a role which ruled out wholesale mechanization, since cavalry and infantry units would be needed to operate in areas where mechanized vehicles and troops would be useless.[5]

The heart of the problem facing the War Office was that of flexibility: how to organize limited forces to enable them to undertake military operations in a wide variety of theatres against opponents of varying military sophistication. The Cardwell system of 'linked battalions' imposed a rigidity on the overall organization which inhibited the recasting of dispositions to meet changing circumstances. With the needs of the Empire having first call on the Army, the expeditionary force was made up of those units of the Home Army in excess of the number required to maintain the Cardwell system. Thus any attempt to plan for a

---

[1] Mowat, *Britain between the Wars*, p. 422.
[2] Taylor, *English History*, p. 367.
[3] Young, *Stanley Baldwin*, p. 177.
[4] 5 *Parl. Debs.* CCCXVII, 1444–5, 12 Nov. 1936. Baldwin's statement, which he made with 'appalling frankness', has been subjected to considerable misinterpretation. See R. Bassett, 'Telling the truth to the people: the myth of the Baldwin "confession" ', *Cambridge Journal*, II (Nov. 1948), 84–95; Middlemas and Barnes, *Stanley Baldwin*, pp. 746–7, 970–3.
[5] *The Times*, 29 May 1933.

continental commitment had either to scrap or radically change the Cardwell system, or to look outside the existing framework to a greatly expanded establishment. In an article entitled 'The Army of Tomorrow' in *The Times*, Liddell Hart wrote that the problem was 'how to render the Home Army more adaptable to its various functions as a strategic reserve without altogether abandoning the Cardwell system.' One solution was to reduce the numbers of troops serving in the colonies by relying more on mechanized units to patrol frontiers and undertake general policing work.[1] This, however, was anathema to military conservatives, who argued that the terrain in many colonial areas was entirely unsuited to the employment of mechanized vehicles. There was as well, perhaps, a romantic prejudice against the use of machines in the place of the cavalry and mounted infantry.[2]

The Cabinet could not ignore the serious warnings it had from the Foreign Office and the Chiefs of Staff and, on 15 November, it laid down that defence expenditure should, for the present, be governed by the requirements of, in order of priority, the defence of British interests and possessions in eastern Asia, commitments in Europe, and the defence of India. No expenditure

[1] *The Times*, 28 Aug. 1933. The article was one of a three-part series, 'The Tasks of the Army'.

[2] Examples of these attitudes, seen through hostile eyes, can be found in Liddell Hart, *Memoirs,* and Kenneth Macksey, *Armoured Crusader: A Biography of Major-General Sir Percy Hobart* (London: Hutchinson, 1967). Hobart was one of Britain's most brilliant and innovative tank commanders during the 1930s, but his ideas were too advanced for his superiors, and he was retired. Churchill rescued him from the Home Guard during World War II, and he was responsible for designing the special tanks used in the Normandy invasion, June 1944.

An amusing, though seriously intended, illustration of the cavalry fixation appeared in the *Journal of the Royal Artillery,* in the form of an article reprinted from *The Cavalry Journal* (April 1937). The author claimed that

the success of the British Regular Army in the past has been largely due to the fact that its officers have been drawn from a class brought up in an atmosphere of country, hunting, fishing, and shooting . . . . In this connection it is only necessary to name a few famous Commanders of the past such as Marlborough, Wellington, Roberts, Haig, Beatty, Allenby . . . .

In deploring the attempts of 'destructive critics' to do away with horses for the Army, the author went on:

It is surely more in the National interest to have good officers to lead our mobile arms, than no officers at all, or to be forced to accept officers of an inferior quality.

'You have been warned: the Army, the Officers, and the Horse', *Journal of the Royal Artillery*, LXIV (no. 3, 1937–8), 323–39.

was to be incurred exclusively for defence against attack by the United States, France, or Italy. Thirdly, it concluded that the Chiefs of Staff, together with representatives from the Treasury and the Foreign Office, should prepare a report with recommendations for a programme to make good Britain's worst defence deficiencies.[1] This was the origin of the Defence Requirements Sub-Committee (D.R.C.).

The chairman of the D.R.C. was Sir Maurice Hankey, secretary of the Cabinet and the C.I.D., and the other members were Sir Robert Vansittart (Permanent Head of the Foreign Office since 1930), Sir Warren Fisher (Permanent Secretary to the Treasury since 1919), Sir Ernle Chatfield (First Sea Lord), Air Marshal Sir Edward Ellington (Chief of the Air Staff), and Field-Marshal Sir Archibald Montgomery-Massingberd (C.I.G.S.). They deliberated for three months, and presented their report to the Cabinet in February 1934.[2] They painted an alarming picture of the state of Britain's defences, and recommended a massive rearmament programme.

The world-wide nature of Britain's responsibilities, both imperial and commercial, coupled with the financial impossibility of maintaining forces capable of providing security against every potential enemy, made it imperative that Britain should seek to establish friendly relations wherever practicable. For this reason, the committee attached great importance to the need for 'getting back . . . to . . . our old terms of cordiality and mutual respect with Japan', which might thereby be dissuaded from seeking closer ties with Germany.[3] While Japan's armed strength, especially in relation to Britain's eastern defence capabilities, made her the immediate danger, the committee looked upon Germany as 'the ultimate enemy against whom our "long range" defence policy must be directed'.[4] The committee took as the basis of its rearmament programme a five-year period, although it warned that certain deficiencies that had accumulated during the imposition of the ten-year rule could not be remedied within that time.[5]

[1] Cab. 23/77, Minutes 62(33)5, 15 Nov. 1933.
[2] C.I.D., Defence Requirements Sub-Committee, 'Report', 28 Feb. 1934. C.P. 64(34), Cab. 24/247. Hereafter cited as D.R.C., 'First Report'. References are to paragraph numbers.
[3] D.R.C., 'First Report', 8–9.
[4] Ibid., 11.
[5] Ibid., 14.

In examining the 'test of the German menace', the committee found that in many respects the situation was like that of 1908, when there were still many factors that were uncertain. However, it maintained that in the next war the armed forces would fulfil basically the same roles that they had in the last: the Navy would be responsible for defending Britain's sea-borne commerce and attacking the enemy's maritime communications; the Army would defend ports and naval bases, provide anti-aircraft defence, and send an expeditionary force to the Continent; while the Air Force would secure the skies, co-operate with the Army and Navy, and provide support for the expeditionary force.[1]

As regards the Army, the committee noted that although coastal defence was completely out of date, and only London had even as much as half the necessary anti-aircraft cover, by far the most important deficiency was the expeditionary force, which within six months of the outbreak of war could reach a strength of no more than six divisions. This had to be substantially upgraded,

> if this country is to be in a position to co-operate with others in securing the independence of the Low Countries. For centuries this has been regarded as vital to our safety, and it is certainly not less true to-day in view of developments in modern armaments. We have fought at regular intervals on the Continent in order to prevent any Power, strong or potentially strong at sea, from obtaining bases on the Dutch and Belgian coasts. To-day the Low Countries are even more important to us in relation to the air defence of this country. Their integrity is vital to us in order that we may obtain that depth in our defence of London which is so badly needed, and of which our geographical position will otherwise deprive us. If the Low Countries were in the hands of a hostile Power, not only would the frequency and intensity of air attacks on London be increased, but the whole of the industrial areas of the Midlands and North of England would be brought within the area of penetration of hostile air attacks.[2]

For these strong reasons the committee found it necessary to advocate that Britain should be able to put into the field within one month of the outbreak of war an expeditionary force of one

[1] D.R.C., 'First Report', 22.
[2] *Ibid.*, 25.

cavalry division, four infantry divisions, two air-defence brigades, and one tank brigade, together with full line of communication troops, all of these to be from the Regular Army. This was in contrast to the existing ability to land one Regular division within the first month. Moreover it was only to be the first contingent, with subsequent contingents to be drawn from the Territorial Army. Such a force, said the committee, if supported by appropriate air units, 'would, as a deterrent to an aggressor, exercise an influence for peace out of all proportion to its size.'[1]

Although technical advances since the war lessened the importance of 'mere numbers', an expeditionary force of the size outlined by the committee was the 'absolute minimum' which could be expected to have 'any hope of operating effectively in conjunction with Allies.' In view of Britain's varied imperial commitments and the Army's share in the defence of ports, the General Staff did not accept that it was either desirable or possible for the whole of the Army to be mechanized, with 'the infantry abolished and replaced by men in fighting machines'. Even if the Army were concerned solely with preparation for a continental war, it was 'far from certain' that a 'highly specialized "robot" army' would be the best system that could be devised.[2] In short, as was to be expected, the committee adopted a conservative approach to the role and organization of the Army.

The problems connected with the expeditionary force were twofold. First, there was the question of creating from the outset and subsequently maintaining a sufficient supply of ammunition; and second, of providing reinforcements for the first contingent, and also troops for subsequent contingents. Both of these problems had been serious ones in 1914, and they attracted considerable attention in the committee's report. It proposed to tackle the first by reducing the gap between the outbreak of war and the time when armament factories would produce ammunition in excess of expenditure, and by maintaining stocks sufficient for the first three months of military operations.[3]

It was not considered possible to withdraw infantry battalions from overseas garrisons to reinforce the expeditionary force as was done in 1914, since it was by no means certain that Russia and Japan would be friendly, and in any case the battalions were

[1] D.R.C., 'First Report', 26.
[2] Ibid., 85, 97.
[3] Ibid., 88-9.

mostly deficient in equipment and personnel. The Territorial Army, therefore, was the only source of reinforcements—at least for the first month of the war, after which, presumably, conscript troops would be available. Such was the poor state of the Regular Army, however, that the committee felt obliged to recommend that all resources be channelled into its improvement; little could be done for the moment for the Territorials beyond allocating an annual sum of £250,000 to rectify 'the more urgent deficiencies'. Further measures regarding the Territorial Army could not be undertaken until the War Office had made a full study of the situation, but the committee warned that 'large expenditure is likely to be required in a not distant future'.[1]

The committee recognized that reasons of economy had restricted the development of anti-aircraft defence. To make a beginning in remedying the lack of searchlights and guns, it proposed that, over the next five years, £1,730,000 be spent to provide adequate defence against a Germany equal in air strength to France. This, however, would leave the industrial Midlands and North of England totally devoid of protection.[2]

The Air Force was to be brought up to a strength of 52 squadrons, this being the requirement for home defence and the provision of an air contingent for the expeditionary force. In terms of numbers, this was the equivalent of 441 aircraft: 88 for the Far East, 110 for home defence, and 243 for the Fleet Air Arm, but as with anti-aircraft defence, this would not be sufficient to provide air cover for areas outside the south-east of England.[3]

In all, the committee proposed a five-year programme involving a capital expenditure of £61,174,600, plus a non-effective expenditure (for personnel and maintenance) of £71,323,580. This did not include the cost of the naval replacement programme —£72,569,000, the upgrading of the Territorial Army, or the £11,057,400 required for projects that could not be undertaken within the five-year period.[4] This huge rearmament programme was presented to the Cabinet at a time when the economic situation was still serious, although improving, and thus raised fundamental questions about government priorities and defence strategy.

[1] D.R.C., 'First Report', 94–6.
[2] Ibid., 118.
[3] Ibid., 28.
[4] See ibid., Table A1.

The D.R.C. Report was presented to the Cabinet on 8 March 1934. After the meeting, Hankey wrote to Vansittart to tell him of its reception:[1]

> I foresee a criticism against the idea that the Expeditionary Force should be equipped to go to France. After the meeting Sam Hoare [Secretary of State for India] said that what had struck him was that we were preparing for a war of exactly the same kind as the last. . . . I have warned General Dill [Director of Military Operations and Intelligence] to have his gun loaded about the Expeditionary Force. I have also spoken to Ellington who will stick up for the Report in that respect. Both lay stress on the importance of the moral effect of the Expeditionary Force and the bad moral effect of not having one to send.

Vansittart was perhaps the strongest proponent of an expeditionary force, for reasons which he explained in a letter to Dill on 12 March. To be without one, he said, 'would be equivalent to isolation', and Britain could not afford to alienate potential allies in the coming conflict with Germany. (A violent Germanophobe, Vansittart was convinced from 1933 that Germany would use force if necessary to reverse the settlement of 1919. His repeated warnings drove both Baldwin and Chamberlain to exasperation, until Chamberlain sidetracked him into a powerless position in January 1938.) 'It seems to me', he wrote to Dill, 'that those who question the necessity of an Expeditionary Force are in danger of following the will o' the wisp that led straight to 1914. We should again be written off—continentally.' It was commonly assumed that Britain could always rely on French support, but he thought that this was by no means certain. France would only support Britain if it was worth her while to do so, and that could only be assured if Britain was in a position to be of positive military value to France if war broke out with Germany:[2]

> To abandon the idea of an Expeditionary Force would lay us open to the same mockery as has always been heaped on France, i.e., that she expects people to love her for herself, whereas most people do not love her at all. De te fabula narratur. . . .

[1] Hankey to Vansittart, 8 March 1934. Cab. 21/434.
[2] Vansittart to Dill, 12 March 1934. Cab. 21/434.

This was the argument that Vansittart constantly put forward for the next four years—that if Britain hoped to have France as an ally, she had to make a sizeable military contribution to the alliance. In Vansittart's eyes, that involved a substantial *land* contribution.

When the Cabinet discussed the D.R.C. Report, it became clear that rearmament involved basic questions of policy. Sir Samuel Hoare insisted that Britain's defensive capabilities could not be discussed without considering what allies Britain might have, and Chamberlain agreed that this problem underlay the whole Report. Even more important, Hoare thought, was the assumption of the D.R.C. that Britain should prepare for war against Germany: that put Britain back in the position she had been in from 1906 to 1914, whereas he could not see that the present situation had yet reached that stage. Other Ministers argued that even if Germany was to be regarded as the ultimate potential enemy, Britain should be wary of accepting any commitment that 'would have the appearance of a military alliance with France', or that, if Britain should have conversations with the French, it should be made clear that 'any unlimited liability on . . . [Britain's] part was out of the question.'[1] The Cabinet by no means uncritically accepted the assumptions underlying the D.R.C. Report, and there was a decidedly lukewarm attitude to the French, which was recorded in the minutes taken by Hankey: 'it was generally recognized that France, by her provocative policy since the War, had done much to bring about the present situation.'[2] The Cabinet appointed a Ministerial Committee to consider the Report which, it was felt, raised questions of broad policy that had to be settled before any final decisions could be taken on rearmament, particularly on the scale envisaged by the D.R.C.

The Ministerial Committee on Defence Requirements spent considerable time discussing the question of an expeditionary force. This had been brought up by Chamberlain, who thought that the D.R.C.'s reference to the need for such a force was a 'fresh and, perhaps, a controversial point'. One of the lessons of the Great War had been that trench warfare inevitably ended in stalemate. Perhaps Britain had been correct in 1914 in preparing to send an expeditionary force to the aid of France, whose army

---

[1] Cab. 23/78, Minutes 10(34)3, 19 March 1934.
[2] Cab. 23/78, Minutes 12(34)1, 22 March 1934.

was inferior in strength to that of Germany, but the situation had changed considerably since then. France had spent huge sums of money on building defensive fortifications on her eastern frontier that were generally considered to be impregnable. The key to the problem, therefore, was Belgium. If the fortifications extended into Belgium, the German penetration would have to be by air. Why then did Britain need an expeditionary force? If Belgium's frontier with Germany was not fortified, an expeditionary force could not possibly prevent a German breakthrough. For these reasons, together with the lessons learned from 1914–18, Chamberlain thought that Britain should concentrate her efforts on building up the Navy and Air Force, and allot an extra-European role to the Army.[1]

In reply, Lord Hailsham, the Secretary of State for War, said that the fortifications had not been extended into Belgium, although the French General Staff were anxious that this should be done. It was vital for Britain that Germany be prevented from establishing submarine and air bases on the coast of the Low Countries, which would be within comparatively short range of Britain. The only way to safeguard this area was to have an expeditionary force to hold Germany back, as was done in 1914–1918. Britain had to try to establish its forward line as close to the Rhine as possible, and for this a strong expeditionary force was needed. The recommendations of the D.R.C. were not designed to create a new or bigger army, but simply to repair the deficiencies that had accumulated under the ten-year rule. The D.R.C.'s investigation had to be related to the hypothesis that Germany was the ultimate enemy against whom Britain's defensive measures had to be directed.[2]

But this, as both Simon and Chamberlain pointed out, did not answer the essential question of why it was necessary to have an expeditionary force. Simon thought that the D.R.C. had worked on the assumption, which they tended to accept automatically, that in the event of war in Europe, Britain would be involved with her land forces. Chamberlain asked for answers from the military experts on four questions that seemed to him to be fundamental to the concept of an expeditionary force:

[1] Air 8/169, Minutes of meeting of Ministerial Committee on Defence Requirements, 3 May 1934, pp. 18–20.
[2] *Ibid.*, pp. 21–7.

1. Could Britain land an Expeditionary Force on the Continent in time to prevent Germany from overrunning the Low Countries, or would the situation develop into a stalemate near the coast as in the Great War?
2. Even if Germany occupied the Low Countries and established bases there, could not Britain—assuming she had sufficient air power—make such an occupation untenable?
3. What did the French think about an Expeditionary Force from Britain? Did they want one, or would they rather have a strong air contribution, together with Britain's naval aid?
4. Would not Britain be better to contribute financially to the building of fortifications on the Belgian–German frontier?

Sir Philip Cunliffe-Lister, Secretary of State for the Colonies, asked whether the four divisions mentioned by the D.R.C. were intended to be the full extent of the expeditionary force, or whether it merely represented the initial contribution until Britain could fight at its 'full strength'. Viscount Halifax, President of the Board of Education, said that in view of the emphasis being placed on the dangers of Germany holding the Low Countries, it should be taken into consideration that the speed and range of aircraft were constantly increasing, and that consequently, before long, Germany would be able to attack Britain directly from her own territory.[1]

Hailsham struggled to reply to these queries, but there was little he could say except that the Cabinet would have to consult its military advisers. On the question of whether an expeditionary force would be able to land on the Continent, and take up defensive positions before Germany broke through, he could only reply—somewhat lamely—that that was 'the one peril which must in any event be guarded against'. He was not prepared to enter into the question of the opinion of the French on a British Expeditionary Force, whereupon Simon drew attention to a dispatch from the British Embassy in Paris, in which General Weygand was reported to have said that unfortunately there was no scheme in existence

[1] Air 8/169, Minutes of meeting of Ministerial Committee on Defence Requirements, 3 May 1934, pp. 27–9.

as there had been before the Great War to set in motion at a moment's notice. As a result, 'it would be months before the power of Great Britain could make itself felt'. J. H. Thomas, Secretary of State for the Dominions, suggested that, whatever the final decision, the Government would have to convince the public of the necessity of sending an expeditionary force to Europe.[1]

To resolve these questions, the Ministerial Committee called on the Chiefs of Staff to detail the reasons for an expeditionary force. The Chiefs of Staff produced a vigorous defence of their original proposals, asserting that if Germany were to gain control of the Low Countries, its air force would be able to deliver an initial attack fully 80 per cent stronger than if compelled to operate from bases within Germany. They did not agree that Belgium could be secured by naval and air forces alone: an expeditionary force was needed for both military and political reasons:

> Assistance on the sea and in the air will always appear to
> Continental peoples threatened by land invasion to be but
> indirect assistance. Refusal on our part to provide direct
> assistance would be interpreted by our ex-Allies as
> equivalent to abandoning them to their fate. The arrival
> of even the small forces proposed would, in the opinion
> of the Chiefs of Staff, have an incalculable moral effect out
> of all proportion to their size.

The key objection that was raised by various member of the Cabinet was still not answered directly. The Chiefs of Staff said that

> if the Belgians and French are encouraged by the
> knowledge that we are coming to their support they should
> be able to hold the Germans sufficiently long for
> reinforcements to reach them, provided that the despatch
> of those reinforcements was prompt.

Technical developments in aircraft increased the importance of defence in depth, and the extreme vulnerability of London made it all the more necessary that Germany be prevented from establishing air bases in the Low Countries. The strength of the

[1] Air 8/169, Minutes of meeting of Ministerial Committee on Defence Requirements, 3 May 1934, pp. 30–4.

French fortifications made it likely that a German attack would move through Belgium and Holland, whose territorial integrity was not as vital to France as it was to Britain. Besides, the French Army could not, unaided, guarantee the security of Belgium; British assistance, *land* assistance, was needed. Thus, the Chiefs of Staff came to the conclusion that for her own security Britain had to have available for use on the Continent an expeditionary force of five divisions, which should be the basis for further expansion according to the needs of the particular situation.[1]

Chamberlain warned the Ministerial Committee that the D.R.C. recommendations presented the Cabinet with a programme that was financially impossible to carry out. He proposed that the expenditure be cut by 30.5 per cent, but added that, even if this were done, he could give no undertaking, either for himself or for his successor as Chancellor, that the money would be found within the five-year period, or in any single year in which money was required for particular projects. He was not prepared to commit himself in advance, saying that the general economic and financial situation would have to be surveyed each year before he would allot money for rearmament.[2] Coming from the Chancellor of the Exchequer (and next Prime Minister) of a country suffering from economic depression, this promised to be a major check on the speed and extent of attempts to repair defence deficiencies, let alone an extended programme of increasing armaments on a significant scale.

Despite this reluctance on Chamberlain's part, a reluctance which the committee noted in its report, it was generally agreed that the Chiefs of Staff had presented a convincing case for the need to have an expeditionary force capable of operating on the Continent. The committee stressed that having such a force did not commit Britain to intervene in the event of a German attack, but it was necessary that the option be there for Britain to exercise. They therefore accepted the recommendations of the D.R.C, relating to an expeditionary force.[3] The problem then became one of translating these general recommendations into a politically acceptable programme.

---

[1] C.O.S., 'The position of the Low Countries: Summary of information obtained from the Chiefs of Staff Sub-Committee', Appendix II of C.P. 205(34), Cab. 24/250.
[2] Ministerial Committee on Defence Requirements, 'Report', para. 47, 31 July 1934. C.P. 205(34), Cab. 24/250.
[3] *Ibid.*, paras 13, 15.

While the Ministerial Committee was considering the D.R.C. Report, the Secretaries for War and Air and the First Lord of the Admiralty presented a memorandum to the Cabinet pointing out that the public was not aware of the dangerous weakness of Britain's defences, and arguing that, if Britain was militarily strong, she might be able to exert a more positive influence in continental circles and world affairs. The situation was so serious that the Ministers thought that the time had come when the Opposition parties should be consulted so that rearmament could be pursued on a truly national basis.[1] Subsequently the Cabinet adopted, at MacDonald's suggestion, a five-year formula for making good the defence deficiencies, after which Britain would be able to face an attack by Germany.[2]

The Government was aware that public opinion, or at least a vocal section of it, would not be receptive to the idea of an expeditionary force. Duff Cooper, Financial Secretary to the War Office, emphasized in a minute that although he agreed with the recommendations of the C.I.G.S. regarding an expeditionary force, expenditure on defensive weapons measures—i.e. anti-aircraft defence—must have first priority in government spending, for there was public unease over the state of A.A. precautions.[3]

In presenting the Army estimates in the House of Commons on 17 March, Duff Cooper played down the possibility of the British Army operating on the Continent. While it was true, he said, that Britain maintained an expeditionary force, it was not necessarily the case, as the proponents of large-scale mechanization failed to realize, that this force 'existed only to fight a war with a great civilized Power, of which the first battle would be fought on Salisbury Plain'.[4] Nobody could predict where the force would be used, and it therefore had to be capable of operating in a variety of conditions. In short, Britain required a 'balanced' army:[5]

> On Salisbury Plain or even on the fields of Flanders the tank is no doubt the most powerful weapon you can possibly use, but it is not necessarily the most powerful in the North-West Frontier, or in the swamps and ditches that surround the suburbs of Shanghai.

[1] Defence Ministers, memorandum, 20 April 1934. C.P. 113(34), Cab. 24/249.
[2] Cab. 23/79, Minutes 18(34)3, 30 April 1934.
[3] Duff Cooper, minute, 9 Feb. 1934. W.O. 32/3486.
[4] 5 *Parl. Debs.* CCLXXXVII, 601–2, 15 March 1934.
[5] *Ibid.*, 615.

Infantry units were needed to protect British interests throughout the world, and the Cardwell system made it necessary that a corresponding number of infantry units be maintained at home. Here Duff Cooper spoke of the important role of the Territorial Army as a source of reinforcements for the Regular Expeditionary Force, and added that, without it, the Government would have 'to review the whole position of . . . [its] voluntary defence scheme. If that were realised, perhaps more would be done for recruiting all over the country'.[1] Here was a threat, none too veiled, that conscription would have to be considered unless recruiting both for the Regular and Territorial armies was improved.

Duff Cooper's cautious references to a European role for the Army were commented upon by a number of members. Sir Francis Acland (Conservative), Financial Secretary to the War Office, 1908–15, asked why the Army had such a large home establishment that was 23 per cent greater than the imperial garrisons. What were these troops needed for?[2] Brigadier-General Makins (Conservative) emphasized that modern armaments made it possible to attack within a few hours of a declaration of war; the mobilization period, therefore, had to be as short as possible.[3]

In a debate on imperial defence several days later the subject of an expeditionary force came in for frequent comment. Lieutenant-Commander Bower (Conservative) said that Britain 'should never again commit itself to taking an active part in a European war', and added, 'Let us get back to our traditional policy upon which the Empire was built.'[4] Brigadier-General Nation argued that 'the great armies, with cavalry and infantry, that we saw in the Great War will never be seen in another war'. If they were, they would quickly be 'bombed out of existence'.[5] Churchill tried to put the role of the Army into the perspective of imperial defence:[6]

> The Army, of course, no longer exists as any appreciable factor in European war until after the lapse of two or three years of national effort. It is no more than a glorified

[1] 5 *Parl. Debs.* CCLXXXVII, 613, 609.
[2] *Ibid.*, 626–7.
[3] *Ibid.*, 641.
[4] *Ibid.*, 1292, 21 March 1934.
[5] *Ibid.*, 1302.
[6] *Ibid.*, 1243.

police force. . . . So far as the Army has any objective it must necessarily and naturally be the defence of the North-West frontier of India against some of the barbarous tribes which I believe lie beyond the Himalayan mountains.

It was clear, then, that the Government had to be wary of arousing public alarm, yet at the same time heed the advice of the military. That they were nervous about a reaction from the public is shown by the decision of the C.I.D. to avoid the use of the term 'Expeditionary Force' both in public and in official documents. This matter had been raised by the First Lord of the Admiralty, Sir Bolton Eyres Monsell, who said that its use would have a 'bad moral effect'.[1]

The largest single test of public opinion on armaments was sponsored by the League of Nations Union in 1934 and 1935. Millions of questionnaires were distributed to householders amid a blaze of publicity. This was the peak of 'Leagueomania', and even though the wording of the questions was such as to prompt the desired answers, the impressive voting figures—over 11.5 million, or 28 per cent of the total number of voters in Great Britain and Northern Ireland over 18—could not be dismissed as entirely worthless. The five questions asked, and the results, were:

1. Should Great Britain remain a member of the League of Nations?

Yes	No	Doubtful	Abstentions
11,090,387	355,888	10,470	102,425

2. Are you in favour of an all-round reduction in armaments by international agreement?

Yes	No	Doubtful	Abstentions
10,470,489	862,775	12,062	213,839

3. Are you in favour of an all-round abolition of national military and naval aircraft by international agreement?

Yes	No	Doubtful	Abstentions
9,533,558	1,689,786	16,976	318,845

4. Should the manufacture and sale of armaments for private profit be prohibited by international agreement?

Yes	No	Doubtful	Abstentions
10,417,329	775,415	15,076	315,345

[1] Cab. 2/6(1), Minutes of the 266th meeting of the C.I.D., 22 Nov. 1934.

5. Do you consider that, if a nation insists on attacking another, the other nations should combine to compel it to stop by (a) economic and non-military measures?

Yes	No	Doubtful	Abstentions
10,027,608	635,074	27,255	855,107

(b) if necessary, military measures?

Yes	No	Doubtful	Abstentions
6,784,368	2,351,981	40,893	2,364,441

On questions 5a and 5b the statement, 'I accept the Christian pacifist attitude', was allowed as an alternative to the answer 'Yes' or 'No'. On question 5a, 14,121 votes of this kind were recorded, and 17,482 on question 5b. The total number of votes was 11,599,165.[1] The interpretations of the Peace Ballot have differed widely. It was not a vote for out-and-out pacifism, although that undoubtedly figured largely in many voters' minds, but an endorsement of the principle of collective security under the aegis of the League of Nations. The significance of the result of question 5b cannot be entirely dismissed as simply a manifestation of 'Leagueomania', nor did the wording of the questions, loaded as it was, necessarily make 'ordinary guileless people think that, as lovers of peace they should naturally answer them all in the affirmative'.[2] If the Government wanted an indication of public opinion, it could surely not ignore the answer to question 4, which showed that at least a substantial proportion of the population would welcome the introduction of restrictions on the activities of private armament manufacturers, which Beverley Nichols had singled out for attention in his book *Cry Havoc!*[3] The Baldwin–MacDonald combination, however, was not one to take the initiative, and with Chamberlain controlling the pursestrings, the National government proceeded along at its own pace, unhurried by the pressure of events or political and public opinion.

On the basis of the D.R.C. recommendations, as modified by the Ministerial Committee, the Government initiated its rearma-

---

[1] Cited in Viscount Templewood (Rt Hon. Sir Samuel Hoare), *Nine Troubled Years* (London: Collins, 1954), p. 128.
[2] L. S. Amery (Conservative), speaking at the Annual Conference of Yorkshire Conservative Women. The Peace Ballot, he said, was part of 'an insidious and unscrupulous campaign to discredit the Government'. *The Times*, 19 Nov. 1934.
[3] Beverley Nichols, *Cry Havoc!* (London: Cape, 1933).

ment programme. The White Paper on defence, which was presented on 11 March 1935, was couched in moderate language, for the Cabinet was particularly concerned lest public alarm be aroused, especially if unduly prominent mention was made of Britain's military obligations and deficiencies relating to the fulfilment of those obligations.[1] As a sign of the seriousness of the situation and of the step which the Government was taking, MacDonald's initials appeared at the end of the statement, an unprecedented personal endorsement from a Prime Minister. In effect the Government proposed to qualify its reliance on collective security and the League of Nations by increasing Britain's military strength. The White Paper noted the deterioration of the world situation and the apparent inability of the League to restrain aggression:[2]

> Hitherto, in spite of many setbacks, public opinion in this country has tended to assume that nothing is required for the maintenance of peace except the existing international machinery, and that the older methods of defence . . . are no longer required. The force of world events, however, has shown that this assumption is premature, and that we have far to go before we can find complete security without having in the background the means of defending ourselves against attack. . . . It has been found that once action has been taken the existing international machinery for the maintenance of peace cannot be relied upon as a protection against an aggressor.

The White Paper referred to Germany's withdrawal from the Disarmament Conference in October 1933, and to Hitler's decision to leave the League of Nations, which Japan had also done. Many other nations were rearming, and the Disarmament Conference had collapsed. In these circumstances the Government could see no alternative to building up Britain's defences, not least because 'the deterrent effect [of the Locarno Treaties] on would-be aggressors . . . is being seriously threatened by the knowledge, shared by all the signatories, that our contribution, in case our obligation is clear to us, could have little decisive effect'.[3] Until war broke out in 1939, deterrence was explicitly stated to be the

[1] Cab. 23/81, Minutes 11(35)1, 25 Feb. 1935.
[2] *Parl. Papers* (*1934–35*), XIII. Cmd. 4827, 'Statement Relating to Defence', para. 4.
[3] Cmd. 4827, para. 8(2).

rationale of British rearmament. For four years, 1935–8, this was so in practice: the Government was more concerned with a 'first-line strength impressive on paper but not necessarily backed by sufficient establishments or by industrial reserves'.[1] The last year of peace was a twilight period for British defence policy, in which the threat of war was always present, unable to be ignored by a Government that was, however, not convinced that it was inevitable, or that successive acts of aggression by the fascist powers made a peaceful solution incompatible with national self-interest or esteem.

As proof of the necessity for rearmament, the White Paper drew attention to Germany's decision to rearm (1934), which threatened to 'aggravate the existing anxieties of the neighbours of Germany, and may consequently produce a situation where peace will be in peril'. This general unrest was increased by the similar rearmament of Russia, Japan, the United States, and Italy. The Government, however, took pains to make it clear that it did not want 'to make the provision for necessary defence merge into a race in armaments strength'.[2]

The debate on the White Paper in the House of Commons was led by Baldwin, who emphasized that the Government was not proposing a rapid expansion of the armed forces; rather it envisaged the reconditioning of a defence system that had been allowed to decline in efficiency. Since 1914–18, for instance, 21 infantry battalions, 61 batteries and artillery companies, 21 companies of engineers, 101 special reserve battalions, and 3 colonial battalions had been disbanded. It was only because of this

[1] M. M. Postan, *British War Production* (*History of the Second World War: United Kingdom Civil Series*, ed. W. K. Hancock. London: H.M.S.O., 1952), p. 12.

[2] Cmd. 4827, para. 12. The D.R.C. had emphasized the gravity of Britain's position by drawing attention to the expenditure on armaments of other countries, based on figures published by the League of Nations.

Increase or decrease of total defence expenditure since 1925 (per cent)

Britain	− 19.6 (to 1932–3)
U.S.S.R.	+197.0 (to 1933–4)
Japan	+110.8 (to 1934–5)*
France	+100.9 (to 1933–4)†
Germany	+ 12.3 (to 1933–4)
U.S.A.	+ 10.3 (to 1933–4)
Italy	+ 9.7 (to 1933–4)

*Excluding additional expenditure on Manchuria.
†Excluding special expenditure on frontier defences.

D.R.C., 'First Report', 156.

decrease in establishment that the Army had been able to do anything more than survive under the financial stringencies imposed by successive treasurers. Baldwin said: 'At the end of the War there were large surpluses and we have been living on these ever since.'[1] Even so, the Government did not plan any increase in the Navy or Army, apart from anti-aircraft defence. Rearmament was to be concentrated on the Air Force, which would be built up to the level proposed in the Air estimates of 1934, 'equality with any Power within striking distance'.[2]

The Opposition parties launched a furious attack on the Government, accusing it of betraying the League of Nations and precipitating an arms race which, apart from its dangerous effect on the world situation, would divert money from essential social welfare projects. Sir Herbert Samuel (Liberal) summed up the Opposition's feelings when he said: 'This White Paper and the whole policy on which it is based are an application of the old maxim "If you wish for peace, prepare for war".'[3] This was to be the reply of the Opposition, and particularly of the Labour party, to the White Papers on defence for the next four years. Labour was in a difficult position. It supported collective security and the use of military force in conjunction with the League of Nations, but when the Government declared that 'the existing international machinery' was no longer sufficient to maintain peace, Labour voted against expenditure on 'national armaments', and continued to vote thus until the outbreak of war. On a point of procedure, this was not necessarily a vote against providing the arms that Britain seemed increasingly to need; it could have been, as Labour's leader Clement Attlee later claimed,[4] a vote of no confidence in the Government's foreign policy, and Labour could justifiably say that the National government had been less than wholehearted in their support of the League machinery which they now found inadequate. Liddell Hart, who frequently advised the Shadow Cabinet throughout the 1930s on defence matters, found them, especially Hugh Dalton, fully aware and seriously responsive to Britain's defence needs.[5] They were placed in a difficult position,

[1] 5 *Parl. Debs.* CCXCI, 56.
[2] *Ibid.,* CCLXXXVI, 207–8, 8 March 1934.
[3] *Ibid.,* CCXCI, 71, 11 March 1935.
[4] Francis Williams, *A Prime Minister Remembers: the war and post-war memoirs of the Rt. Hon. Earl Attlee K.G., P.C., O.M., C.H.* (London: Heinemann, 1961), p. 18.
[5] Liddell Hart to Dalton, 7 July 1957. Liddell Hart Papers, J2.

and it can easily be seen how their tactics infuriated the Government and its supporters, when they continually demanded that Britain 'stand up to the dictators' and yet refused—or so it seemed —to approve the means of giving British foreign policy an effective military backing.

The German government reacted indignantly to the tone and substance of the White Paper. Hitler conveniently caught a chill as an excuse for postponing the visit of Simon and Anthony Eden, who had been invited to Berlin on 7 March to discuss the European situation. On 9 March foreign governments were officially informed that Germany already had an Air Force. When this announcement produced no marked reaction Hitler revealed, on 16 March, his plans to reintroduce conscription, which had been expressly forbidden Germany under the Treaty of Versailles, and to build up a 36-division army of 550,000 men.

In response to sharpening international tensions the British government had begun a programme of rearmament by early 1935 to make good the worst of the deficiencies that had accumulated under the ten-year rule. Rearmament, however, was only a part of wider strategic considerations, and these were not quickly agreed upon. The legacy of 1914–18 was a strong deterrent against an automatic acceptance of the recommendation by the Chiefs of Staff of a continental role for the Army. Financial limitations, particularly with Chamberlain as Chancellor of the Exchequer, reinforced this reluctance to commit the Army to a continental role, or even to give it the capability of operating on the Continent, for there was virtual unanimity in political and military circles that Britain should not enter into any advance commitment as she had done in 1906. For the moment, however, there was no pressing sense of urgency, and these questions continued to be discussed for several years before a firm decision was reached.

3 The debate on defence 1935-6

By the middle of 1935 the question of defence preparations had an added urgency. The deficiencies of the armed forces that had accumulated during the ten-year rule could not be made good at leisure, for the international scene was becoming increasingly tense. The League of Nations, which had failed its first test in the Far East in 1931-2, was faced with the much more difficult and dangerous question of the Italian-Ethiopian war, which threatened to rupture Anglo-Italian relations, the very situation the Defence Requirements Sub-Committee's 'First Report' had warned against. Meanwhile, Germany showed that it would continue to dismantle the Versailles Treaty until it could regain its position as a great power in Europe.

Against these external pressures were the continuing problems of economic recovery. The difficulty facing the Government was that of balance: how to strengthen the country's defences—and to what degree—without overburdening a weakened economy. Financial considerations therefore played an important part in the Cabinet's discussion of the D.R.C.'s rearmament proposals. Criticism increasingly centred on the proposed role of the Army, and the question of an expeditionary force for a continental campaign became the main point at issue between the Cabinet and its military advisers.

The Field Force Committee, which had been set up in the War Office to study the use of the expeditionary force, stated that in the first three months of a campaign, operations were more likely to be of a 'more or less mobile nature'.[1] However, General Sir John Burnett-Stuart, G.O.C.-in-C., Southern Command, told Liddell Hart that a 'Battle of the Marne' mentality prevailed in the War Office, which was still thinking in terms of the last war. In his opinion, the Army should restrict itself to an imperial

[1] Field Force Committee, 'Second Interim Report', part II, para. 13, June 1935. W.O. 32/3458.

role, and avoid the entanglements that inevitably arose when British troops landed on the Continent. The duties of an expeditionary force should be given to the Air Force which, in view of post-war technical developments, could best handle the problems involved in operations on the Continent. Burnett-Stuart said he had written a paper along these lines for the War Office, where at first it had been 'hailed with scorn', although after a time the authorities there had admitted that 'there was something in it'. The trouble was, he said, that the political masters made no effort to find out what their military advisers were really thinking. Hailsham, for example, had been at the War Office for several years, and even then had no idea of the state of things.[1]

It needed a strong Secretary of State for War to break through the conservatism of the War Office and institute fresh thinking on military problems. The Army Council rarely met in the early 1930s,[2] and the Secretary for War tended to rely upon the advice of the C.I.G.S., or such reports as the latter allowed to reach him. When Duff Cooper became Secretary of State for War after the general election and Cabinet reshuffle in October 1935, he told Liddell Hart that any Secretary for War was 'shut off from unofficial advice, and his judgment was apt to suffer thereby—it had not a broad enough basis. ... The soldiers at the top were themselves shut off.'[3]

Several weeks prior to this meeting, Liddell Hart had talked with Lieutenant-General Sir Hugh Elles, Master General of the Ordnance, who had displayed just those symptoms of blinkered vision that Duff Cooper spoke of. Liddell Hart recorded their conversation in detail.[4] Elles said that

---

[1] Liddell Hart, notes of conversation with Burnett-Stuart, 26 Aug. 1935. Liddell Hart Papers, B2/1.

[2] It met three times in 1932. Halifax, minute, 23 March 1935. W.O. 32/2561.

[3] Liddell Hart, notes of conversation with Duff Cooper, 14 Dec. 1935. Liddell Hart Papers, B2/1.

[4] Liddell Hart, notes of conversation with Elles, 22 Nov. 1935. Liddell Hart Papers, A2/2. Until the Chamberlain Papers are open for inspection, it cannot be determined how far Chamberlain was influenced by Liddell Hart's writings. By 1937, however, he was familiar with them, and wrote to congratulate Liddell Hart on *Europe in Arms*. See below, p. 102.

Brigadier-General S. E. Massey Lloyd, Chairman of the Militia Club, called for the reintroduction of the militia system as the way to recruit more infantrymen: 'No war can be won and no country defended without the infantryman—the man with the rifle and bayonet, plus the ability to use them.' Letter, *JRUSI*, LXXX (Feb. 1935, no. 517), 174–5.

although small parts of the Army would become mechanized the bulk would remain infantry of the old style—the manhood of the nation would be mobilized if war came. I said that under modern conditions such masses would be of little value, while increasing the danger of air attack. He declared—'Mass will always be.' He went on to talk of the predominance of the infantry for garrisoning the Empire, repeating—'It is the man with the bayonet you want—you'll never change that.' (Prodding me in the waistcoat frequently to emphasise his point.)

Liddell Hart countered publicly with a series of three articles in *The Times* on 'The Army To-day', arguing that, since it could not at present be predicted with any confidence that armies would regain their offensive power, it would be foolish to plan on the basis of sending an army expeditionary force into the field, especially since the necessary armaments for such a force existed only in imagination. Until it became clear that an expeditionary force was or was not a practical proposition, it would be better for Britain to delegate the old expeditionary role to the Air Force.[1]

The editorial column of the *Army Quarterly*, which tended towards the conservative viewpoint, dismissed this argument: air forces alone could not prevent the advance of a modern army, and, in any case, 'Still more difficult is it to believe that France or any other country, which happened to be our ally and to whose assistance we were going, would be satisfied with nothing more than air support in the early stages of a war.' The provision of a well-equipped, though not necessarily large, force, which was available for immediate despatch, would 'heighten the morale of our ally and . . . prove to the aggressor that Great Britain was determined to play her full share in the contest'.[2]

The debate in professional military circles over Britain's proposed military policy continued most noticeably in the *Journal of the Royal Service Institution*, which rarely published an issue without a contribution to the controversy. Major W. G. Carlton Hall threw out a direct challenge to the 'advanced thinkers' by postulating as the ideal standard an army equal in 'strength and in relative efficiency, allowing for changed conditions, to that of 1913'. It was nonsense, he wrote, to suggest that technical developments automatically decreased the size of armies; on the contrary,

[1] *The Times*, 25 Nov. 1935.
[2] *Army Quarterly*, XXXI (Jan. 1936), 201-2.

Germany would simply use armament innovations the better to equip greater numbers of soldiers, and other countries would be forced to follow suit. If Britain was to reach the 1913 standard, it was essential that the Territorial Army be reconstituted along compulsory lines, since Britain could no longer afford the fad of voluntary service, an 'insular peculiarity' that in 1914-18 had cost the country a million lives. With this sort of military force, Britain would be in a good position to defend her interests, but an 'extra margin of safety' would be hers if she had the support of reliable allies, such as France and Japan. It was necessary to understand, however, that though these two nations had in the past shown themselves willing to make alliances with Britain, they would only do so again if Britain could make a tangible military contribution to any such alliance. 'Only fools ally themselves with the weak.'[1]

Lieutenant-Colonel J. K. Dunlop (Territorial Army) replied that conscription was unsuited to Britain's needs, besides being alien to her tradition. The rate of deployment of British forces depended not only on mobilization arrangements, but on the availability of transport. What was needed was a flexible organization that would enable the Army to adapt its manpower and structure to any one of a number of theatres of war. Those who looked to conscription as the answer to the Territorial Army's weakness had 'lost their sense of proportion'. The cost of introducing conscription would be at least as great as had been estimated by Arnold Forster in 1909—£25.9 million—and a fraction of that sum would provide the Territorials with a nucleus of officers, N.C.O.s, and instructors who would form the basis of a wartime expansion in accordance with the needs of the moment.[2]

Dunlop developed further his objections to conscription in a lecture at the Royal United Service Institution on 'The Territorial Army', on 20 March 1935. Conscription, he said, provided a solution to two, and only two, military problems, neither of which faced Britain: the provision of manpower to guard a frontier, or to invade a neighbouring country. Unless conscription were applied uniformly and universally, it tended to create divisions and jealousies in the country, and particularly in the industrial sphere. The answer was to improve conditions of service, and

[1] W. G. Carlton Hall, 'British Rearmament', *JRUSI*, LXXX (Aug. 1934, no. 514), 595–9.
[2] J. K. Dunlop, letter, *JRUSI*, LXXX (Feb. 1935, no. 517), 175–6.

thus stimulate recruitment to both the Regular and Territorial Armies.[1]

The Government was confronted by the problem of how to raise the efficiency and readiness of the Territorial and Regular forces without producing alarm in the country or presenting the Opposition with an electoral issue to campaign upon. Chamberlain advised Baldwin to take the 'bold course' of appealing to the voters on a defence programme. The international situation was such that Britain had to rearm: this could neither be concealed nor postponed until after the election, and the best course, therefore, was a direct challenge to the electorate to face the realities of the situation.[2] Baldwin, however, remembered only too well the example of East Fulham, and preferred to take the safest political course. The Government emphasized its allegiance to the principles of the League of Nations, and despite the controversy over the Italian-Ethiopian war and the decision to impose sanctions on Italy, the election campaign was dull.

The outcome was a great victory for the coalition, which, although it retained the name 'National', became more and more Conservative in character. The coalition parties won 432 seats, Labour 154, and the Liberals 21. In the Cabinet reshuffle, Baldwin replaced MacDonald, long since a spent force, as Prime Minister. Simon moved into the Home Office, and Sir Samuel Hoare became Foreign Secretary. Yet even with one of the largest Parliamentary majorities in British history—over 250—Baldwin could not afford to ignore public opinion, especially when it coincided with that of Parliament. When details of an agreement between Britain and France over the Ethiopian problem were leaked to the press, the resulting furore in Britain forced Baldwin to jettison Hoare to save his government.[3] Anthony Eden, Minister without Portfolio for the League of Nations, succeeded Hoare as Foreign Secretary.

[1] J. K. Dunlop, 'The Territorial Army', *JRUSI*, LXXX (May 1935, no. 518), 308-27. The necessity of determined government action to fill the ranks of the Territorial Army was stressed in a report by its Director-General, who pointed out that its important roles—manning coastal and A.A. defences, and providing the second and subsequent contingents for the expeditionary force, made it imperative that it be brought up to strength. D.G.T.A., 'Report on the Territorial Army', Oct. 1936. W.O. 32/2679.
[2] Feiling, *Neville Chamberlain*, p. 266. Diary entry, 2 Aug. 1935.
[3] See Baldwin's comments on the reaction to the Hoare–Laval Pact in Thomas Jones, *Diary with Letters 1931–1950* (London: Oxford University Press, 1954), pp. 158–61.

The election was barely over when the Defence Requirements Sub-Committee presented its third report[1] to the Cabinet. The report drew attention to the terms of reference under which it had worked. Whereas its first report was based on the desirability of repairing Britain's worst deficiencies within a five-year period, the third report was required to present a programme 'on the assumption that by the end of the financial year 1938-9 each Service should have advanced its state of readiness to the widest necessary extent in relation to the military needs of National defence and within the limits of practicability'.[2] The international situation had seriously deteriorated since 1934. Germany continued to rearm, and her new military strength, together with the breakdown of the Stresa front (the Anglo-French-Italian solidarity declared in April 1935), attracted smaller nations into her camp. Germany was aiming at domination of Europe, and might easily succeed in eastern Europe, while Japan ruled eastern Asia. Italy had become hostile to both France and Britain over the Ethiopian war, and France was rent by internal political quarrels. Britain, therefore, could not count on any other nation for definite support, especially since her own military weakness, which had been exposed by the necessity to concentrate naval forces in the Mediterranean, undermined her value as an ally. The position had become so serious, the D.R.C. warned,[3] that:

> We consider it to be a cardinal requirement of our national and imperial security that our foreign policy should be so conducted as to avoid the possible development of a situation in which we might be confronted simultaneously with the hostility, open or veiled, of Japan in the Far East, Germany in the West, and any Power on the main line of communication between the two.

The requirements of providing for war against Germany and Japan were so great, however, that the D.R.C. could not make additional recommendations to provide against a hostile Italy, although it was the obvious threat to Britain's communications between Europe and Asia. The alternative was for Britain to make special efforts to re-establish good relations with Italy.

[1] Defence Requirements Sub-Committee, 'Third Report', 21 Nov. 1935. C. P. 26(36), Cab. 24/259. Hereafter cited as D.R.C., 'Third Report'. References are to paragraph numbers.
[2] *Ibid.*, 123.
[3] *Ibid.*, 16.

Emphasizing that its recommendations were based on a conservative estimate of what was necessary for security, the D.R.C. advised that Britain should achieve a new naval standard such that she could maintain a fleet in the Far East of full defensive capability and strong enough to deter any potential aggression, while at the same time having a force able to take part in a war against Germany in European waters, as well as adequate protection for colonial territories and sea-borne trade. The Army was to maintain imperial garrisons at their existing levels, take its due share in home defence, and provide an expeditionary force to protect Britain's vital interests and/or to operate on the Continent in co-operation with other signatories of the Treaty of Locarno, which action would include the occupation of the Low Countries in order to deny their use as an advanced air base to the enemy. The Air Force should be expanded to attain the minimum level agreed to by April 1937, i.e. 123 squadrons (or 1,512 first-line aircraft), but since this figure was based on the assumption that Germany would have 1,500 first-line aircraft—an assumption that could not be guaranteed to remain valid—the position would have to be kept under constant review. In addition, the R.A.F. should be able to provide the necessary air assistance for the expeditionary force, and build up its strength overseas, particularly in the Far East, where it should be ready to meet the requirements of war against Japan. Wartime industrial needs of the three services were to be ensured by the creation of 'shadow' industries which could be quickly switched over to war-production when necessary.[1]

The question of an expeditionary force again came in for close examination, and the report included a detailed study by the C.I.G.S. of the Army's requirements.[2] As in the first report, attention was drawn to the dangers that had arisen in 1914 because of the shortage of ammunition and especially because of the lack of any adequate reinforcements for the original commitment. The C.I.G.S. reached the conclusion that four months was the longest period for which the original expeditionary force could be left without reinforcements, which should then follow fully equipped on the scale:

[1] D.R.C., 'Third Report', 140(8).
[2] *Ibid.*, Schedule II, 'Suggested programme for meeting the deficiencies now existing in the defence services: note by the Chief of the Imperial General Staff on Army requirements.'

4 divisions four months after embarkation of the original force,
4 divisions after six months,
4 divisions after eight months.

Two Territorial divisions would be used for the air defence of Great Britain (A.D.G.B.), leaving twelve to provide reinforcements for the expeditionary force.[1] The personnel situation of the Regular Army, and even more of the Territorial Army, gave cause for alarm, for, on this projected scale, the Regular and Territorial Armies had a deficit of 46,000 and 318,000 respectively.[2] If serious preparations for the employment of an expeditionary force were to be made, therefore, it was clear that considerable attention would have to be given to the problems of providing reinforcements on a sizeable scale. The Army Council planned to encourage recruiting, but the deficit was of such proportions that nothing less than a national campaign would meet the needs of the Regular and Territorial Armies.[3]

The provision of equipment for training and mobilization for the twelve divisions of the expeditionary force would entail an expenditure over a five-year period of £26.08 million, in addition to the annual sum of £250,000 for improving the training and efficiency of the Territorial Army. The total projected expenditure for the Army over the five-year period was £146.778 million, including £13.65 million for air defence.[4]

When the report was presented to the Cabinet, Chatfield was dismayed to find that its recommendations were not apparently to be examined on their merits, but were to be subjected to detailed financial scrutiny by Lord Weir, government adviser on air rearmament. Chatfield's dismay was the greater because, as he wrote to Hankey, Weir had told him that he was reluctant to approve rearmament measures that would disrupt the normal functioning of civil industry.[5] With Chamberlain keeping such a tight rein on government expenditure, particularly on rearmament, additional pressure of this sort was certain to have a considerable influence on the Cabinet's decision.

[1] *Ibid.*, Schedule II, 13, 14.
[2] *Ibid.*, Appendix VII, 1–3.
[3] *Ibid.*, Appendix VIII, 3.
[4] *Ibid.*, Schedule II, Appendix I.
[5] Chatfield to Hankey, 4 Jan 1936. Cab. 21/422A. See W. J. Reader, *Architect of Air Power: The Life of the first Viscount Weir of Eastwood* (London: Collins, 1968), pp. 180–225.

Meanwhile Hankey was trying to show Baldwin that the Cabinet reaction to the report was of vital importance to the future of the nation. He put particular emphasis on the need for an army fit for action on the Continent, saying that 'the wrong decision today will result in a force which will neither deter war nor avert defeat'. If war came, Britain would have to be allied at least with France and Belgium, neither of which were convinced that air action alone could successfully defend against an invasion. Britain, therefore, had to have an army, not necessarily large, to contribute to the defence of Belgium, for without a land contribution from Britain, France would not go to the defence of Belgium, which would then be overrun, thus exposing the British Isles to intensified air attacks from advanced German bases in the Low Countries. If Britain lacked the ability to make a land commitment to the defence of western Europe, her potential allies, Hankey stressed, 'will feel we do not mean business'. His final appeal to Baldwin warned of the dangers of imbalance if the needs of defence were consistently and unduly subordinated to financial considerations. Unless the Government took a broad view of Britain's role, Bacon's observation (*Of Vicissitudes of Things*) would come true: 'When a war-like State grows soft and effeminate they may be sure of war. For commonly such States are grown rich in the time of their degenerating; and so the prey inviteth and their decay in valour encourageth a war.'[1]

Such sentiments would not have appealed to Chamberlain, who was gradually coming out in opposition to the D.R.C.'s recommendations on the role of the Army. He was wary of making his doubts known in case he should be accused of merely wanting 'defence on the cheap', but by the beginning of February he had come to the decision that the basic strategic question had to be squarely faced. He wrote in his diary: 'I cannot believe that the next war, if it ever comes, will be like the last one, and I believe that our resources will be more profitably employed in the air, and on the sea, than in building up great armies.'[2]

The Government had to reach a firm decision on the role of the Army, both Regular and Territorial, in a future war. Chamberlain was clearly by this stage opposed to the employment of large numbers of British troops on the Continent, preferring to rely on the traditional use of British sea-power and the new weapon

[1] Hankey, 'Memorandum for the Prime Minister', 15 Jan. 1936. Cab. 21/434.
[2] Feiling, *Neville Chamberlain*, p. 314. Diary entry, 9 Feb. 1936.

of air-power. In February he submitted a paper to the Cabinet along these lines, pointing out that all the available evidence indicated that if Germany attacked in the west, it would be in the form of a swift thrust around the line of fortifications, followed by the speedy establishment of air bases. In such circumstances, it was extremely doubtful whether a British Expeditionary Force could be landed on the Continent in time to prevent or contain a breakthrough.[1]

Halifax raised the question of the balance between Britain's forces with Liddell Hart, asking whether a proportionately greater air contribution would be preferable to a land expeditionary force. Liddell Hart explained that if it was to be of any use, the expeditionary force would have to arrive very soon after hostilities broke out, and that if it was decided to send a force, several mechanized divisions would be worth far more than large numbers of infantry. Even better, the old duties of the expeditionary force should be handed over to the Air Force, and industrial production concentrated on building up air power, which could be deployed immediately in the decisive opening stages of a war. Liddell Hart thought that Halifax, who seemed already to have doubts about the direction of policy on this vital question, agreed with his line of reasoning.[2]

Liddell Hart also discussed the problem with Duff Cooper who, far from questioning the need for a land contribution, wondered if two or four divisions would be sufficient. He foresaw difficulties if Britain limited itself to providing assistance in the air, because the French, he said, would demand troops. Liddell Hart emphasized the dangers that had arisen in the last war when Britain's expeditionary force had been attached to the French operational plan rather than going into Belgium. The result had been that Britain was tied to a futile strategy, which robbed her Army of any initiative it might have been able to take.[3]

The recommendations of the D.R.C. relating to the role of the Army were accepted by the Cabinet, with 'certain reservations' regarding the provision by the Territorial Army of reinforcements

---

[1] Chamberlain, 'Memorandum on defence co-ordination,' 11 Feb. 1936. C.P. 28(36), Cab. 24/260.
[2] Liddell Hart, notes of conversation with Halifax, 21 Jan. 1936. Liddell Hart Papers, B2/2.
[3] Liddell Hart, notes of conversation with Duff Cooper, 18 Jan. 1936. Liddell Hart Papers, B2/2.

for the expeditionary force.[1] There was little that could be done to provide modern equipment for the Territorials during the next three years, and the Government faced some political difficulty over the question of publicly announcing the nature of the role that the Territorial Army would fulfil during wartime. Territorial recruitment had long been affected by fears that when war came, Territorial units would be split up and used to make good wastage in Regular units, i.e., to act as drafts. This was a delicate problem that the Government was anxious to avoid until absolutely necessary. Shortages of equipment, and the consequent inability to announce concrete measures to improve seriously the lot of the Territorials, enabled the Government to delay final consideration of the whole question. In the meantime, the Cabinet decided to announce that if Territorial units were sent abroad as part of an expeditionary force, those units would be maintained, and not used as drafts for the Regular Army. It was also decided to stress in Parliament that the rearmament measures which the Government had agreed upon would be carried out without infringing upon social services or interference with normal industry and trade.[2]

This was done at the insistence of Chamberlain who, backed by Weir, was determined to limit rearmament expenditure to levels such that the most pressing needs of the services could be met without committing the Government to a vast programme of rearmament.

During the last few months of 1935 and the early part of 1936, there was widespread discussion in political and public circles on the question of the co-ordination of defence. There were fears that defence planning had failed to keep up with technical developments which cut across traditional service lines and made it vital that there should be close co-operation between the three services. Closely connected with this was the question of maintaining supplies in war, and having sufficient supplies ready before war broke out. It was suggested that there was no government machinery to co-ordinate the inter-connected activities of the armed forces, which were in danger of duplication and insufficient inter-service planning. The Cabinet and the C.I.D. discussed the problem at great length, and a ministerial committee appointed to consider the various proposals recommended that the traditional responsibilities

---

[1] Defence Policy and Requirements Sub-Committee, 'Report', 12 Feb. 1936. C.P. 26(36), Cab. 24/259; Cab. 23/83, Minutes 10(36)f, 25 Feb. 1936.
[2] Cab. 23/83, Minutes 13(36)2, 2 March 1936.

of the Prime Minister and the Service Ministers be retained, but more clearly defined. The Prime Minister, however, was judged to be so heavily overburdened that he could not give the necessary time to defence matters. The committee therefore proposed that a minister be appointed to act as his deputy in the C.I.D. and to co-ordinate the executive action of the Defence Policy and Requirements Committee relating to the rearmament programme.[1]

There was wide speculation that Churchill would be chosen to fill the position, but such an appointment would have been too much for Baldwin, who was continually plagued by Churchill's criticism of his handling of foreign affairs and defence. Besides, he feared that Churchill's dynamic manner would disturb the tenor of the Cabinet. Instead, he chose Sir Thomas Inskip, a somewhat ponderous lawyer, whose chief claim to fame was that he had led the campaign in Parliament in 1927–8 to oppose the revision of the Anglican Prayer Book. With one room, two secretaries, and very little executive power, Inskip set out to 'co-ordinate' defence.

A second White Paper on defence was released on 3 March 1936.[2] The Government again noted with concern the rising rearmament expenditure in Germany, Russia, and Japan, and emphasized that Italy had been on a war footing for six months. In response to these pressures, further defence increases in Britain were proposed. Two battleships, an aircraft carrier, and nineteen cruisers were to be added to the Navy, while the R.A.F. was to have its first-line home defence strength increased to 1,750, with an additional twelve squadrons distributed throughout the Empire.

The role of the Army was clearly defined:[3]

> It has to maintain garrisons overseas in various parts of the Empire, to provide the military share in Home Defence, including anti-aircraft defence and internal security, and, lastly, in time of emergency or war to provide a properly equipped force ready to proceed overseas wherever it may be wanted.

[1] Ministerial Committee, 'Report on a Ministry for Co-ordination of Defence', 20 Feb. 1936. C.P. 51(36), Cab. 24/260
[2] *Parl. Papers (1935–36)*, XVI, Cmd. 5107, 'Statement Relating to Defence'.
[3] *Ibid.*, para. 31.

To this end the Government planned to raise four new infantry battalions, about 4,000 men in all, which would 'to some extent mitigate the difficulties of . . . imperial policing duties.' It was considered 'urgently necessary' to recondition the Army's equipment, and the White Paper noted with some satisfaction that 'particular attention is being given to our Field Artillery equipments, which will be thoroughly modernised.'[1]

Limited industrial resources, however, ruled out the possibility of doing much about the sorry state of the Territorials, who would have to make do with insufficient equipment and inadequate facilities for training.[2] Thus the Government's response to the potential dangers throughout the world was a limited one, and its projected level of rearmament was planned to be achieved without discarding the 'business as usual' policy. Yet without a concerted effort to upgrade the Territorials substantially—which could not be done without significantly increasing defence expenditure and introducing controls over civil industry—the concept of an expeditionary force was not a viable one, since it was planned that the Territorials would supply the vital supporting contingents subsequent to the embarkation of the first (Regular) contingent.

Meanwhile the situation in the Mediterranean had reached a critical point, with Italy deeply embroiled in the Abyssinian invasion and the League members debating the question of oil sanctions on Italy. Hitler took advantage of the international preoccupation with the Mediterranean, and three days after the White Paper was issued, German troops marched into the demilitarized zone of the Rhineland. Britain refused to join in a plan for action against Germany, which thus scored its first major success in foreign ventures under the Nazi government.

When the Army estimates were presented later in the month, Duff Cooper, Secretary of State for War, spoke at length on the public debate over the role of the Army: whether Britain could ever again revert to its 'traditional strategy' of relying on seapower and restricting its assistance to continental allies to subsidies, refraining from any large-scale land commitments. While he recognized the serious doubts that some members entertained on this question, he assured them that the professional heads of the services were unanimous in agreeing that, despite advances in weapon technology, Britain could never discount the possibility

[1] Cmd. 5107, para. 32.
[2] *Ibid.*, para. 33.

that she would have to send an expeditionary force to the continent. The sea no longer provided a completely safe barrier, and the advent of air-power enhanced the strategic importance of the Low Countries. In answering the general question of whether it would be possible to land an expeditionary force on the Continent in time to be of use to Britain's allies, he said that the foreknowledge that such a force was to be sent would encourage a stronger defence. In any case, advances in mobility were not confined to the new arms, for 'the mobility of the infantry is being increased all the time'. There was also an important psychological consideration. If Britain was involved in war on the Continent, it would certainly be in league with allies, among whom the knowledge that 'our contribution towards such a war was to be limited solely to naval and air action ... would immediately spread a considerable feeling of despondency'.[1]

Duff Cooper's sentiments found support among several speakers. Sir Hugh Seely (Conservative) not only agreed that Britain could not rely alone on her Navy and Air Force, but argued that ultimately defence depended on the Army, 'for that is where you get the greatest number of men, who eventually win the war'.[2] This was not an argument for a highly trained mechanized force, but a mass army on the lines of 1914–18.

Leo Amery pointed out that the expeditionary force was bound to a system, i.e. Cardwell's linked battalions, that bore no relation to the present-day realities. He was not clear whether it would be possible to limit Britain's continental involvement to naval and air support, but if not, he thought that the country would have to be prepared to send 'something substantially larger than the six divisions of 1914, something less fully trained but at any rate numerically larger'.[3] The old habits of thinking, and especially of equating manpower with fire-power and mobility, were strongly entrenched.

The German reoccupation of the Rhineland weakened the defensive position of France and the Low Countries, and with the increasing fear of further German ventures, the question of closer military ties with France was raised. When the C.I.D. discussed staff conversations on 3 April, Simon emphasized the dangers

[1] 5 *Parl. Debs.* CCCIX, 2353–6, 12 March 1936.
[2] *Ibid.*, 2379.
[3] *Ibid.*, CCCIX, 2381–3.

involved, in that broad discussions could turn into a firm commitment on Britain's part. Even if the British representatives refrained from giving any definite undertakings, the expectation of assistance from Britain would cause the French to adjust their own dispositions to accommodate the British forces. Britain would again, as in 1914, find herself involved in operations she had not planned. The C.I.D. agreed that the British representatives should be empowered to discuss only technical matters, and that they should make it clear to the French and Belgian representatives that any mention of the size of a British force to be sent to the Continent should not be taken to imply that such a force would be necessarily dispatched. That was a decision which would be taken by the government of the day after considering the particular circumstances. Similarly the British representatives were advised that discussion of the size of Britain's air, naval, and land forces was outside the scope of the talks.[1]

The Government was clearly wary of becoming closely involved militarily with France and Belgium. Memories of 1914 were strong, and the talks took place in a confined atmosphere, with noticeable Cabinet reluctance. Lloyd George had voiced publicly the widespread fears in an article in the *New York American*, which was published shortly after the White Paper and Hitler's reoccupation of the Rhineland. He suggested that the British General Staff were laying plans for eventual participation in a continental war against Germany. The White Paper, he said, 'takes us back in one sudden leap to that old policy of military understandings, which proved so fatal to millions of the youth of Europe', and he warned: 'Professionals do not care to waste time, thought and energy on plans that are destined to accumulate dust in pigeon holes. They always pine for an opportunity to see them in action.' The Foreign Office commented that the article was 'pernicious stuff to deal out to the Americans'.[2]

Yet, reluctant as the Government was to countenance formal military ties with France, there was some recognition of the fact that geographical factors played at least as great a part as the prevailing political climate in determining British policy. As Orme Sargent pointed out in a Foreign Office minute, vital British interests would compel Britain to assist France in the event of an

---

[1] Cab. 2/6(1), Minutes of the 276th meeting of the C.I.D., 3 April 1936.
[2] The article, together with the Foreign Office comment, is in F.O. 371/19903. C 2967/4/18.

invasion by Germany, irrespective of the rights and wrongs of the particular circumstances. The complication lay in the fact that war would most likely break out as a result of trouble in eastern Europe, where France had extensive commitments. An automatic British guarantee to defend France had to be related, therefore, not so much to the possibility of a direct attack on France but to the need for a British *droit de regard* over French policy in eastern Europe.[1]

The Anglo-French-Belgian talks took place in London on 15 and 16 April. The British representatives were careful, both in the opening meeting and in subsequent conferences, to stress the limitations imposed by their political chiefs. General Dill referred to the large forces which Britain was maintaining in the Mediterranean in connection with the Italo-Ethiopian war: until these could be reduced, the expeditionary force would be severely limited. Secondly, equipment changes would take some time to effect, and the expeditionary force would not therefore be ready for action in the near future. The British aimed to dispatch fourteen days after mobilization a corps of two infanty divisions with the necessary supporting units.[2]

The French representative, General Schweisguth, advised the British that the French were 'well able without assistance' to defend the French border from Switzerland to Belgium, and that, 'although he would always be happy to see a British flag on French territory he would prefer to see the British troops lend assistance to the Belgians'.[3]

This was virtually the limit of the conversations. The British delegation adhered to its instructions not to commit the government to any specific course of action, although the French report noted that whereas the British military representatives had been given very little latitude by the Foreign Office, the General Staff wanted 'much closer relations than were at present permitted by a government that was very conscious of public opinion, uninformed though that was'.[4]

---

[1] Orme Sargent, minute, 16 March 1936. F.O. 371/19895. C 2967/4/18. Sargent was in the Central Department of the Foreign Office. He served as Permanent Under-Secretary of State for Foreign Affairs, 1946–9.

[2] '*Procès-verbal:* conversations held in London between the British, French, and Belgian General Staffs on the 15th and 16th April, 1936.' F.O. 371/19904. C 3422/4/18.

[3] *Ibid.*

[4] France, Ministère des Affaires Étrangères, *Documents diplomatiques français, 1932–39,* 2ᵉ serie (1936–9), II (Iᵉʳ Avril—18 Juillet 1936), (Paris: Imprimerie nationale, 1964), 97.

There were further indications that the talks had not been entirely satisfactory. The Secretary of State for Air, Viscount Swinton, told the Cabinet that it had become evident during the conversations that the French were 'much alarmed' at the poor state of Britain's military forces, and especially over the undue concentration of strength in the Mediterranean, which left western Europe relatively weak.[1] It was the general view of the Cabinet that whilst the present military distribution created problems, any significant change in the balance in favour of western Europe 'would have the worst possible effect on uninstructed opinion in this country'. Without suggesting any steps that might be taken to educate the public, the Cabinet concluded that 'the dangers from public opinion at home and abroad outweighed the very real difficulties of the Admiralty'[2] (and the other services). The Belgians were also unhappy about the state of affairs, as revealed in the conversations, at least according to Colonel Bernard Paget and Lt.-General Ronald Adam. They told Liddell Hart that the Belgian General Staff had made it plain that British troops were vital to their defence, and that they would not rest easy until a British Field Force was dispatched and landed in Belgium.[3]

The staff conversations, therefore, settled nothing: they merely raised basic questions and left them hanging in the air—to the satisfaction of no one, except perhaps Baldwin. Public opinion, however, could not be ignored, and in the latter half of 1936 the Government was forced to face up to many of the questions it had prevaricated upon for so long.

On 28 and 29 July, the Prime Minister, accompanied by Sir Thomas Inskip, received a deputation of Conservative M.P.s and peers. The group, which included Winston Churchill and Austen Chamberlain,[4] had requested a meeting to discuss serious defence

---

[1] Cab. 23/84, Minutes 31(36)4, 29 April 1936.
[2] *Ibid.*
[3] Liddell Hart, notes of conversation with Paget and Adam, 15 May 1936. Liddell Hart Papers, B2/2. Paget was a General Staff Officer at the War Office, and became Commandant of the Staff College, Camberley, in 1938. Adam was Deputy Director of Military Operations at the War Office, and served as Deputy C.I.G.S., 1938–9.
[4] The deputation consisted of: L. S. Amery (First Lord of the Admiralty, Oct. 1922–Feb. 1924; long-standing interest in defence); Austen Chamberlain (Secretary of State for Foreign Affairs, Nov. 1924–June 1929); Winston Churchill (First Lord of the Admiralty, 1910–15; Secretary of State for War, 1918–21; Chancellor of the Exchequer, 1924–9); Sir John

problems which, they felt, were not being given adequate consideration. Baldwin agreed to meet them, but, no doubt anticipating more of the criticism to which he had been exposed continuously in Parliament, he came armed with a memorandum, prepared by Hankey, on the collective responsibility of some members of the deputation for the ten-year rule. Hankey advised him, if he became irritated beyond endurance, to 'answer' the critics by pointing out their share of responsibility for the state of things.[1] How typical of Baldwin!

Discussions on the Army centred around the question of an expeditionary force.[2] Sir Edward Grigg suggested that the fear of Britain being dragged into another continental campaign because of pre-war commitments—i.e. a repetition of 1914—was the greatest single deterrent to recruiting. He would not rule out the possibility of an expeditionary force being sent to France after the outbreak of war, depending on the need and Britain's ability to maintain large military forces on top of a Navy and an Air Force, but unless the Government categorically stated that no automatic commitment existed, the recruiting situation would continue to deteriorate. Not only would the Army be further weakened, but Britain's position in Europe would be undermined:[3]

> We have got to go through an interim period of very great danger and suspense, i.e. until rearmament measures begin to take effect, and we shall have to depend during those two or three years on making the impression abroad

---

Gilmour (Secretary of State for Scotland, 1928–9); Sir Edward Grigg (long-standing interest in imperial (Governor of Kenya, 1925–31) and defence matters); Captain F. E. Guest (various Admiralty posts, 1917–18; Secretary of State for Air 1921–2); Admiral Sir Roger Keyes (distinguished naval career; retired 1931); Lieutenant-Colonel Sir Henry Moore-Brabazon (long connection with aviation); Brigadier-General Sir Henry Page Croft (member, Hertfordshire Territorial Force Association); Earl Winterton (member, Sussex Territorial Force Association; M.P. since 1904); Viscount Wolmer; Viscount Fitzalan (Viceroy of Ireland, 1921–2); Lord Lloyd (a distinguished imperial administrator); Field-Marshal Lord Milne (C.I.G.S., 1926–33); Marquess of Salisbury (Lord President of the Council, 1922–4; Lord Privy Seal 1924–9); Lord Trenchard (Marshal of the Royal Air Force; Chief of Air Staff 1918–29).

[1] Hankey, memorandum, 24 July 1936. Cab. 21/437.
[2] The full minutes of the meeting are found in D.P.M.2, 'Deputation to the Prime Minister on defence questions, July 28, 1936'. Cab. 21/437. Hereafter cited as D.P.M.2. References are to page numbers.
[3] D.P.M.2, 37–38.

throughout Europe that this country is alive to the danger and is determined to deal with it. Recruiting is really vital from that standpoint. Europe judges the spirit of a country very largely by that. I do not believe there is a single European nation that will believe this country is in earnest until men begin to come into the ranks.

At the second meeting, on 29 July, Grigg returned to the question of an expeditionary force by quoting from a confidential memorandum by the former C.I.G.S., Montgomery-Massingberd, which clearly implied that Britain was committed to sending an expeditionary force to defend the Low Countries. It was precisely this fear, Grigg emphasized again, that was holding down recruiting. Baldwin spoke firmly to reassure the deputation that, apart from the mutual obligations incurred under the Locarno Treaty (which he hoped might 'possibly come to an end in two or three months'), Britain had given no undertakings whatever regarding the dispatch of troops to France. At the same time he did not want to give a public pledge that Britain had no obligations, nor was he prepared to rule out the deployment of a British Army on the Continent once war had broken out. Churchill agreed with him, saying that France and Belgium should be under no illusions as to their responsibility—and theirs alone—to provide forces sufficient for the defence of their frontiers. At all costs Britain should avoid committing a certain number of divisions to carry out a specified role in the French plans.[1]

These objections and *caveats* were reasonable enough, but no one raised the crucial issue: given the fact that Britain was prepared to contemplate the use of troops in Europe, but without a firm and automatic commitment, to what extent could the French and Belgians rely upon, and therefore be reassured by, possible British support? To say that the French were not to be allowed to rely upon British troops to man part of their frontier defences merely begged the question, especially when staff conversations had revealed the number of divisions that Britain 'might' send. The Government tried to avoid anything approaching a commitment, and to keep its options entirely open, by taking the line that it could not discuss hypothetical situations. But staff talks automatically shifted the discussion from the realm of hypothesis to that of reality, albeit indeterminate in time.

[1] D.P.M.3, 1–3, Cab. 21/438.

The need to show potential allies and enemies that Britain 'meant business' was a theme that recurred more and more frequently in the years to come. The Government vacillated and procrastinated over rearmament and the formulation of strategic policy until, in April 1939, the international situation had deteriorated to such an extent that the demands of Britain's allies for reassurances forced the Government to take the very step it had sought to avoid.

The War Office prepared a lengthy reply to the criticisms made by the deputation.[1] The report referred to a memorandum of the Chiefs of Staff sub-committee of 8 May 1934, which stated that an expeditionary force was needed (1) for its moral effect on Britain's allies, (2) because all continental powers agreed that an army was essential if a decisive victory was to be achieved, (3) to prevent Germany establishing submarine and air bases in the Low Countries, and (4) to provide Britain with greater depth in air defence by holding Belgium and Holland.[2] Since the German General Staff would, in all probability, plan for a short war, it was likely that an intensive air attack would be launched against Britain at the same time as a bridgehead into France and/or Belgium was seized. Once the air assault against Britain had been concluded, successfully or otherwise, Germany would proceed with a land attack on France. Should the French and Belgians draw back, they would do so on divergent lines, and British troops would be needed— as in 1914—to plug the gap, for without this intervention, German forces would have an open road to the Channel ports, with all that implied for British security. In one breath the War Office deplored the fact that 'public opinion is too prone to think of the next war in terms of 1914', and then asserted: 'It may well be . . . that the intervention of the British Field Force will alone suffice, as in 1914, to turn the scale in favour of the Allies and save France from defeat.'[3] Whether Germany chose to attack France or Britain first, there was an absolute need for a British Expeditionary Force, equipped and ready to go to the Continent. Only if the Government was convinced that Germany would first launch an air attack against Britain that would eliminate her from the war could Britain dispense with an expeditionary force; and obviously no govern-

---

[1] D.P.M.2 Annex II, 'Reasons for the despatch of a Field Force to the continent in the event of a war with Germany'. References are to paragraph numbers.

[2] *Ibid.*, 1.

[3] *Ibid.*, 7.

ment could plan that on assumption. At the same time, however, the War Office emphasized—as if the point needed making again:[1]

> An engagement such as we had to France in 1914 must be avoided at all costs. Not only was the British Expeditionary Force committed to a plan of which we did not know the full implications, but we could not influence in any way the French plan of campaign.

The two-division contingent that was discussed at the staff conversations was a token force only, and therefore had to be capable of immediate and adequate reinforcement unless it was to be sacrificed—as happened to the B.E.F. in 1914. Government policy was that in the post-mobilization period the Territorial Army would be used to reinforce the expeditionary force. The War Office stressed that since the allies would need armies as well as navies and air forces, Britain could not enter a war on the basis of limited liability on land.[2]

It was possible to argue, the War Office conceded, that the most valuable part Britain could play in an allied defence effort would be to contribute a large, efficient, and well-equipped Navy and Air Force, leaving the provision of land forces to other members of the alliance. However, the demands for manpower and war material of the Navy and the Air Force were limited, thus leaving a 'residuum' free for other uses. This rested on the assumption that the whole manpower of the nation would be conscripted in time of war. Using the figures for 1918, and doubling the size of the Air Force, the War Office arrived at a residuum of about five million men, once the needs of the Navy, Air Force, and munitions industry had been satisfied. Of this number, the War Office said:[3]

> If the war is not already lost before this residuum can be brought into play, then it must be employed; there is bound to be a wide public demand that it should be employed. There is only one way in which this surplus effort can be used in the common cause—in the Army.

Even if, therefore, military reasons for a large Army and an expeditionary force were not completely convincing, public opinion, which would demand that everyone should 'do their bit',

[1] D.P.M.2, Annex II, 12.
[2] *Ibid.*, 15(d).
[3] *Ibid.*

would win the day. The War Office anticipated a huge Army—because that, it said, was what the public would want. The drain on war material, the provision of skilled military personnel to train this mass of conscripts—these adverse factors were either forgotten or ignored on the basis of a dubious reading of 'public opinion'. 'Limited liability on land' had no place in the War Office lexicon.

Meanwhile the recruiting position in the Regular Army gave cause for alarm, and the War Office warned that unless the voluntary system produced the necessary numbers, some form of compulsory military service would have to be introduced. However, it thought that if the issue was clearly presented to the public, the voluntary system would be able to satisfy the Army's needs.[1] Again, public opinion was to be the arbiter of policy.

The same deputation met a third time with Baldwin and Inskip on 23 November 1936.[2] Inskip repeated the arguments of the War Office regarding the expansion of the expeditionary force, but the deputation was not satisfied. When Inskip mentioned the Government's pledge that Territorial units would be preserved intact and not used as drafts for the Regular Army, both Lord Winterton and Lord Salisbury pointed out that there was a crucial gap in the Government's plans. Assuming that conscription was introduced after the outbreak of war, it would be at least six months before the first conscripts had completed training. During this time the Regular Army (or the expeditionary force) would be fighting, but the reserve and supplementary reserve units would, on the basis of the 1936 figures, be sufficient to make good the wastage for only five weeks. If the pledge to maintain Territorial units intact was to hold good, the Army was faced with a period of about five months during which Regular formations would be without reinforcements. How did the Government propose to solve this problem?[3]

Inskip admitted the difficulty, but was unable to detail any plans that the Government had, except to reiterate that Territorials would not be drafted as reinforcements for Regular units.[4] Captain Guest sought a reassurance that there would not be a repetition of the experience of the Great War, when the Regular

[1] D.P.M.2, Annex II, 15(e).
[2] See D.P.M.4, Cab. 21/439. References are to page numbers.
[3] Ibid., 34–8.
[4] Ibid., 37.

Army fought during 1914 and 1915 awaiting the arrival of trained conscripts.[1] Baldwin emphasized that the Government was making an intensive study of the manpower situation, and added that: 'I imagine the whole nation would have to be conscripted in one form or another—and everybody expects it.'[2] Amery suggested a system of 'voluntary conscription' to build a special reserve, but Churchill pointed out that the size of the Army that Britain could maintain was governed by the production capacity of the munitions industry: it was no good expanding the establishment if the necessary equipment was not available.[3] The discussion closed with the problem exposed but not solved. Baldwin summarized the Government's position with the comment: 'It is an extraordinarily difficult subject.'[4]

The deputation had dwelt at length on the supply of reinforcements and the associated question of recruiting. This latter problem had become increasingly severe during 1935 and 1936, to the extent that, by the beginning of 1936, the Regular Army had a deficit of 10,000 in its peace establishment. Duff Cooper presented a paper to the Cabinet, explaining that, at the existing rate of recruiting, the annual intake would fall short of the requirement by 3,352. Over a five-year period—the basis of the D.R.C. programme—the accumulated deficit would be 16,760. There was no reason to think that, under the present system, recruiting and retention figures would improve; in fact, discharge applications (on compassionate grounds or by purchase) were rising above the norm, and the desertion rate was steadily increasing. Since the Army was wholly dependent upon the voluntary system, immediate steps had to be taken to remedy the situation.[5]

The Territorial Army, which constituted the second, third, and fourth contingents of the expeditionary force postulated by the D.R.C., was in a similarly alarming situation. Requirements for a five-year period ending 31 March 1940 were 42,000 a year, but the average annual intake during the previous ten years (1926–1935) had been only 27,800.[6] The Adjutant-General, Sir Harry

[1] *Ibid.*, 38–9.
[2] *Ibid.*, 39.
[3] *Ibid.*, 40.
[4] *Ibid.*
[5] Duff Cooper, 'Recruiting for the Army', 2 April 1936. C.P. 92(36), Cab. 24/261.
[6] *Ibid.*

Knox, felt that the voluntary method would not suffice to meet the Territorial requirements, especially those of the Territorial Reserve.[1]

Any discussion of recruiting problems inevitably raised the question of conscription. The political and industrial implications of any move to introduce compulsory military service were laid squarely before the Cabinet by Ernest Brown, Minister of Labour. He referred to the D.R.C.'s recommendation regarding 'business as usual', and stressed that 'the goodwill of the Trade Unions is of the highest importance to the smooth working and the ultimate success of the scheme'. Any step in the direction of military or industrial conscription would throw the entire armament industry into chaos, which would have far more serious effects on the defence situation than would a temporary shortage of recruits. It would be shortsighted in the extreme to jeopardize the very basis of the rearmament programme for the sake of expediency.[2]

The question of conscription was disposed of—seemingly with finality—by Baldwin when, on 1 April, he pledged unequivocally in the House of Commons that the present government would not introduce conscription in peacetime.[3] When he informed the Cabinet earlier in the day of his intended announcement, there was no dissent.[4] It appeared that conscription would not become an issue, but in fact the announcement settled nothing. It was accepted, certainly by the Government, and apparently by the public, that in a future war there would be compulsory military service—once war had begun. Even when it pointed to gaps in the Government's manpower planning, the deputation did not press peacetime conscription upon Baldwin as a solution to having a trained reserve ready to reinforce the first contingent upon its despatch to the Continent.

Six months later, however, the recruiting figures had not improved, and Duff Cooper again raised the question in the Cabinet. The effect of the manpower shortage in the Army was not confined to the Army itself. The inability of the Army to attract the requisite numbers had serious implications for British policy: 'As the figures of recruitment in this country became

[1] Knox, memorandum, 30 April 1936. W.O. 32/4246.
[2] Brown, 'Defence programme: labour issues involved', 26 March 1936. C.P. 96(36), Cab. 24/261.
[3] 5 *Parl. Debs.* CCCX, 1992.
[4] Cab. 23/83, Minutes 25(36)1.

known, those nations in Europe who rely upon our support are alarmed, while those who hope that our strength is gradually decaying find grounds for encouragement.[1] For this reason it was imperative that the Government take steps to improve conditions of service, especially those relating to 'take home' pay, housing, and overseas tours of duty. In these fields, life in the Army had little, if anything, to recommend it over civilian life, and any moves to better conditions would have political benefits, both domestic, in electoral terms, and foreign, by impressing other countries with the 'determination of His Majesty's Government to make good ... deficiencies in men as well as in equipment.'[2]

In view of the gravity of the situation, it was questionable whether Britain could afford the luxury of the voluntary system, especially when every other European power not only had compulsory military service in one form or another, but was relying on such service to increase the size of their armed forces. The Government, however, had pledged itself against peacetime conscription, and it was therefore necessary to examine all other possibilities.[3]

Casting about for solutions to the problem, Duff Cooper picked out two factors for criticism: the attitude of the Ministry of Labour, and the strong pacifist sentiment in the country.

The first of these had involved him throughout 1936 in a long wrangle with Ernest Brown. The Ministry of Labour put severe restrictions on the display of recruiting posters in labour exchanges, and absolutely forbade employment officers to suggest enlistment in the armed forces to men on the dole. Duff Cooper found it difficult to understand why unemployed men could not have their attention drawn to the possibility of enlistment.[4] The danger was, as Brown pointed out, that any suggestion of military service would be interpreted as a form of indirect conscription, whereby those attending labour exchanges would be under the impression that if they did not enlist when no other suitable job was available, their unemployment benefits would be cut off. The fact that refusal to enlist did not constitute proper cause to withhold benefits was beside the point: anything, such as greater prominence for military posters or a deliberate effort to single out a military

[1] Duff Cooper, 'Recruiting for the Army', 16 Oct. 1936. C.P. 322(36), Cab. 24/265.
[2] Ibid., p. 9.
[3] Ibid., p. 3.
[4] Ibid., p. 5.

career, that tended to link enlistment with unemployment, would give the Government's political opponents an effective electoral weapon.[1]

A more serious obstacle to recruiting, Duff Cooper thought, was the prevailing attitude in the country at large. Both in the Cabinet and in public, he attacked the spread of pacifist ideas by the nonconformist churches, intellectuals, and a large section of the Labour party.[2] Yet while it was true that many advocates of pacifism and disarmament showed a remarkable ability to avoid the realities of the situation, Duff Cooper himself was often far off the mark in his criticism and appraisal of the public mood:[3]

> The great majority of young Englishmen today are not unnaturally reluctant to join the Army, and when they are informed on high intellectual and spiritual authority that sentiment that might have been mistaken for laziness or cowardice is really due to the promptings of their higher nature they are readily inclined to recognize the authenticity of such information.

The reasons for lack of interest in the Army, Liddell Hart suggested, were rather more immediate. Poor conditions of Army life were not an attractive advertisement, and the military had yet to demonstrate conclusively that they had learned the lessons of the last war. He wrote to the C.I.G.S., Field-Marshal Sir Cyril Deverell, explaining the importance of the latter:

> No-one who is so placed as I am to hear the views of all sorts and classes of people can help realising what lasting harm the memory of the Somme and Passchendaele has done to the cause of defence and the attitude of people towards it.

He told of one Territorial commander who asked his N.C.O.s why recruiting had fallen off, and got the same reply from them all: 'What can you expect, the boys now growing up are the sons of the infantry in the last war.'[4]

These sentiments were echoed by such M.P.s as L. S. Amery, who said that recruiting would be enormously improved and

---

[1] Brown, 'Recruiting for the Army and the Ministry of Labour', 30 Nov. 1936. C.P. 327(36), Cab. 24/265.
[2] See *The Times*, 24 March 1936.
[3] Duff Cooper, C.P. 322(36).
[4] Liddell Hart to Deverell, 25 Nov. 1936. Liddell Hart Papers, J2.

Britain's international position strengthened if the Government made it clear that Britain would never again be dragged into European entanglements by committing ground troops to the Continent.[1] Sir Francis Acland argued that if conscription was introduced as a result of war arising out of special alliances, then popular feeling against it 'might amount to revolution'.[2]

During 1935-6, the issues involved in the formulation of a viable defence policy began to emerge. The Locarno Treaty collapsed when German troops marched into the Rhineland in March 1936, and Anglo-French-Italian solidarity, which enjoyed a brief, if ineffective, revival at Stresa in April 1935, foundered as Italy became embroiled in war with Ethiopia. French fears of a resurgent Germany were compounded by the possibility of war on two fronts, and Britain was faced with the very situation the D.R.C. had warned against—a hostile Germany, Japan, and Italy.

This gave an added urgency to the proposals that the D.R.C. made, which, on its own reckoning, were a conservative estimate of what was needed for British security. Just at the time, however, when international developments seemed to support the D.R.C.'s plans, Chamberlain was tightening his grip on the Treasury control of expenditure, and hence of defence policy and capability. Although he had not yet enunciated his principle that finance was the 'fourth arm of defence', he was moving in that direction. The concept of limited liability on land took shape in his thinking as his strength in the Government increased. Although he was not able to reduce drastically the expenditure recommended by the D.R.C., he managed to hold back on issuing modern equipment to the Territorial Army. This indirectly delayed a full consideration of the role of the Army *vis-à-vis* the Continent, for an expeditionary force that lacked reinforcements (for the first contingent, and the second, third, and fourth contingents, drawn from the Territorial Army) was operationally impracticable.

The deputation to Baldwin and Inskip had revealed the inconclusiveness of the Government's position. Baldwin could not give definite answers to the questions on the role of the Army and how it would be fulfilled, particularly to those questions that centred on reinforcements for the first contingent, and the manning of subsequent contingents, of any expeditionary force that might be dispatched to the Continent. Given the assumption of the War

[1] *The Times*, 20 Nov. 1936.
[2] *Ibid.*, 9 July 1936.

Office that, at least in the opening stages of a future war, time, and hence speed, would be of the essence—much more so than in 1914—if Britain was to send an expeditionary force to the Continent, she could not count upon having enough time to train conscripts after the outbreak of war to act as reinforcements. There were two alternatives: either Territorials could be posted to fill gaps in Regular units, or conscription could be introduced in peacetime in order to have a pool of trained manpower available on the outbreak of war. Both of these, however, had been specifically rejected by the Government, which was pledged to maintain Territorial units intact, and not to introduce conscription in peacetime. The way out of this impasse was either to renege on one of these undertakings, or to abandon the concept of dispatching a significant expeditionary force to the Continent. It was, as Baldwin said, an 'extraordinarily difficult subject'.

4 'Will Britain fight to the last French soldier?'

Discussions on rearmament and strategic policy continued at length throughout 1936, but no firm decisions were reached, that is, apart from a general determination to avoid any agreement of the pre-war type that would involve Britain in the automatic commitment of land forces to a continental campaign. However, this determination, which had the unanimous support of the political and military hierarchy, did not necessarily mean that Britain would not send troops at any time; it merely refused to countenance an *automatic* commitment. Still less did it imply any limit on the size of a commitment the government of the day might see fit to make. These latter questions were not decided until 1937. Discussion of them revealed a fundamental difference between the Government and its military advisers.

With Baldwin continuing to show little determined interest in foreign affairs and related areas such as rearmament, Chamberlain increasingly emerged as the strong man of the Cabinet. His control of the Treasury gave him a powerful voice in the formulation of policy, the more so since the Cabinet had agreed[1] that

> the plan of defence requirements must be carried out
> without restrictions on the programmes of social services
> and that the maintenance of the general industry and trade
> of the country must be maintained: indeed it was an
> essential element in the financing of the reconditioning
> of the Services.

It would be wrong, however, to suggest that Chamberlain was preoccupied with financial considerations to the exclusion of all else. His reputation for being less than competent in the great affairs of state is perhaps well founded on the basis of his handling of the successive crises of 1938 and 1939, but in the earlier period he showed a commendable perception and willingness to question 'expert' advice.

[1] Cab. 23/83, Minutes 13(36)3, 2 March 1936.

He realized that if he disagreed with the views of the military, he might well be accused of 'advocating the cheapest way of defence, instead of the best',[1] but he felt strongly that policy should be based on the assumption that, in a future war, Britain would limit her contribution to the provision of a powerful Navy and Air Force, rather than 'building up great armies'.[2] Limited liability on land was central to his strategic thought—and to his fiscal policy.

As the discussions continued throughout 1936, he became more and more impatient with the lack of firm decisions, especially relating to the roles of the Regular and Territorial Armies. Until the Cabinet decided what these roles were to be, he could not plan with any certainty the expenditure and industrial capacity needed for the rearmament programme. His own mind was clear: the Government should scrap any ideas of a million-man army, and aim at building up four Regular divisions and one mobile division, to be maintained by drafts as needed. This should be the limit of Britain's troops for 'overseas work' (i.e. for an expeditionary force). Territorials, he was convinced, should be kept for anti-aircraft defence.[3]

The War Office disagreed. Its arguments for employing the residuum of five million men had been presented to Inskip who repeated them verbatim to the deputation on defence in November.[4] Liddell Hart had also been told of the War Office's plans by Deverell, the C.I.G.S., and Haining, Director of Military Operations and Intelligence. Haining stressed that if war broke out, Britain 'must be prepared to go all out with all the resources of the nation'. The Navy and the Air Force alone could not win a decision, and a strong Army was therefore a prerequisite of victory. In any case, he said, there would be five million men left over once the needs of the other services and industry had been satisfied, and it was unthinkable that we should not use them for the Army. The French would expect a substantial military contribution,

---

[1] Feiling, *Neville Chamberlain*, p. 313.

[2] *Ibid.*, pp. 313–14. Diary entry, 9 Feb. 1936.

[3] Feiling, *Neville Chamberlain*, p. 314. Diary entry, 25 Oct. 1936. A short diary entry cannot be conclusive, but it is interesting to note that Chamberlain showed no recognition here of the difficulty of relying on drafts to provide reinforcements—a difficulty that was discussed at length during the November meeting of the Conservative Parliamentary deputation with Baldwin and Inskip. See above, pp. 74–5.

[4] See above, pp. 72–4.

which Britain would have to provide to maintain French morale.[1]

Liddell Hart replied that this was a dubious reading of French military opinion among the officers rising to senior command—those who would be at the top when a war came. *They* much preferred Britain to provide air assistance, which was capable of immediate intervention, than to send land forces, which would undoubtedly arrive late and interfere with the French operational plans. He recorded despairingly:[2]

> It seems clear that the General Staff want a field force that can be sent across the Channel, as a preliminary to the creation of a large national army. But one cannot discover that they have any clear idea what the force can achieve, and how it can act, when it gets there. . . . The force itself has no structural plan other than a vaguely general modernising of the five Divisions we happen to have. There is no sign that they have tried to *think out* the problem of its form, use and effect—in all its implications.

The difficulty, as Liddell Hart realized, was that of reconciling the General Staff's reluctance to enter into close ties with the French with their apparent faith in their ability to land on the Continent, shortly after the outbreak of war, a force that could at once move into the field. Again there was evidence that aside from strictly military reasons, the General Staff would point to the need to satisfy French opinion, both military and public, by sending substantial numbers of ground troops.

Further pointers to the prevailing attitude in the War Office came from talking to Major-General R. H. D. Tompson, commander of the 1st Anti-Aircraft Division. He told Liddell Hart that the home-defence system was in a hopeless position, with the Greater London area having only 120 of the recommended 1,056 searchlights—little better than a 10 per cent coverage. He had pressed Duff Cooper and Deverell to remedy the situation, but they did not seem to be able to appreciate how serious it was. Liddell Hart noted[3] that Tompson

---

[1] Liddell Hart, notes of a conversation with Deverell and Haining, 12 Nov. 1936. Liddell Hart Papers, B2/2.

[2] *Ibid.*

[3] Liddell Hart, notes of a conversation with Tompson, 19 May 1936. Liddell Hart Papers, B2/2.

feels that they are disproportionately concerned with creating an Expeditionary Force, while failing to realise that the first few days of war would be crucial and that there is heavy risk of the Expeditionary Force never even starting to get abroad—if our internal arrangements are dislocated.

Liddell Hart's diagnosis was basically correct: the War Office showed little sign of having thought out all the implications of its projected policy.

It was in November that Duff Cooper openly revealed to the Cabinet the trend of War Office thinking. He asked the C.I.D. to recommend to the Cabinet that the twelve Territorial divisions should be used in the field. Britain's expeditionary force was very small, and in his opinion five Regular divisions and twelve Territorial divisions would be the *minimum* that Britain could put into the field. He said that 'he could not imagine anyone limiting the Field Force to five Regular divisions'.[1] He did not believe that limited liability was a viable policy. Chamberlain did.

There was a hint of the War Office position in a memorandum it submitted to Baldwin in connection with the defence deputation. Speaking of the rate of modernization, the memorandum said: 'We are aiming at completing the equipment of the regular forces in April 1939 and providing them by the same date with the war reserves necessary for the first contingent on a European scale of war.'[2] The clear implication was that, when circumstances permitted, the second, third, and fourth contingents of the expeditionary force would also be attuned to a 'European scale of war'.

Duff Cooper presented his proposals to the Cabinet in December.[3] He argued that 'in a war of any magnitude' Britain could not fight on the principle of limited liability, and he quoted Inskip as saying: 'Great Britain can never give up until she is safe again. That means, however much we may regret it, that we shall have

[1] Cab. 2/6(2), Minutes of the 284th meeting of the C.I.D., 19 Nov. 1936.
[2] War Office, 'Statement by a Deputation to the Prime Minister: Note by the War Office', section 4, 'The Deficiencies in Army Equipment', p. 4. 21 Nov. 1936, Cab. 21/437.
[3] Duff Cooper, 'The Role of the British Army', 3 Dec. 1936. C.P. 326(36), Cab. 24/265. See also 'The Organization, Armament, and Equipment of the Army', 4 Dec. 1936. C.P. 325(36), Cab. 24/265.

to make the maximum effort until the victory is complete.'[1] For this reason, he sought Cabinet approval for the immediate modernization of the equipment of the Territorial Army, a move that had previously been postponed because of shortage of funds and industrial capacity.[2] The Cabinet was asked to accept in principle and in practice an expeditionary force of seventeen divisions.

This provoked a firm response from Chamberlain,[3] who questioned Duff Cooper's interpretation of decisions previously reached by the Cabinet. The D.R.C., he said, had proposed a scheme whereby the first contingent of the expeditionary force—five Regular divisions—would subsequently be reinforced at intervals of four, six, and eight months by the second, third, and fourth contingents, each of four Territorial divisions. Duff Cooper, however, was now arguing that there would not be time to build up these latter contingents after the war had begun, and that consequently they had to be ready before the outbreak of war. In other words, Britain's initial commitment should not be five divisions, but seventeen. Such a reversal of policy needed the most careful consideration by the Cabinet.[4]

Putting aside the question of whether Britain had the financial and industrial capacity to build up and maintain such a force, Chamberlain suggested that the creation of a seventeen-division expeditionary force was not necessarily the best means of utilizing Britain's resources. Britain's geographical position meant that she did not have to maintain a large standing army to defend her frontiers. She therefore had the choice of diverting a much larger proportion of her defence resources into the Air Force than could continental countries. Air-power had emerged in recent years as 'a factor of first-rate, if not decisive, importance'. If the Government concentrated their efforts on building up a powerful Air Force, Britain would be correspondingly much stronger than if she increased the number of divisions she could put into the field, a number that would still be small compared with the armies of continental powers.[5]

Chamberlain saw the illogicality of Duff Cooper's reference to limited liability. He admitted that in a major war Britain could

[1] 5 *Parl. Debs.* CCCXVII, 732, 10 Nov. 1936.
[2] See above, p. 65.
[3] Chamberlain, 'The Role of the British Army', 11 Dec. 1936. C.P. 334(36), Cab. 24/265.
[4] *Ibid.*, para. 2.
[5] *Ibid.*, para. 12.

G

not hold back its resources, but he pointed out that this imposed the necessity of making the best use of those resources. The Government should prepare the country's resources in peace, so that when war came they could be most effectively used, a degree of flexibility having been built in to provide against changing circumstances.[1] Unlimited liability on land was no substitute for a rational distribution of resources.

Political factors also had to be taken into consideration. Chamberlain was prepared to admit that in certain circumstances the ability of Great Britain to land a powerful army on the Continent might have a deterrent effect, and would strengthen Britain's European influence, but the Cabinet should realize that the prevailing opinion in the country was 'strongly opposed to Continental adventures'. If war did break out, the public might be persuaded by the course of events that Britain should send substantial land forces to Europe, but 'they will be strongly suspicious of any preparation made in peace time with a view to large scale military operations on the Continent, and they will regard such preparations as likely to result in our being entangled in disputes which do not concern us'. It was debatable whether this view showed 'a sound perception of the principles upon which our foreign policy should be founded', but it was widely held, and as such could not be ignored by policy-makers.[2]

While Duff Cooper prepared an answer to Chamberlain's paper, the Foreign Office received an indication that the French were dissatisfied with Britain's military policy. On 8 December Vansittart talked with Paul Reynaud, Deputy for Paris, who was a firm anti-Nazi and an intelligent observer of military developments. Reynaud suggested that Franco-Soviet staff talks should begin, but Vansittart warned that this would give the German government a pretext for breaking off all negotiations with France, and allow them to impute all the blame for the deterioration in relations to France. This would come at a time when public opinion in Britain was steadily moving in France's favour. Reynaud agreed with Vansittart's reasoning, but stressed that France had to provide herself with the best possible military assistance in time of war. Britain's military power was 'practically non-existent'. (This evaluation provoked the marginal comment from Eden: 'What rubbish!') If France was involved in a continental war,

[1] Chamberlain, C.P. 334(36), para 13.
[2] *Ibid.*, paras. 14–16.

Britain could, on existing estimates, send only two divisions, which would be in 'nothing like the trim of 1914', and which would arrive after a considerable delay. Time was of the essence, especially since the likelihood of war was increasing. In fact, the French Embassy in Berlin thought that war would break out in 1937.[1]

When Eden read Vansittart's account, he was irritated by the reference to Britain's 'non-existent' military strength. He pointed out that Britain had the strongest navy in Europe, with a margin of superiority over the Germans that was much greater than in 1914. Within a year the R.A.F. would probably surpass the French Air Force. It was only the British Army that was much below the standard of 1914, but the Army had never been a 'formidable factor in British aid'. He concluded: 'It might do the French good to be reminded of these things.'[2]

Vansittart replied that Reynaud's comment referred only to the British Army, and that Reynaud had fully agreed with his evaluation of the strength of Britain's Navy and Air Force. He then warned Eden:[3]

> This is a fresh sign—if any were needed—that the French count, and always will count, on us for a substantial supply of *ground troops*, even if not on the same scale as in 1914–18. They don't go as far as that, but they do expect from us a 'military' contribution. . . . We shall not be able to keep on close terms with the French—and so shall drift towards isolation—unless we are able to make a real, even though reduced, 'military' effort, as well as at sea and in the air—our next task at sea will not be very formidable or exacting. Nor do the French need our fleet quite so much as they did, for they are now 40% stronger than the Germans instead of being 40% weaker as in 1914. I have a strong feeling that many of your colleagues in the Cabinet do not grasp this when they talk of limiting the role of the army in future.

Britain was in no position to dictate terms to France since, as Vansittart had already stated,[4] she would never again be strong

[1] Vansittart, notes of a conversation with Reynaud, 8 Dec. 1936. F.O. 371/19916. C 8892/4/18.
[2] Eden, note on Vansittart's minute, 8 Dec. 1936. F.O. 371/19916. C 8892/4/18.
[3] Vansittart, minute, 11 Dec. 1936. There was apparently no reply from Eden, except for the note: 'Seen by S/S, 12/12/36.' F.O. 371/19916. C 8892/4/18.
[4] Vansittart to Dill, 12 March 1934. Cab. 21/434. See above, p. 39.

enough to maintain a position of 'splendid isolation'. If the security of France and the Low Countries was vital to Britain— and British defence policy rested on the assumption that it was— Britain could not take half measures to ensure that security. Clearly there was room for argument as to the nature of British support, but that support could not be offered on a non-negotiable basis. Given the dependence of British security upon France, British policy had to be correspondingly co-ordinated with French plans. The Government did not have the range of options that ministers such as Chamberlain seemed to think.

Duff Cooper presented his reply to Chamberlain's criticism on 14 December.[1] He explained that whereas the Cabinet had decided to postpone the re-equipment of the Territorial Army because of the lack of money and industrial capacity, he now found that modernization could go ahead at once: indeed, it had to begin immediately, since the delay in deciding how the Territorials should be re-equipped was holding back the rearmament of the Regular Army. The War Office had found that it would be impracticable to maintain two levels of preparedness, i.e. between the Regular divisions of the first contingent of the expeditionary force, and the Territorial divisions that made up the second, third, and fourth contingents. The General Staff preferred to re-equip the whole Territorial Army, with the understanding that some equipment would have to be transferred to particular divisions earmarked for the expeditionary force. While the War Office agreed that the lessons of the last war were not necessarily an infallible guide to the conditions of the next, it had been the view of successive Chiefs of Staff and Secretaries of State that in the event of the most likely situation arising—an attack by Germany on France and Belgium—Britain would be required to send an expeditionary force to the Continent. Recent technological developments made it certain that the opening moves would occur more quickly than in 1914, which therefore necessitated a greater degree of preparedness.[2]

Duff Cooper then raised an even more basic question. If the Cabinet took the view that in no circumstances should Britain send land forces to the Continent, and that the possibility of such a move should be excluded from all policy-making considerations,

[1] Duff Cooper, 'The Role of the British Army', 14 Dec. 1936. C.P. 337(36), Cab. 24/265.
[2] Ibid.

the whole of Britain's military policy would have to undergo fundamental revision. However, policy had always been based on the assumption that such a possibility did exist, and there was no reason to think that the Chiefs of Staff would be prepared to discount it. Chamberlain had suggested that the 'competent authorities' should examine all possible choices, but this had already been done: the Chiefs of Staff had not reached their decision lightly. As long as the possibility of a continental campaign existed, that was the contingency towards which all strategic planning had to be directed.[1]

Duff Cooper found a ready ally in Vansittart. Upon reading the paper, Vansittart wrote a memorandum for Eden, emphasizing that vital issues of foreign policy were involved in any decision on the role of the Army. If it were to become known that Britain would limit its contribution to a continental war to a force of the size suggested by Chamberlain, the country would drift into a position of isolation, which would demand much greater armament efforts than were being sought by Duff Cooper. It was not necessary to postulate a contribution on the scale of 1914–18, but if Britain wished to retain any continental influence, it was vital that the Army be increased in size and upgraded in efficiency.[2]

The opposing arguments were discussed by the Cabinet on 16 December. Duff Cooper again deplored the delay in authorizing the re-equipment of the Territorial Army, which was affecting the Regular Army and causing unrest in the Territorial Army. He stressed the fact that the Chiefs of Staff had examined the assumptions of the continental policy a number of times, and he asked the Cabinet to approve the programme outlined in his two papers.

Chamberlain replied that the opinions of the Chiefs of Staff and successive Secretaries of State for War did not impress him; they were far from being impartial, in fact they were the interested party. There was a much larger question at issue: whether by equipping twelve Territorial divisions they would be making the best possible use of limited resources. Had the Chiefs of Staff looked at it from this much wider perspective? He then urged the Cabinet to make an entirely new appraisal of its policy of using Territorial troops for the second, third, and fourth contingents of the expeditionary force, and instead examine the possibility of

[1] Duff Cooper, C.P. 337(36).
[2] Vansittart, memorandum, 14 Dec. 1936. F.O. 371/19882. C 9094/6761/62.

relying on air power, even if that entailed an increase in the size of the Air Force. It was a matter of working from first principles: 'Our aim should be to deter war, and this might be better accomplished by increasing the Air Force than by equipping the Territorial Army.' There was a tendency to approach the question from the point of view of the last war, but this was a dangerous method. In answer to the assertion that the French might not be satisfied unless Britain sent land forces, Chamberlain replied that 'it was not for France to dictate to us the distribution of our Forces'. In his mind there was a *prima facie* case for a careful re-examination of the whole policy of a large expeditionary force.

When such basic issues were raised, no quick decision could be reached, and the Cabinet resolved to ask the Chiefs of Staff to make a further study of the role of the Army in light of the criticism that had been made.[1]

While the Chiefs of Staff were preparing their paper for the Cabinet, Vansittart continued to pressure the Secretary of State for Foreign Affairs to bring home to the Cabinet the importance of the issue at stake. The essence of his argument, which, he stressed, he had presented many times during the previous years, was that an expeditionary force was the foundation of Britain's military-diplomatic policy:

> It is eventually certain that if we were really to let the
> French know that we would do nothing more on land
> beyond the despatch of five regular divisions, their whole
> confidence in us would be shaken and they would be
> inclined to make their own terms with Germany, to which
> they are continually being solicited. . . .

Chamberlain's objection that France had no right to dictate the distribution of Britain's military forces missed the whole point of Vansittart's advice. Sea-power was no longer the prime concern that it had been in 1914, since the French were now much stronger at sea compared with the Germans, and a limited British offer, restricted to the sea and the air, was therefore of doubtful value. Vansittart warned: 'This question, if it is to be seriously pushed in the direction of restriction, may well bring us within sight of the parting of the political ways.' Britain was not strong enough, and never would be, to assume an isolationist position, yet she would be pushed into it if she persisted in offering France an alliance of

[1] Cab. 23/86, Minutes 75(36)6, 16 Dec. 1936.

limited military value.[1] The choice that the Cabinet was considering was not really a choice at all.

Meanwhile the Cabinet reviewed the political and military situation in Europe. Looking at Germany, Eden said that Britain should stand firm against the aggressive Nazi party, but always be ready to talk, especially with the more cautious and restrained elements in Germany—the Army and the Foreign Office. This delicate balancing manoeuvre would be facilitated if the Government could show that it was determined to push ahead with rearmament, and that the programme was at present in a satisfactory state. A show of resolve of this sort would have a 'steadying effect'.[2]

Indications were, however, that the rearmament programme was far from making satisfactory progress. The Director-General of Munitions Production drew attention to the grave consequences that would arise from any further postponement of a decision on the role and equipment of the Army.[3] A Cabinet committee on the armament industry noted that it was time that the Government faced the problem of wartime conscription of industry as recommended by the Royal Commission on the production of arms.[4] Another Cabinet committee, on the recruiting situation of the Army, warned that the problem had reached 'formidable' proportions, and added that 'it may be that it will prove to be insoluble by voluntary means'. However, since the Government had pledged itself against peacetime conscription, any talk of compulsory service, which would in any event be 'extremely unpopular', would be difficult to justify, unless every other step had been taken to get the necessary numbers by the voluntary system. The committee agreed with the Secretary of State for War that the Government should try to improve conditions of service, with an increase of pay being the last resort short of conscription itself. Only 'action on a large scale' would do anything to solve the problem.[5] Without a solution, Eden and the Foreign Office would look in vain for evidence that rearmament was proceeding satisfactorily.

[1] Vansittart, memorandum, 18 Dec. 1936. F.O. 371/19882. C 9096/6761/62.
[2] Cab. 23/87, Minutes 1(37)2, 13 Jan. 1937.
[3] Director-General of Munitions Productions, minute, 5 Jan. 1937. Circulated in C.P. 41(37), Cab. 24/267.
[4] Hankey (Chairman), 'Private Manufacture of and Trading in Arms: Report of an Inter-Departmental Committee on the Report of the Royal Commission', 22 Jan. 1937. C.P. 34(37), Cab. 24/267.
[5] 'Report of the Cabinet Committee on Recruiting for the Army', 14 Jan. 1937. C.P. 11(37), Cab. 24/267.

The Chiefs of Staff submitted their paper on 28 January 1937.[1] The most likely situation in a major European war, they said, would be an attack by Germany on France or Belgium, either case involving Great Britain. Whether the initial attack was launched against France, or Britain was first subjected to an intensive air attack, Britain would have to be prepared to assume an offensive role. Some critics suggested that Britain could limit that role to the sea and air, but it was not possible, in the absence of any modern campaigns, to say that air-power could defeat armies. This being the case, Britain and her allies had to be capable of deploying large land forces if they were to defeat a German army. Limited liability was therefore implicitly ruled out for military reasons. Political objections made it even more unsound:

> However strong may be the arguments in favour of such a
> course from our own standpoint, we must have regard to
> the reactions that it would cause upon our Allies. We are,
> for instance, credibly informed that the French would be
> prepared to support the Belgians with eight infantry
> divisions and one mobile division, on condition that a
> British Field Force were despatched to the Continent; and
> though it is undesirable that we should accept such a
> commitment in advance, circumstances at the time may
> well demand that we should do so. Moreover, it is probable
> that the French would press us strongly to take some share
> in the war on land.

As long as the possibility of a continental campaign existed, therefore, Britain had to be prepared to send land forces to Europe.[2] Yet the Chiefs of Staff added:[3]

> We think it is right to say that we should strongly
> deprecate the development of such a land campaign, so
> far as this country is concerned, on the scale experienced
> in 1914–18 with large national armies. It is, of course,
> impossible to dogmatize on such a matter in advance, but
> we think that our effort on land, so far as peace
> preparations are concerned, should be strictly limited to
> the Regular Field Force supported by the Territorial Army.

[1] C.O.S., 'The Role of the British Army', 28 Jan. 1937. C.P. 41(37), Cab. 24/267.
[2] *Ibid.*, paras 11–15.
[3] *Ibid.*, para. 16.

This 'strong deprecation', however, was qualified by the reference to peacetime preparations. The General Staff was still thinking of using the five-million-man residuum for the Army, and presumably they were not contemplating an inactive role for such a large force.

Once Regular troops had been committed to the Continent, the twelve divisions of the Territorial Army would be mobilized as reinforcements, this being the minimum number necessary for the reasonable support of the expeditionary force. However, the Territorial divisions would not be ready to take the field before four months had elapsed, and this delay was computed on the basis of a higher degree of preparedness than presently existed. It was vital, therefore, that the equipment of the whole of the Territorial Army be improved as Britain's industrial capacity and the demands of the other services allowed. Until the Cabinet had decided the role that the Army was to assume, the War Office could not proceed with the planning necessary to enable the Army to fulfil its appointed task. For their part, the Chiefs of Staff had no doubt that Britain needed an expeditionary force capable of swift intervention in a continental campaign. Seventeen divisions, five Regular and twelve Territorial, should be the basis of peacetime preparation.[1] This appeared to be a crushing reply to Chamberlain and the theory of limited liability.

Vansittart again added words of strong support for the Chiefs of Staff paper. Political considerations made it imperative that Britain be capable of sending substantial land forces to Europe. Britain's allies would not consider sea and air assistance alone to be effective, especially as 'no continental opinion now regards the air and sea factors as being in any way decisive'. Since France could not shoulder the entire burden of land warfare, there was the danger that, if Britain limited her role to the sea and air, both France and Belgium, particularly the latter, might, 'in certain eventualities, prefer to make the best terms they could with Germany beforehand and to leave Great Britain to face Germany alone'.[2] The logical conclusion, therefore, was that 'continental opinion' should decide the nature of Britain's defence contribution. If France and Belgium demanded a British land commitment, Britain would have to comply.

British military policy had even wider implications than the

[1] C.O.S., C.P. 41(37), paras 19–24.
[2] Vansittart, memorandum, 1 Feb. 1937. F.O. 371/30746. C 928/928/18.

defence of western Europe. The Little Entente countries of eastern Europe would resist German expansionist pressure only to the extent that they felt they could rely upon French guarantees being backed by British military power, since there was 'a general feeling [in the Little Entente] that unless France in her turn can count upon the effective collaboration of Great Britain, in the event of her finding herself in danger, she may hesitate to honour her obligations'. If Germany thus gained control through intimidation of Europe, Britain would find herself in a position of 'impotent and precarious isolation'.[1]

Political considerations aside, military reasons demanded that Britain maintain efficient land forces for deployment on the Continent. The Chiefs of Staff said that it was an open question whether or not air-power could stop armies, but Vansittart entertained no such doubts: 'No, they cannot. *Vide* Spain. The Germans are now quite convinced that the air is overrated. The Germans and Italians have learned from the Spanish experience that infantry is still the dominant factor.'

Everyone wished to avoid a repetition of the warfare of 1914–1918, but that was really beside the point. A sound perception of the basic principles of British foreign policy would more reliably keep Britain out of another war of such magnitude than would the glib advocacy of false limited-liability doctrines. Any thought of leaving the burden of the fighting on land to the French was 'most certainly out of the question, for on that basis we should have no allies'. On that premise, therefore, a four-month delay before the Territorial divisions could be deployed in the field was intolerable. The Chiefs of Staff noted that Britain might not be able to land its forces on the Continent before Belgium had been overrun, but Vansittart protested: 'We *ought* to be able to guarantee to be in time to *assist*: if we can't we shall lose our own clients. Four months is far longer now than in 1914. Time has no longer the same meaning.' Vansittart's comments foreswore the caution expressed by the Chiefs of Staff. He had no hesitation in stating categorically that the political facts of the case were 'incontestable' and that the military basis of the paper was 'elementary fact'.[2] The Chiefs of Staff had produced a 'masterly understatement' of the position, and it was up to the Foreign

---

[1] F.O. 371/20746. C 928/928/18.
[2] F.O. 371/20746. C 928/928/18 contains a copy of C.P. 41(37) with extensive handwritten comments by Vansittart.

Office to give them the necessary support.[1] Vansittart's paper was submitted to Eden for use in the Cabinet when the question of the role of the Army was raised again.

The political importance of a British land contribution was also emphasized in a minute by Orme Sargent, who wrote that the staff conversations of April 1936 were 'merely eyewash, since our representatives were only allowed to dole out information and not exchange plans'. The Chiefs of Staff were understandably reluctant to continue the staff talks to cover joint plans involving predetermined commitments, especially where such discussions centred on the role of the Army, which was in no condition to accept any obligations. Conditions had changed, however, and Britain had to be prepared to outbid Hitler by offering Belgium a guarantee backed up by meaningful staff conversations which would have the effect of 'giving to Belgium that sense of security which she at present lacks, without the feeling of humiliating dependence on France, from which she has hitherto suffered'.[2] Between them, the service chiefs and the Foreign Office appeared to exert irresistible pressure on the Cabinet.

In February 1937 Baldwin made one of his last public statements on defence. Since the abdication crisis of December 1936 he had left the bulk of the work on rearmament to Inskip and Chamberlain, a delegation of responsibility that had prompted Chamberlain to record in his diary: '. . . another case of my doing the P.M.'s work, but as he won't or can't do it himself, someone must do it for him.'[3] By the beginning of 1937 Baldwin was merely waiting for George VI to be crowned before he retired from public life. In the Defence Loans debate in February, Baldwin justified the Government's proposal to borrow £1,500 millions for rearmament by saying:[4]

> With all this planned increase in expenditure . . . there is
> no thought and no intention of aggression by this country.
> We want to put ourselves in a position to deter aggression.
> Deterrence is our object, and if you believe that deterrence
> possible you will believe that ineffective deterrence is
> worse than useless.

[1] Vansittart, memorandum, 1 Feb. 1937. F.O. 371/20746. C 928/928/18.
[2] Orme Sargent, minute, 30 Jan. 1937. F.O. 371/20738. C 1142/271/18.
[3] Quoted in Iain Macleod, *Neville Chamberlain*, p. 194.
[4] 5 *Parl. Debs.* CCCXX, 1508, 18 Feb. 1937.

The White Paper on defence released in connection with the Defence Loans debate outlined a further acceleration of the rearmament programme. As in previous years, the greater share of expenditure was allotted to the Navy and the Air Force. The Army, admittedly small in comparison with continental forces, would be strengthened by two tank battalions, and greater emphasis would be placed on mechanization.[1] These statements had a reassuring air about them; they gave the appearance that the Government was making marked progress in its efforts to improve the efficiency of the armed forces. The real position, however, was far from impressive or reassuring.

Inskip informed the Cabinet that in the event of war, either in Europe or the Middle East, Britain could dispatch a maximum of two divisions together with ancillary units. This force *could* have one battalion of light tanks, but in May 1937 it would be deficient in equipment to the order of: infantry tanks—100 per cent; mortars—25 per cent; Bren guns—100 per cent; anti-tank rifles—75 per cent; and anti-tank guns (2-pounders)—80 per cent. The tank situation was serious for, apart from light tanks, no tanks were on order because designs had not been finalized, pending decisions on the deployment of the Army.[2] The Chiefs of Staff added further details. There was also a deficiency of all kinds of ammunition, and the two divisions that Inskip mentioned could only be mobilized by drawing on the personnel and equipment of the other Regular units in the United Kingdom. The twelve Territorial divisions that would make up subsequent contingents of the expeditionary force were under strength, had no modern equipment, and would lack war reserves of many kinds.[3] Military forces of this order added up to an effective deterrent that was 'worse than useless'.

The Cabinet continued to discuss the role of the Army in April. With Baldwin on the brink of retirement, Chamberlain, his successor as Prime Minister and firm controller of government expenditure, was in a powerful position to urge his views on his colleagues. He warned the Cabinet that the time was rapidly coming when the Treasury would have to impose an absolute ceiling on

[1] *Parl. Papers (1936–37)*, XVII, Cmd. 5374. 'Statement Relating to Defence Expenditure.'
[2] Inskip, 'Progress in Defence Requirements', 2 Feb. 1937. C.P. 40(37), Cab. 24/267.
[3] C.O.S., 'Comparison of the Strength of Great Britain with certain other Nations as at May, 1937', 9 Feb. 1937. Appendix II. C.P. 58(37), Cab. 24/267.

defence expenditure. The financial question was so important that strategic policy would have to be considered from the military, financial, and manpower point of view. There could not be an unlimited build-up of the services without serious disruption to industry, which was the very basis of British prosperity and security.[1]

Sir Thomas Inskip stressed that it was not a viable policy to contemplate an expeditionary force of four divisions without simultaneously making provision for reinforcements. If the expeditionary force was dispatched to the Continent at the outbreak of war without substantial reserves being in existence, a considerable delay would elapse before any Territorial divisions would be ready for deployment in the field, especially since the Air Force would draw heavily on war industry after the commencement of hostilities. Inskip suggested—it was really a false alternative[2]—that the Government could dispatch the five Regular divisions on the understanding that they constituted the total British commitment and would not be reinforced. If, however, reinforcements were to be sent, then the War Office insisted that four Territorial divisions was the minimum number that was practicable. At this point Inskip disagreed with the Chiefs of Staff on the grounds that their proposals to equip the Territorial Army so that it would be ready for war after four months would impose too heavy a burden on the country's finances and industry. He thought it would be enough to fully equip the Regular Army and the two Territorial anti-aircraft divisions, while giving the rest of the Territorial units sufficient equipment to enable them to follow the same training procedures as the Regular Army. If this were done, one or more Territorial divisions would be ready to join the expeditionary force after four months.[3]

Duff Cooper said the problem confronting the Cabinet was not the role of the Regular Army—that was settled—but that of the Territorial Army. At present the War Office was restricted to providing training equipment for the Territorials, but that policy severely handicapped the Army and could not be allowed to continue. It would be better to decide how many Territorial divisions should be dispatched to the field after a certain period,

---

[1] Cab. 23/88, Minutes 19(37)5, 28 April 1937.
[2] The Chiefs of Staff had long maintained that once British troops were committed to a continental campaign, there could be no limited liability. See above, chap. 2.
[3] Cab. 23/88, Minutes 19(37)5.

and plan on that basis. The Chiefs of Staff were adamant that the minimum was four divisions after four months.[1]

Chamberlain returned to the attack on 5 May. He disagreed with Duff Cooper's implication that the Cabinet was simply considering a military question, on which they should accept the advice of the Chiefs of Staff: 'he himself definitely did challenge the policy of their professional military advisers.' When the country was faced with maintaining a large navy, a strong air force—a new arm in defence—it was wrong to assume automatically that Britain should also have a continental army, especially when demands on the armament industry would be so heavy—from Britain's allies as well as her own forces.[2]

> He did not believe that we could, or ought, or, in the event, *would be allowed by the country*, to enter a Continental war with the intention of fighting on the same lines as in the last. We ought to make up our minds to something different. Our contribution on land should be on a limited scale.
> It was wrong to assume that the next war would be fought by ourselves alone against Germany. *If we had to fight we should have allies, who must in any event maintain large armies.*

This latter assumption—that in any war against Germany, Britain would necessarily have strong allies—was precisely that which Vansittart had so consistently criticized: Britain could not expect others to love her, and therefore fight for her, simply because she was Britain.[3] Chamberlain had either missed the point, or dismissed it as untrue. In any case, British public opinion must prevail over allied opinion—military and public. In place of a hasty decision, he proposed the examination, 'in comparative leisure, of the proper role of the Army in the light of other considerations'.[4] This despite the fact that the War Office and the Foreign Office had warned of the grave consequences of delay in reaching a decision on the Army.[5]

So strong was Chamberlain's objection to the proposals of the Chiefs of Staff that he virtually won the day. The Cabinet agreed

[1] Cab. 23/88, Minutes 20(37)4, 5 May 1937.
[2] *Ibid.*
[3] See above, p. 39.
[4] Cab. 23/88, Minutes 20(37)4.
[5] *Ibid.*

that the Regular Army and the Territorial anti-aircraft divisions should be provided with 'the most complete and efficient equipment with the necessary war reserves'. This section of the rearmament programme was to be completed if possible by April 1940, but Chamberlain reserved the right to change the schedule according to the financial situation. The remainder of the Territorial Army was to be given equipment of the same type sufficient to enable all twelve divisions 'to be trained in peace'. The Defence Plans (Policy) Committee of the Cabinet was made responsible for reviewing the debate on the role of the Army.

In effect Chamberlain won a delaying action. The Cabinet did not explicitly accept his theory of limited liability, but neither did it settle the crucial issue of reinforcements for the Regular Army. Were the five Regular divisions to be the extent of Britain's commitment to the Continent—a policy that Duff Cooper, Vansittart, and the Chiefs of Staff firmly rejected—or would they be reinforced? If so, by how much, and when? The extent and timing of the reinforcement of the first contingent dictated the role of the Territorial Army in war, and therefore the preparations that would have to be made in peace to enable it to fulfil that role. Alternatively, it pointed to the training of a large pool of manpower—from sources outside the Territorial Army—that could provide reinforcements for the first (Regular) contingent. The third possibility was that proposed by Chamberlain: a limited commitment on land, with the bulk of Britain's effort going into a naval and air contribution. These questions continued to be debated throughout 1937.

5   Limited liability 1937

On 28 May 1937 Neville Chamberlain succeeded Baldwin as Prime Minister. The Government continued to call itself 'National' although by this time there was nothing to distinguish the non-Conservative members from the rest. Sir John Simon became Chancellor of the Exchequer, and Sir Samuel Hoare was brought back into the ministerial ranks and installed in the Home Office. Anthony Eden remained in the Foreign Office, while Duff Cooper was moved to the Admiralty. The only new appointment of any interest was that of Leslie Hore-Belisha as Secretary of State for War. It did not quite fit the image of the Government— an image that was administratively efficient, but stolid and unimaginative.

Leslie Hore-Belisha had been only nine months old when his father died, and not until he was in his teens did his mother get married again, to a distinguished civil servant, Adair Hore, who was later knighted. Lady Hore took the name of her husband, but her son added his step-father's name to his own, thus Hore-Belisha. He was deeply attached to his mother, surrounding himself with countless portraits of her after she died in 1936; he did not marry until late in life, in 1944. He was educated at Clifton College, the Sorbonne, and Heidelberg. When war broke out in 1914 he was studying at St John's College, Oxford. He immediately joined the Army, and after three months' training, was granted a commission in the Royal Army Service Corps. He was promoted to captain in the autumn of 1915, and he served in France for two years. In 1917 he was transferred to General Milne's headquarters in Greece, and sent on missions to Egypt and Cyprus. This brought him promotion to major, mention in dispatches, and malaria, which caused him to be invalided back to England. After the war Hore-Belisha returned to Oxford, where he neglected his studies in favour of the Oxford Union, the Archery Club, an intense interest in athletics, and a social life that was active and extravagant. Despite this, he was admitted to the Bar in 1922.

He first stood for Parliament as a Liberal in 1923, and the following year, in the general election of October, successfully opposed a Conservative M.P. of thirteen years' standing, and was elected Member for Devonport. The same year he began writing for the Beaverbrook papers, the *Evening Standard*, the *Daily Express* and the *Sunday Express*. This association lasted six years, and gave him a keen insight into the methods of Fleet Street and the value of good public relations.

In 1931 he was made Parliamentary Secretary to the Board of Trade, and a year later he was moved to the Treasury, where he became Financial Secretary. This brought him to the notice of Chamberlain, who was impressed with his ability to tackle problems at the root cause, and he became very much a 'Chamberlain man'. In 1934 he was appointed Minister of Transport. It was there that he developed his imaginative ability and drew upon his Fleet Street experience to reduce the rate of road accidents. His flamboyant methods—as in the case of his famous 'Belisha beacons'—produced results, and Hore-Belisha became known as a man who got things done. His achievements, however, were not without cost. He was often insensitive towards those he worked with, and he undoubtedly aroused hostility in public circles, where many considered him vulgar and ambitious, and where the fact that he was Jewish did not help him. Inevitably, both the man and the causes he espoused suffered.[1]

At forty-four Hore-Belisha was one of the youngest men ever to be Secretary of State for War, and he was one of the few members of the Cabinet to have served in Britain's military forces in wartime. Chamberlain chose Hore-Belisha as a man of action. He told him that he wanted to see 'drastic changes', adding that 'the obstinacy of some of the Army heads in sticking to obsolete methods is incredible'.[2] He went on to encourage Hore-Belisha to keep him well informed of what his department was doing and what it intended to do: he had no intention of letting things drift as Baldwin had done.[3]

During the first nine months of his new appointment, Hore-Belisha worked closely with Liddell Hart as his unofficial adviser. Liddell Hart had long had access to the War Office, and Duff Cooper told him that 'a Secretary of State was shut off from

---

[1] The material for this biographical sketch is drawn from R. J. Minney, *The Private Papers of Hore-Belisha* (London: Collins, 1960), pp. 13–30. Additional information was provided by Sir Basil Liddell Hart in conversations with the author.

[2] Quoted in Liddell Hart, *Memoirs*, II, 2.

[3] Minney, *Hore-Belisha*, p. 16.

unofficial advice and his judgment was apt to suffer thereby'.[1] Chamberlain was familiar with Liddell Hart's books, and in March 1937 wrote to congratulate him on *Europe in Arms,* with the comment: 'I am quite sure we shall never again send to the Continent an Army on the scale of that which we put into the field in the Great War.'[2] When Hore-Belisha became Secretary for War, Duff Cooper introduced him to Liddell Hart, who showed him a copy of a paper he had written at the request of Sir Thomas Inskip. Inskip had asked him to give particular attention to the role of the Army in imperial defence, since this, rather than a large-scale continental involvement, would be the policy of the Chamberlain government.[3]

Within weeks of becoming Secretary for War, Hore-Belisha had embarked on an intensive study of the problems confronting the Army. Foremost among these was the difficulty in attracting sufficient recruits, a problem that had received considerable attention both from the War Office and the Cabinet for several years past. By the beginning of August he was ready to announce the first steps of his plans to improve conditions of service: serving soldiers would be allowed to extend their service after completing the normal seven years, and men in the reserve for five years following their service could rejoin the Regular Army. The response was immediate and gratifying: within two weeks, over three thousand reservists had signed up.[4]

Yet on other, perhaps more substantial, issues, Hore-Belisha met firm opposition. The debate on the role of the Army had not progressed since May, but it was clear that the Cabinet was moving towards complete acceptance of Chamberlain's ideas. After one meeting of the Cabinet, Hore-Belisha recorded his disappointment in his diary:[5]

> My proposal for the provision of war equipment, war reserves and maintenance for four Territorial divisions was turned down today. . . . At some time a decision will have to be made that some of the T.A. divisions will have to be fully equipped, and there are many reasons why it would be advantageous to make a decision now. . . . I

[1] Quoted in Liddell Hart, *Memoirs,* I, 300.
[2] *Ibid.,* 386.
[3] *Ibid.,* II, 2–3.
[4] Minney, *Hore-Belisha,* pp. 42–3.
[5] *Ibid.,* p. 35. Diary entry, 13 July 1937.

argued with Simon, but he was quite firm that at present there should be no increase in the cost of the Army's programme.

Simon, in fact, had argued in the Cabinet that the Government had to impose an absolute ceiling on defence expenditure. On the assumption that existing high rates of taxation and economic expansion were maintained, he estimated that for the five years 1937–42 the Government could allot £1,100 million for the armed forces, with an additional £400 million being raised under the Defence Loans Act. But whereas the White Paper issued on February 16[1] had spoken of £1,500 million as the minimum to be made available, Simon now asserted that this figure had to be regarded as the maximum.[2] Hore-Belisha pointed out to the Army Council that if a rationing system were introduced covering defence expenditure, the Council would be obliged to see that 'only schemes of the highest priority were put forward'.[3] The imposition of a ceiling was a further move to restrict the role of the Army, and now that Chamberlain was Prime Minister, he could show just how little weight the opinions of the Chiefs of Staff carried with him.

Basic to the question of a continental commitment—or lack of one—was the manpower issue. As the rearmament programme was stepped up, greater attention was paid to the problem of mobilizing the resources of the nation in time of war. The Chiefs of Staff had continually stressed that in a future war the time factor would be of the utmost importance: victory might well come to the side that was best prepared. For this reason it was essential that mobilization take place as quickly as possible and that the industrial capacity of the country be immediately switched over to war production. The question then was—how best to organize human resources in peace to facilitate this transfer in war?

The method most commonly discussed was the so-called 'National Registration'. Under this system the Government would compile a register of all the nation's citizens, listing their special qualifications that would be useful in time of war, so that

[1] Cmd. 5374.
[2] Simon, 'Memorandum on Defence Expenditure', 25 June 1937. C.P. 165(37), Cab. 24/270.
[3] W. O. 163/43, Minutes of the 390th meeting of the Army Council, 29 June 1937.

when war did break out and emergency services had to be set up at once, the situation would not arise whereby—as happened in the 1914–18 war—highly skilled industrial craftsmen were put in the Army with complete disregard for the needs of industry. In embryonic form the system was simple enough, but when it came to setting up a national register, there were many difficulties. Was the Government to make registration compulsory, or was it to leave the decision to register up to the conscience of the individual? The mere mention of a register would raise doubts in the public mind: was the Government trying to sort out at leisure military needs from industrial ones? Did a register foreshadow a measure of compulsion? The political implications of these questions were enough to make any government hesitate.

National registration was discussed by the Committee of Imperial Defence in July. Duff Cooper assumed that if war broke out, Britain would rely on the voluntary system to provide the requisite numbers. Lord Swinton, however, emphasized that compulsory service would be introduced from the outset. Unless that was understood, every decision made by the C.I.D. would have to be reviewed, since the Man-Power Sub-Committee had based its estimates on the assumption that all the resources of the nation would be mobilized upon the outbreak of war. Hore-Belisha said that so far as the Army was concerned, it needed only about 270,000 men, and these could be obtained without a system of national registration. Hankey pointed out that the Government had to take a much wider view of manpower requirements, and had to avoid unnecessarily plundering one sector of the nation to boost another. The C.I.D. agreed that it would be politically impossible for the Government to introduce compulsory national registration in peacetime for any reason whatsoever, 'except as the result of prior consultation with, and the assent of, the Leaders of the Opposition Parties.'[1] So far as the Labour party was concerned, there was little chance that its leaders would agree. The Labour movement tended to look upon any form of registration as the prelude to military and industrial conscription, and the Trades Union Congress (T.U.C.) had, for two years running, passed motions pledging absolute resistance to any move by the Government to interfere with the rights of trades unions. The Minister of Labour had stressed to the Cabinet that industrial harmony was essential to the progress of the rearmament programme, and

[1] Cab. 2/6(2), Minutes of the 295th meeting of the C.I.D., 1 July 1937.

Chamberlain himself was unwilling to antagonize Labour's supporters. The C.I.D. also decided that, as regards recruiting for the armed forces, peacetime national registration was unnecessary. It was, however, 'impressed by the fact that the principal military Powers of the Continent are able (owing to conscription) to allocate in peacetime personnel to war posts in industry, to the great advantage of their arrangements for industrial mobilization'.[1] Political considerations prevented Britain from following a similar course. Inskip informed the Cabinet that the Government had three choices: it could adopt a scheme of registration which had been suggested by the Registrar-General; it could postpone registration until war seemed imminent; or it could do nothing. The disadvantage of the first scheme was that 'it would be interpreted in some quarters as a prelude to the introduction of conscription', while the second course would—at a time when tensions were extreme—'appear to be almost tantamount to mobilization'.[2] The third course seemed to be the safest for the present.

During the middle of 1937 there was little direct discussion of the question of the role of the Army. There were signs, however, that the senior levels of the Army were becoming increasingly discontented over the lack of a firm decision. Major-General Sir Edmund Ironside, G.O.C.-in-C., Eastern Command, discussed the problem with Deverell, and recorded in his diary: 'Once again I came home profoundly sad at the state to which the Army has been brought.'[3] The Army was suffering because of the indecision surrounding its future; what was needed was a public statement from the Prime Minister on the role of the Army—without it, the recruiting situation would not improve.[4] Shortly afterwards, he wrote despairingly:[5]

> I cannot say what Hore-Belisha will do or what I think of it. He is only 41 and full of energy. . . . We are at our lowest ebb in the Army and the Jew may resuscitate us. I

[1] Cab. 2/6(2), Minutes of the 295th meeting of the C.I.D., 1 July 1937.
[2] Inskip, 'National Registration: Note by the Minister for Co-ordination of Defence', 3 July 1937. C.P. 177(37), Cab. 24/270.
[3] Roderick Macleod and Denis Kelly (eds), *Time Unguarded: The Ironside Diaries 1937–1940* (New York: McKay, 1962), pp. 21–3. Diary entry, 13 May 1937.
[4] *Ibid.*, p. 23. Diary entry, 23 May 1937.
[5] *Ibid.*, p. 24. Diary entry, 29 May 1937.

hope that he hasn't been ordered to cut us down, and yet surely we can be cut down in our overhead expenses.

When there was still no decision by August, he complained: 'The nation does not believe an Army is necessary and the Government, so democratic is it, will not make up the nation's mind for it.'[1]

In fact, the Government was moving towards a decision. The C.I.D. took note in July of the recommendation by the Defence Plans (Policy) Sub-Committee that, after consultation with the Treasury, the War Office should base its plans on a re-equipped Regular Army, four Territorial infantry divisions, and two Territorial anti-aircraft divisions.[2] Limited liability had not yet been explicitly declared the basis of British policy, but the Government was heading in that direction.

The Chiefs of Staff had presented their arguments, but these had not been accepted by Chamberlain. In July, the Foreign Office received a report from Colonel F. Beaumont-Nesbitt, British Military Attaché in Paris.[3] His observations tended to support the Chiefs of Staff against the Cabinet:

> The opinion of the average Frenchman as to the value of the British Army is inclined to be critical. And this is no doubt due to the fact that the British Army is numerically small, and has of late been further discredited by its inability to obtain recruits.
>
> This view is not shared by the General Staff, which realises that, though the initial British contribution may indeed be a small one, British expansion is potentially unlimited.

The Chiefs of Staff had said that Britain could not send troops to the Continent on the basis of limited liability; the French understood that once Britain had committed any number of troops, she could not put a ceiling on that commitment. Beaumont-Nesbitt pointed to certain weaknesses in the French Army, but ended on an optimistic note: 'the French Army is a highly efficient machine,

[1] Macleod and Kelly, *Ironside Diaries*, p. 26. Diary entry, 11 Aug. 1937.
[2] Cab. 2/6 (2), Minutes of the 297th meeting of the C.I.D., 15 July 1937.
[3] Colonel F. Beaumont-Nesbitt, 'The Present Military Situation in France compared with that in Germany, as disclosed by the Annual Report on Germany, 1936', 5 July 1937. F.O. 371/20694. C 5048/122/17.

undergoing constant revision and improvement, to fit it to meet the problems with which it is confronted.'[1]

Hore-Belisha formed a similar opinion when he visited the French Army and attended its manoeuvres in September. He was impressed by the professionalism of the officers and men, and after being shown the still incomplete Maginot Line, he recorded in his diary:[2]

> I was informed that the Maginot Line only required 100,000 men to hold it, which left a large reserve for the French Field Army. When the French realise that we cannot commit ourselves to send an Expeditionary Force, they should be all the more induced to accelerate the extension of the Maginot Line to the sea.

Beaumont-Nesbitt reported to the Foreign Office that the French had been most impressed by Hore-Belisha, and that his visit had produced good, though unspecified, results.[3]

Throughout the autumn of 1937 there continued to be a marked indecision over the role of the Army. In August the Government received a report by Ogilvie-Forbes of the British Embassy in Berlin, detailing the state of German anti-aircraft defences, which had developed a high degree of efficiency, especially compared with those in Britain.[4] The Foreign Office reacted sharply to the report, and Vansittart urged that the Cabinet be informed of the alarming disparity between the two systems, saying: 'If the nation knew the truth there would surely be righteous anger. The whole of our passive air-defence needs entirely and vigorously recasting. Otherwise we are simply courting eventual destruction.'[5] Here was further weight to the view that the War Office should concentrate its resources on improving the equipment and efficiency of the two Territorial anti-aircraft divisions rather than equip the twelve infantry divisions. The Treasury made it clear that it would not sanction greater expenditure: what was needed was a recasting of priorities. 'Our general economic strength is not merely the condition of continued prosperity but as a deterrent to a would-be aggressor it is little less important than ships and aeroplanes and

[1] Beaumont-Nesbitt, 'The Present Military Situation in France'.
[2] Minney, *Hore-Belisha*, p. 59.
[3] See minute by William Strang, 4 Oct. 1937. F.O. 371/20694. C 6821/122/17.
[4] Ogilvie-Forbes, 'A Comparison of Germany's A.A. defences with those of Britain', 18 Aug. 1937. F.O. 371/20746. C 6100/1421/18.
[5] Vansittart, minute, 2 Sept. 1937. F.O. 371/20746. C 6100/1421/18.

guns.'[1] Improvements in defence were not to be at the expense of 'business as usual'.

There were indications, however, that the General Staff had not reconciled itself to a limited continental role. Although Deverell wrote to Liddell Hart that 'any idea of our small Army attacking a first-class continental Army has never entered my head',[2] he told Ironside that Britain could not send an expeditionary force to France in time unless it was dispatched before the outbreak of war. The expeditionary force would have to be prepared to carry out a counter-offensive against a German attack that would consist of 'a mass of aeroplanes backing up the machines attacking the Maginot Line, followed by mechanized troops and lorried infantry'.[3] Ironside related how he had told Hore-Belisha that 'as a matter of policy' Britain could not announce that she would not send an expeditionary force to the Continent: 'that if we did say so, France would lie down and defend herself no more . . . and we shouldn't have a single friend in Europe.' Hore-Belisha had not seemed impressed with this argument, and stressed the importance of British naval and air support.[4] Ironside wrote in his diary: 'we don't want Belisha or any other politician to make a decision as to our future based upon insufficient evidence.'[5] Unfortunately, Chamberlain and—increasingly—the rest of the Cabinet thought the evidence of the Chiefs of Staff insufficient to support their recommendations.

It was in December 1937 that the Cabinet reached a decision on the role of the Army. On 8 December it considered a secret report by the Chiefs of Staff on the comparative strength of Britain with other world powers as of January 1938. The Chiefs of Staff warned that Britain's armed forces were not sufficiently strong to protect her world-wide interests against simultaneous attack by Germany, Italy, and Japan. Even allowing for assistance from France and other allies, the Chiefs of Staff could not foresee when this situation would change. The position was clear:[6]

[1] Treasury 'Defence Programme: Financial Aspects', 30 Oct. 1937. W.O. 32/4600.
[2] Deverell to Liddell Hart, 15 Nov. 1937. Liddell Hart Papers, A4/15.
[3] Macleod and Kelley, *Ironside Diaries,* pp. 37–8. Diary entry, 1 Dec. 1937.
[4] *Ibid.*
[5] *Ibid.*, p. 35. Diary entry, 21 Nov. 1937.
[6] C.O.S., 'Comparison of the strength of Great Britain with certain other Powers, January 1938'. 'Most Secret Report', C.I.D. Paper 1366–B. See Cab. 23/90A, Minutes 46(37)10, 8 Dec. 1937.

We cannot, therefore, exaggerate the importance, from the point of view of Imperial defence, of any practical or international action that can be taken to reduce the numbers of our potential enemies and to gain the support of potential allies.

The responsibility for the success of British policy depended on British diplomacy.

Chamberlain did not attach much weight to possible assistance from allies. France, Britain's 'most important friend', was defensively strong with a powerful Army, but her Air Force was in a 'far from satisfactory' state, and it would be a long time before she could give Britain any effective air backing. The smaller powers could add little to Britain's offensive or defensive strength. Theoretically it might be possible to drive a diplomatic wedge between Germany, Italy, and Japan, but the danger was that this could only be achieved at the expense of humiliating and damaging concessions that would destroy the confidence of Britain's allies. Consequently the Foreign Office was trying to prevent the situation arising wherein all these powers would simultaneously be at war with Britain.[1]

The following week Inskip presented a major paper on defence to the Cabinet. He went to considerable lengths to stress the importance of the financial framework of defence planning: it was such an 'essential element in [Britain's] defensive strength' that it could 'properly be regarded as a fourth arm in defence'. Britain's traditional stability, its demonstrable ability to solve problems and face difficulties by peaceful means, was a powerful deterrent to a potential aggressor. This deterrent, however, would lose its effectiveness if Britain showed 'signs of strain'.[2]

At the same time there had to be proper balance between long-term 'staying power' and the strength to withstand a sudden sharp blow, which would probably be the form of an attack launched against Britain. And not only should Britain be strong enough to counter such an attack, she had to *be seen* to be strong enough. If other nations believed that Britain was militarily weak, then her diplomatic influence on the course of world events would decline. Thus there was a direct and vital link between

[1] Cab. 23/90A, Minutes 46(37)10, 8 Dec. 1937.
[2] Inskip, 'Defence Expenditure in Future Years: Interim Report by the Minister for Co-ordination of Defence', 15 Dec. 1937. C.P. 316(37), part II, paras 9–11. Cab. 24/273.

military strength and diplomatic effectiveness, with an added factor of economic stability to underline and encompass the connection.[1]

The rearmament programme had to be planned on the basis of four defence needs. In order of priority, these were: the security of the United Kingdom (including the maintenance of productive capacity and economic prosperity) and its imperial communications; the defence of British imperial possessions; and lastly, 'co-operation in the defence of the territories of any allies Britain might have in war'. The latter objective could only be met after the first three had been satisfied, and since the third demanded 'considerable reinforcements' for imperial garrisons, there seemed little chance that Britain, in its existing poor state of defence preparedness, could do very much towards achieving the capability to assist allies.[2]

So far as the Army was concerned, its primary responsibility was imperial and home defence, including anti-aircraft protection, which was to be given top priority. Accordingly, the 'continental hypothesis' was ranked last in priorities. The rationale for this was that there were heavy burdens imposed on Britain's industry and manpower by the demands of increased anti-aircraft defence, as well as the cost of maintaining a large navy and air force. External developments reinforced this reasoning. There was evidence that France no longer relied upon Britain to provide large-scale land assistance, Germany had guaranteed the integrity of Belgium, and it seemed likely that in a future war imperial responsibilities would absorb the greater part of Britain's military resources.[3]

This was a major change in policy, and Inskip drew attention to its implications:

> I must, however, warn my colleagues of the possible consequences of this proposal in order that they may share my responsibility for the decision to be taken with their eyes open. Notwithstanding recent developments in mechanised warfare on land and in the air, there is no sign of the displacement of infantry. If France were again to be in danger of being overrun by land armies, a situation might arise when, as in the last war, we had to improvise an army

[1] Inskip, C. P. 316(37), part II, paras 12–13.
[2] *Ibid.*, part IV, paras 12–13.
[3] *Ibid.*, part V, paras 68–71.

to assist her. Should this happen, the Government of the day would most certainly be criticised for having neglected to provide against so obvious a contingency.

Nevertheless, because of its already heavy commitments, the Government had no choice but to adopt a policy of limited liability as regards the Army's involvement on the Continent.[1]

With the concept of a continental commitment all but scrapped, the role of the Territorial Army was changed. Henceforth it was to be responsible for anti-aircraft defence and the 'maintenance of order and essential services [in Britain] in time of war'. Thirdly, 'units of the Territorial Army should be regarded as available to support the Regular Army in their primary role of Imperial Defence overseas as soon after the outbreak of war as their training and equipment permits'.[2] The whole focus of British defence policy was swung around to a concentration on British security protected by British-based forces. Continental ventures were virtually abandoned.

When the Cabinet discussed the paper on 22 December, Hore-Belisha admitted he was relieved that the ambiguity over the role of the Army would finally be resolved. He personally had no doubt that it was correct to give the continental hypothesis the lowest priority. The situation had changed since 1914: British public opinion was against sending land forces to Europe; there was the new factor of air warfare; and, unlike 1914, Italy and Japan were now hostile. Most important of all was the fact that the French, after providing for the manning of the Maginot Line, had a large reserve for their field army. If the French were told of the rejection of the continental hypothesis, they would not count on a British land commitment, and would therefore accelerate the completion of the Maginot Line. It would be even better if staff talks could cover world-wide defence, for once the extensive nature of Britain's responsibilities and defence priorities had been made clear, there could be no reason for France to rely on a British Expeditionary Force.[3]

Inskip was also supported by Sir Samuel Hoare, the Home Secretary, who appreciated the effect the proposals would have in simplifying the provision of equipment. The threat from air

[1] Inskip, C. P. 316(37) part V, para. 75.
[2] *Ibid.*, part V, para. 79.
[3] Cab. 23/90A, Minutes 49(37)1.

attack was so great that he thought the Territorials should be given training in air-raid precautions work.[1]

The only doubts were expressed by the Secretary of State for Foreign Affairs, Anthony Eden, and the Lord President of the Council, Lord Halifax. Eden confessed to 'some apprehensions' over Britain's inability to provide assistance on land for her allies in Europe, but said that on balance the arguments presented by Inskip were 'irresistible'. Nevertheless he could not dispel his doubts: the report postulated an entirely defensive role for the Army. It was disturbing to think that British public opinion was opposed to the use of land forces on the Continent, for the situation might arise where British assistance was vital. It was true that the French had said that they expected only two mechanized divisions from Britain, but that was on the assumption that the Belgians could defend themselves. What if Germany invaded Belgium and Holland? The Channel ports would fall, and France would be directly threatened. The Chiefs of Staff had consistently maintained that this was the method Germany would use to attack France, yet—if Inskip's report was adopted—Britain would be incapable of sending land forces to France. Similarly Halifax said he hoped the Cabinet would not ignore Inskip's warning on the situation that would arise if circumstances demanded that Britain provide assistance on land for France. Wise policy allowed for all contingencies, kept all options open as long as possible.[2]

Such was the force of Chamberlain's arguments and his dominant position within the Government that he carried the Cabinet with him. Limited liability was adopted as the formula governing future defence planning. It appeared that a continental Army policy had finally and decisively been abandoned. Chamberlain's arguments had prevailed against the combined advice of the Chiefs of Staff and the Permanent Head of the Foreign Office.

This change in policy was accompanied by a change in personnel, as Chamberlain and his ministers reconstructed the Government with advisers who were attuned to the new policies. Duff Cooper, who had consistently opposed the concept of limited liability, had already been moved to the Admiralty. In the War Office, Hore-Belisha embarked on a programme of reform, and subjected many long-standing practices to critical examination.

[1] Cab. 23/09A, Minutes 49(37)1.
[2] *Ibid.*

A drive to improve recruiting based on more attractive conditions, the use of Fleet Street methods to promote the Army's cause, the scrapping of regulations that unduly restricted the soldier's private life: these moves were opposed as unworkable and unnecessary. But they did work, and the increase in enlistments seemed to indicate that they were necessary.[1]

There was greater opposition when Hore-Belisha tackled basic Army policy, especially the difficult question of the role of the Army. Here he came up against the conservative military establishment, which was unwilling to admit that changing circumstances had rendered invalid many of the assumptions of Army policy. This led increasingly to disagreements, and when Hore-Belisha began to urge the need for greater mechanization, Elles resigned on the grounds that he could not keep up with the pace. As Hore-Belisha developed closer ties with Liddell Hart, who became his unofficial adviser, tensions built up within the War Office. But Hore-Belisha was in a strong position: he had been sent to the War Office with a mandate to carry out drastic change, and, in March, Chamberlain had written to him[2] to draw his attention to Liddell Hart's latest book, *Europe in Arms*. Chamberlain especially recommended a chapter entitled 'The Role of the British Army', in which Liddell Hart argued that 'the balance seems to be heavily against the hope that a British field force on the Continent might have a military effect commensurate with the expense and the risk'.[3] Hore-Belisha read the chapter and wrote to Chamberlain that he was 'impressed by his [Liddell Hart's] general theories'.[4]

In October and November Hore-Belisha called for an examination of the disposition of British forces, particularly in India. The C.I.G.S. told him that the heavy commitment of troops to India had always been accepted as necessary, and that the reasons for this commitment still held true.[5] It was becoming clear that Deverell was not the man to carry out a policy of change within the Army. There was similar resistance from the Adjutant-General, Sir Harry Knox. By the end of November Hore-Belisha had reached the conclusion that there would have to be a clean sweep of the War Office. He wrote to Chamberlain:[6]

[1] See Minney, *Hore-Belisha*, pp. 38–49.
[2] *Ibid.*, p. 54.
[3] Liddell Hart, *Europe in Arms* (London: Faber, 1937), p. 130.
[4] Minney, *Hore-Belisha*, p. 54.
[5] *Ibid.*
[6] *Ibid.*, p. 69.

> My view, after the fullest survey, including a visit to France, is that our Army should be organised to defend this country and the Empire, that to organise it with a military prepossession in favour of a Continental commitment, is wrong. The C.I.G.S., although he may overtly accept this view, does not accept it in fact or practice, and he has told me that he is unable to advise any modification in our organisation.

Deverell and Knox were not called upon to advise much longer. Letters asking for their resignations were dispatched from the War Office on 1 December, and they resigned the following day, with considerable bitterness on Deverell's part. To replace Deverell, Hore-Belisha chose Lord Gort, his Military Secretary. Gort had an excellent record as a fighting soldier, he held the Victoria Cross, and his peerage gave him an extra touch of influence. He had impressed Hore-Belisha as a keen military mind that was bent on change and rethinking. It was not until after he was installed as C.I.G.S. that Hore-Belisha found this inclination to be a shallow one, and Gort became no less staunch than his predecessor in defending the *status quo*. Hore-Belisha later admitted he had made a bad choice, but said that 'having sacked the Army Council once, I could not do it again'.[1] Despite sweeping changes in personnel at the War Office, Army thinking on the role of the Army was not changed so easily.

There was also a change in the Foreign Office. Vansittart, who had been one of the prime advocates of a strong land commitment to France in case of war, was replaced by Sir Alexander Cadogan[2] as Under-Secretary, and sidetracked into a powerless position— Chief Diplomatic Adviser to the Government—in which he was not permitted to see many important papers before they had been discussed and decided upon by the Cabinet.

By the end of 1937 then, the Government, under Chamberlain's firm hand, was committed to a policy of limited liability on land, despite the fact that its military and diplomatic advisers had warned against the effects of such a policy on Britain's relations with potential allies.

[1] Minney, *Hore-Belisha*, p. 89.
[2] Cadogan was Under-Secretary from 1938 until 1946.

6 'An unforgettable past, an unpredictable future' December 1937–March 1938

During the first few months of 1938, the Government worked on the details of the new policy of limited liability. The rearmament programme had to be readjusted, Army estimates drawn up on the new assumption that Britain would not commit itself to a continental campaign on land, and the French had to be informed of the Cabinet's decision. Yet barely had these steps been taken when the whole tenor of the international scene was changed by Hitler's march into Austria. Wise policy, as Halifax had pleaded, allowed for all contingencies.

The Cabinet agreed in December 1937 that the French government should be informed of the decision that had been reached regarding the role of the Army, since this would undoubtedly lead to further requests from the French for staff conversations to discuss the new situation.[1] The British Chiefs of Staff maintained their reluctance to engage in close talks with the French on the grounds that this would involve the British in unforeseen commitments. The Foreign Office pointed out that the British government had originally agreed to talks on a restricted basis only because it was hoped, in 1936, that the five Locarno powers (Britain, France, Germany, Italy, and Belgium) would be able to conclude a mutual defence and guarantee pact. Since this was now no more than a remote possibility, there was no reason why the scope of future staff conversations had to be severely limited.[2] Eden suggested that the various military attachés be authorized to engage in talks on a wide basis, even if—for domestic parliamentary reasons—the pretence of close restrictions had to be maintained in public.[3] When the Chiefs of Staff failed to respond favourably, Eden wrote in exasperation to Chamberlain ('Personal and strictly confidential'):[4]

[1] Cab. 23/90A, Minutes 49(37)1, 22 Dec. 1937.
[2] Strang to Hankey, 16 Dec. 1937. Cab. 24/274, Annex 1.
[3] Cab. 24/274, Annex 1.
[4] Eden to Chamberlain, 1 Jan. 1938. F.O. 371/21593. C 362/36/17.

I cannot help believing that what the Chiefs of Staff would really like to do is to re-orientate our foreign policy and to clamber on the band wagon with the dictators, even though that process meant parting company with France and estranging our relations with the United States. I believe, moreover, that there is a tendency among some of our colleagues to understate the strength of France. The recurrent political crises in that country seem to us evidence of fundamental weakness. . . . I am myself convinced, however, and Phipps [British Ambassador in Paris] and others better qualified than I to express an opinion share that conviction, that the French Army is absolutely sound.

The Foreign Office insisted that there be staff talks with France, especially since Britain's assistance to France was henceforth to be confined to the sea and the air, the latter making close co-operation before the outbreak of war vital: unless there was agreement as to the role of British air-power, its effectiveness in the opening stages of a war that was expected—at least by the French General Staff[1]—to be short and swift would be considerably reduced. Cadogan accused the Chiefs of Staff of ' "hanging back" on *political grounds*', which were outside their sphere of responsibility. He suggested that the Foreign Office advise that from the political point of view there were no objections to staff talks, so long as they did not involve Britain in any commitments.[2] Vansittart sent a strongly worded memorandum to Eden, and urged the necessity of conversations with the French:[3]

I most earnestly hope that we shall insist on having these Staff conversations with the French. At present the position is briefly this. We are proceeding on two assumptions, both of which I am sure will be falsified: first, that France can hold out on two or perhaps even three frontiers with no expeditionary force from us. It is completely out of the question that she should be able to

[1] The British Air Attaché in Paris had advised the Foreign Office (14 Jan. 1938) that the French General Staff thought that war with Germany was inevitable, but that it would not break out until Germany felt confident of victory within a matter of weeks: 'Never again, according to the French Staff, will Germany run the risk of a long war.' F.O. 371/21593. C 362/36/17.
[2] Cadogan, Memorandum, 24 Jan. 1938. F.O. 371/21593. C 362/36/17.
[3] Vansittart to Eden, 27 Jan. 1938. F.O. 371/21593. C 362/36/17.

do so. Secondly, we are assuming that the war, if it comes, will be a long one and we must therefore lay great stress on conserving our staying power. This really means spending less in the crucial years ahead. I, on the contrary, am convinced that the Germans at least will not risk a war unless they are practically sure of being able to make it a short one, and there is much in modern warfare which makes this a conceivable proposition. I do not believe that we shall again see so protracted a war as that of 1914–18.

If in addition to these two main conceptions, both of which I am sure are ill-founded, particularly the first, we add the third error of making no preparation at all with the French even where we might be able to help, that is in the air, the cumulative effect may well prove fatal to us.

Despite the firm Cabinet decision on the role of the Army, Vansittart was not convinced of the soundness of its reasoning, and continued to fight a rear-guard action against scrapping a continental role for the Army.

The Chiefs of Staff restated their objections to staff conversations in a paper that was a direct reply to the Foreign Office views.[1] Their long-standing opinion—that staff conversations (a term that had a 'sinister purport') would involve Britain in an automatic commitment—had not changed. The new policy regarding the role of the Army had, in fact, weakened the case for staff talks with the French, although the increased importance of Britain's air contribution logically pointed to closer military ties. However, the admittedly strong reasons for air conversations were outweighed by political factors:

The temptation to arrange a leakage of the information that such collaboration was taking, or had taken place would, in our opinion, prove irresistible to them [the French] in order to flaunt an Anglo-French accord in the face of Germany. Apart from the deplorable effect of such a leakage upon our present efforts to reach a *detente* with Germany, it is most important, from the military stand-point, that at the present time we should not appear to have both feet in the French camp. We consider,

[1] C.O.S., 'Staff Conversations with France and Belgium', 4 Feb. 1938. C.O.S. Paper No. 680, Cab. 24/274.

I

therefore, that the military advantages of closer collaboration with the French regarding concerted measures against Germany, however logical they may appear, would be outweighed by the grave risk of precipitating the very situation which we wish to avoid, namely, the irreconcileable suspicion and hostility of Germany.

This was too much for the Foreign Office. Calling it 'an astounding document', Strang wrote that 'in presenting a report of this kind, the Chiefs of Staff are exceeding their function'.[1] Eden was 'certain that we must have staff conversations with the French'.[2] The question then became one of timing.

The Chiefs of Staff, however, had not lost on all counts. They realized that limited liability was essentially an artificial policy. As they pointed out in a memorandum, any commitment to France would involve British forces in a continental campaign, for casualties and the need for reinforcements would compel Britain to increase the size of its expeditionary force. This was the situation that had arisen in 1914, and the French General Staff and the French people were aware that it would be repeated in a future war.[3] Liability could only be limited in proportion to the limitations imposed on aims: the means of achieving those aims could be directed and channelled, but not limited. If allied opinion demanded liability of a particular sort, then no government in Britain could attempt to withhold that liability. Ironside said as much to a conference of senior commanders:[4]

Our wretched little Corps of two divisions and a mobile division was unthinkable as a contribution to an Army in France. . . . Let us make Imperial plans only. After all, the politicians will be hard put to it to refuse to help France and Belgium when the 1914 show begins again.

Despite the Government's action, the range of options open to Britain was much narrower than it was prepared to admit.

[1] Strang, minute, 8 Feb. 1938. F.O. 371/21653. C 841/37/18. Strang was Head of the Central (i.e. European Department in the Foreign Office, and served as Assistant Under-Secretary of State for Foreign Affairs, 1939–43.
[2] Eden, minute, 31 Jan. 1938. F.O. 371/21593. C 362/36/17.
[3] C.O.S., 'Staff Conversations with France and Belgium', Memorandum No. 707. F.O. 371/21653. C 3129/37/18.
[4] Macleod and Kelly, *Ironside Diaries*, pp. 47–8. Diary entry, 5 Feb. 1938.

In February 1938, the Cabinet reviewed the role of the Army in light of the limited-liability decision of the previous December. Hore-Belisha presented a paper in which he reviewed the duties of the Army and the reorganization which the new role both implied and made necessary. On the home front, the primary duty of the Army was anti-aircraft defence. The ideal scheme involved 1,264 A.A. guns, 4,684 searchlights, and 93,000 personnel. At that time approximately half the equipment and personnel were being deployed to cover the area from Portsmouth to Newcastle, with special detachments to protect outlying ports. This involved two Territorial divisions, with an additional two divisions needed to fulfil the requirements of the ideal scheme. Two Regular anti-aircraft groups provided protection for the Regular Army, and were available for use as a mobile reserve for (Territorial) A.D.G.B. formations. Hore-Belisha recommended that further anti-aircraft measures be restricted to the implementation of the second and third stages of the ideal scheme—the protection of the Tyne, Clyde, and Forth—which entailed the use of one-third of a division. This, he thought, should be the extent of immediate action regarding A.D.G.B., since industrial resources were limited, and rearmament in other fields was already being delayed because of the emphasis that had been placed on anti-aircraft defence.[1]

British imperial commitments, exclusive of India and Burma, absorbed the equivalent of two and a half infantry divisions, plus one mobile division that it was planned to organize out of troops in Egypt. The ideal reorganization would permit this to be increased by an additional mobile division, an infantry division, and five battalions. India and Burma absorbed 45 of the 138 battalions of the Regular Army, a number that imposed an undesirable 'and perhaps dangerous restraint' on the employment of British troops in other theatres. Hore-Belisha urged that the Government approve talks between the War and India Offices with a view to reaching an agreement on the redistribution of British forces and the acceptance by the Indian government of a greater share of the cost of maintaining troops in India.[2]

Under the new role of the Army, it was proposed that Britain be able to send overseas within three weeks two Regular divisions and a mobile division, *equipped for an eastern theatre*. These

[1] Hore-Belisha, 'The Organization of the Army for its Role in War', 10 Feb. 1938. C.P. 26(38), Cab. 24/274.
[2] *Ibid.*

119

would be followed, if necessary, by a further two divisions within forty days of the outbreak of war. Hore-Belisha emphasized 'that their equipment and war reserves will not be on the Continental scale,' and he added:

> I suggest that it is of great importance that our potential allies should be left in no doubt as to the possibilities of direct assistance on our part and that the various alternative operations, whether in defence or in local offence, which our available reserves may have to undertake should be covered by any discussions or interchange of information which take place.

The abandonment of the continental concept made it possible and necessary to reorganize the divisions that were being prepared for an expeditionary role on the Continent. It was intended to reduce the size of the existing divisions and build up a larger number of smaller units, in which the emphasis would be on increased fire-power and mobility, to be achieved through a greater degree of mechanization. In this way the effectiveness of Britain's 200,000-man Army, which Hore-Belisha took as the peacetime limit, would be maximized.[1]

The reorganization of the Army was largely predicated upon the assumption that it would have to operate in an eastern theatre, most probably in defence of Egypt, although, as Inskip said, this would have to be reconsidered if there was any permanent improvement in Anglo-Italian relations.[2] The mention of a specific area was criticized in the Cabinet. Simon thought it tended to commit Britain and would complicate attempts to reach settlements with Italy. For that reason he preferred that a phrase such as 'for general purposes' be used to describe the role of the Army. Likewise he objected to Hore-Belisha's proposal to use some of the industrial capacity released by the abandonment of the continental hypothesis for the rearmament of Belgium, on the grounds that any discussions with Belgium might involve Britain in a commitment that could be invoked in unforeseen circumstances. Even though, as Eden pointed out, Belgium was a special case since Britain already had a political commitment there, Simon stressed that

[1] Hore-Belisha, C.P. 26(38).
[2] Inskip, 'Defence Expenditure in Future Years: Further Report by the Minister for Co-ordination of Defence', 8 Feb. 1938. C.P. 24(38), Cab. 24/274.

the Government could not judge in advance the events surrounding the outbreak of a particular war: better to avoid even the slightest hint of a commitment that could turn into a repetition of 1914. From the political point of view, Eden could see objections to the reference to an eastern theatre, since knowledge of this preparation would inevitably complicate negotiations with Italy. As such, it was 'politically undesirable'. The Cabinet agreed, and it was decided that in future there should be no references to an eastern theatre, the phrase 'for general purposes' to be used instead.[1]

Halifax drew attention to the position of the Territorial divisions, the greater part of which would not be able to take the field until ten months after mobilization. It was questionable, therefore, whether it was worth maintaining so many Territorial units. Hore-Belisha agreed, but added that 'public sentiment' would react unfavourably to any move to reduce Britain's already small armed forces. At the same time considerations of cost prevented the conversion of more Territorial divisions into A.A. units. Financial considerations continued to play an important part in the rearmament programme, and the abandonment of the continental hypothesis had resulted in a possible reduction of Army expenditure of only £14 million.[2]

The Cabinet agreed that the French government should be informed of the recent decision regarding the role of the Army, and told that, if Britain did decide to send a force to the Continent, it would consist initially of two infantry divisions and a mobile division. The Secretary of State for Foreign Affairs was instructed to make it clear that these forces would *not* be equipped with special reference to a continental campaign, and to stress the importance of Britain's sea and air contribution. The French were to be left in no doubt as to the policy and mood of the British government.[3]

Hore-Belisha's paper was then examined by a sub-committee of the C.I.D., consisting of Inskip as chairman, with the Secretaries for India, War, and Air, the First Lord of the Admiralty, and the Chiefs of Staff as members. They noted that the proposed restriction on anti-aircraft defence was dictated by financial and industrial considerations alone, and important as the latter were, the fact remained that air defence, which the Cabinet had

[1] Cab. 23/92, Minutes 4(38) and 5(38), 9, 16 Feb. 1938.
[2] Cab. 23/92, Minutes 5(38), 16 Feb. 1938.
[3] *Ibid.*

determined would have the highest priority, would continue to be inadequate.[1]

Hore-Belisha explained to the sub-committe that under the new arrangements proposed by the War Office, Britain would be able to send to the Continent, twenty-two days after the outbreak of war, two Regular divisions and one mobile division, together with full war reserves, and equipped for war on a continental scale. Within forty days of the outbreak of war these could be reinforced by two further infantry divisions, but if this was done, no more contingents could be dispatched for some considerable time, possibly as long as ten months. He made it clear that it was not the policy of the War Office to lay the foundations in peacetime for the creation of a large national Army after war had broken out. But, Inskip argued, whereas the Cabinet had given first priority to the defence of Britain, and fourth (and last) priority to assisting in the defence of ,the territory of allies, Hore-Belisha's paper reversed these, or at least diminished the first in favour of the last.[2] The difficulty was that unless the Government was willing to abandon completely the possibility of having to send troops to the Continent (and this clearly was the contingency that Inskip was thinking of), then that possibility would tend to exert an influence disproportionate to the actual priority it held in Army policy.

A White Paper on defence[3] was presented to Parliament on 7 March 1938. Drawing attention to the increasing cost and complexity of modern armaments, the Government warned that the total defence expenditure would exceed the figure of £1,500 million mentioned in the 1937 White Paper as the estimated cost of defence for the five-year period 1937–41. Again Chamberlain outlined the priorities governing defence policy:

> The cornerstone of our defence policy must be the security of the United Kingdom. . . . Therefore, our first main efforts must have two main objectives: we must protect this country and we must preserve the trade routes upon which we depend for our food and raw materials. Our third objective is the defence of British territories

[1] Inskip, 'The Organization of the Army for its Role in War', 8 March 1938. D.P.(P.) 21, Cab. 24/275.
[2] *Ibid.*
[3] *Parl. Papers (1937–38)*, XVII, Cmd. 5682. 'Statement Relating to Defence'.

overseas from attack, whether by sea, land, or air. . . .
That makes it necessary for us to have available forces
which can be despatched on what may be called Imperial
police duty. In war time there would undoubtedly be
substantial demands for reinforcements to be sent to these
strategic points, but, taking them in order of priority, they
are not as vital as the defence of our own country, because
as long as we are undefeated at home, although we sustained
losses overseas, we might have an opportunity of making
them good thereafter. The fourth and last which I will
mention can be stated quite shortly, namely cooperation
in the defence of the territories of any allies we might
have in case of war.[1]

As Vansittart had so often argued, it was this very reluctance to
countenance assistance to Britain's allies that endangered the
support of those allies. Chamberlain's policy virtually guaranteed
that Britain would not have any allies in case of war.

Chamberlain made it clear that in setting up these priorities,
financial considerations had weighed heavily, and he spoke of the
economy as being the fourth arm of defence:

The fact is that wars are not won only with arms and men;
they are won with the reserves of resources and credit.
That is what we mean when we speak of the staying power
of a nation. . . . The economic stability of a country . . . is
recognized to be a powerful deterrent against attack.

Since it was doubtful if it was possible to win a war with a sudden
'knock-out' blow, a potential aggressor, even though militarily
stronger, would think twice before attacking an opponent who
was capable of prolonged resistance because of its overall economic
staying power. Such was the importance of this fourth arm that
the rearmament programme had to maintain a careful balance
between military expenditure and general economic prosperity
and stability. The Government was confident that rearmament was
contributing to peace: 'The sight of this enormous, this almost
terrifying, power which Britain is building up has a sobering
effect, a steadying effect, on the opinion of the world.'[2]

[1] 5 *Parl. Debs.* CCCXXXII, 1561–2.
[2] *Ibid.*, 1566.

In the debate on the White Paper, a number of speakers referred to the role of the Army. Sir Archibald Sinclair, leader of the Liberal party, sought an assurance from the Government:[1]

> I hope the Government has abandoned the idea of waging warfare on land on the Continental scale, as in the last war. If we are prepared to send an expeditionary force to the Continent, it should be sent not by the War Office but by the Air Ministry.

Sir Edward Grigg (Conservative) thought it unlikely that the British Army would be engaged in Europe in the early stages of a war. He did not exclude the possibility of conscription in Britain in the future, but it was made unnecessary at the moment by the fact that France had compulsory military service. Britain's most pressing need was to organize a more effective defence against air attack.[2] The only doubts voiced over the Government's Army policy were those of Harold Nicolson (National Labour), who said:[3]

> What is still more serious is that the very function of the Army is not decided upon. . . . It should be explained [to the electorate] that in the event of war, we cannot limit our liability to a small token force fighting on this front or on that front.

The general opinion as expressed in the debate, however, was favourable to the principle of limited liability as it applied to the Army's role in a continental war.

Hore-Belisha presented his first Army estimates to the House of Commons on 10 March 1938. In noting that the War Office proposed to spend £43 million on military stores, a sum that exceeded the complete Army estimates for any one year 1926–34, he took some time detailing the place that the Army held in the defence system. At home it was responsible for coastal and anti-aircraft defence, and overseas it bore the heavy burden of imperial defence. These duties, and the vastly changed conditions of warfare, necessarily qualified the use of the Army's strategic reserve. With reference to the nature of the British land commitment to France in 1914 he said:[4]

[1] 5 *Parl. Debs.* CCCXXXII, 1584.
[2] *Ibid.*, 1621.
[3] *Ibid.*, 1646.
[4] *Ibid.*, 2138.

History, it is true, sometimes repeats itself, but rarely in the same context. The assumptions of an unforgettable past are not always the surest guide to an unpredictable future. They tempt us to leave out of account certain only too obvious tendencies, developments and modifications. . . . The extent to which we might be required to send, or have available, assistance for an ally, and what form it should take, must be related to these considerations. It must be remembered that support on land is not the only support we can offer.

Here, in broad outline, were the objections that Chamberlain had consistently made against a continental policy: the development of air-power and offensive mobility undercut the need for a British land commitment to the Continent. Britain's contribution to the defence of France and the Low Countries could best be made in other areas—on the sea and in the air.

In the debate that followed, the House gave warm support to Hore-Belisha's pronouncement on the question of an expeditionary force. Sinclair again denounced the concept, saying that any attempt to organize a continental-style Army would be a 'disastrous blunder'.[1] Leo Amery, a keen advocate of conscription as a means of building up the Army, nevertheless put the emphasis on air support:[2]

The mere addition of a large mass of British troops and a still larger mass of transport, say, to the French Army, would be of infinitely less help to them than the direct and immediate service of the whole of our Air Force. . . . In putting the strategical problems . . . [Hore-Belisha] quite rightly gave priority to one entirely new problem . . . the defence of this country against air attack.

Only Major-General Sir Alfred Knox (Conservative) was not convinced by Hore-Belisha's arguments, and referred to the huge armies that were being built up on the Continent: 'It is not done for fun, and there must be something in that idea of these big armies still.'[3]

Chamberlain was now in a strong position. The Cabinet was

[1] 5 *Parl. Debs.* CCCXXXII, 2162.
[2] *Ibid.*, 2169–70.
[3] *Ibid.*, 2174.

behind him, Vansittart had been ousted from power, and Anthony Eden had resigned in February in disagreement with Chamberlain's conduct of talks with Italy. His successor as Foreign Minister, Lord Halifax, was in close sympathy with the Prime Minister's foreign policy, and henceforth Chamberlain played an even more active role in foreign affairs. On the military side, the senior levels in the War Office had been purged by 'his man', Hore-Belisha. Moreover the House of Commons and the press reacted favourably to the policy of limited liability.[1]

In his speech on 10 March Hore-Belisha referred to an 'unpredictable future'. Two days later German troops marched into Austria.

---

[1] See e.g. *The Times, Daily Telegraph, Manchester Guardian*, 11, 12 March 1938.

7 'An obligation of honour, a counsel of expediency' March–September 1938[1]

After long discussion within the Cabinet, and between the Cabinet and its advisers in the War Office and the Foreign Office, a decision regarding the role of the Army had finally been made in December 1937, and put into practical terms in the Army estimates introduced on 10 March 1938. Within two days German troops occupied Austria, giving Germany a door to eastern expansion and undermining the strategic security of eastern Europe, especially Czechoslovakia, with its large German population in the Sudetenland. The problem facing the British government was to determine how far the German action undercut the assumptions upon which British policy was based, and to delineate an appropriate response to that action. Within six months the Government was confronted by a major crisis over Czechoslovakia, a crisis in which it chose what was fundamentally a diplomatic solution. Only later did it come to the realization that in so doing it had itself destroyed the assumptions upon which its policy rested.

The day after German troops crossed the Austrian frontier, Chamberlain was moved to write that 'force is the only argument Germany understands', and that only 'collective security' backed by 'a visible force of overwhelming strength . . . [and the] determination to use it' would deter Hitler from further ventures. Britain's response had to be firm and show that she could not be bullied; 'announcing some increase or acceleration in rearmament' would achieve this.[2] On 22 March the Cabinet decided that non-interference with trade need no longer be the basis of defence programmes.[3] However, this decision was taken in principle only,

---

[1] 'Mr. Hore-Belisha said it was not only an obligation of honour, but also a counsel of expediency that we should inform the French of the recent decision as to the role of the British Army'. Cab. 2/7, Minutes of the 318th meeting of the C.I.D., 7 April 1938.

[2] Feiling, *Neville Chamberlain*, p. 342.

[3] Cab. 23/93, Minutes 16(38)3, 22 March 1938.

for when, two days later, Chamberlain announced the Government's proposals, he emphasized that there would be no compulsion or government dictation to industry. Steps were to be taken to accelerate the provision of equipment for the R.A.F. and anti-aircraft defence.[1] There was little in such measures to impress Hitler with Britain's 'determination not to be bullied'.

In fact, a continental commitment was the key to British security, for Britain's defence policy rested upon deterrence and collective security. Without such a commitment, France could not be relied upon to resist German overtures, and collective security would disintegrate piecemeal as each nation looked to its own immediate interests. Unless Britain could be seen to be willing to play its part fully in the defence of Europe, its deterrent power, and, conversely, its contribution to collective security, would be weakened. The French thought of a British commitment in terms of land forces, but, without a large increase in military manpower, Britain was not in a position to make a commitment to France. The test—in French eyes—of Britain's determination to fulfil a commitment to France was her ability to raise large land forces. In the last resort, if Britain continued to avoid facing the realities of defence, conscription would be the final gauge of willingness to accept her responsibilities, and not to 'fight to the last French soldier'.

Once the Cabinet had agreed to a limited role for the Army, this decision had to be communicated to the French, but the Chiefs of Staff were reluctant to exchange information with the French on an official level in case this was construed as a commitment by Britain. On the same day that Austria was occupied, however, the French Ambassador called on Halifax to suggest Anglo-French consultations.[2] In view of the German action and of the need to inform the French of the decisions affecting the British Army, the Government could hardly refuse. Nevertheless, before talks could be held, the Cabinet had to discuss the full implications of the role assigned to the Army.

Although he accepted that the first duty of the Army was home defence, Hore-Belisha argued that the provision of anti-aircraft equipment should not be given absolute priority to the

---

[1] 5 *Parl. Debs.* CCCXXXIII, 1410–11, 24 March 1938.

[2] Great Britain, *Documents on British Foreign Policy, 1919–1945*, edited by E. L. Woodward and Rohan Butler (Third Series, 1938–9; 12 vols; London; H.M.S.O., 1949–55), 1, 35–6. Halifax to Phipps, 12 March 1938. Hereafter all references to *Documents on British Foreign Policy* are to the Third Series, cited as *DBFP*. References are to page numbers.

detriment of other roles, particularly the expeditionary force, which was virtually without field artillery. Both Inskip and Hoare questioned his proposals to limit the A.D.G.B. programme to the second and third stages of the 'ideal' scheme on the grounds that this would be counter to the Cabinet decision that the defence of Great Britain should be the first duty of the Army. Hore-Belisha stressed that the order of priorities laid down by the Cabinet was not meant to preclude the proper consideration of all those priorities, rather than the fulfilment of the first at the expense of the rest. The C.I.D. therefore agreed to accept the proposals put forward by the War Office that the initial contingent of the expeditionary force comprise two Regular divisions and one mobile division, together with full war reserves of ammunition, capable of embarkation within twenty-one days, with a second contingent of two Regular divisions ready to embark within forty days, both contingents to be equipped for warfare on a *defensive* continental scale only. Furthermore, the C.I.D. noted that the expeditionary force was markedly inferior in artillery to any potential first-class enemy, and it therefore approved the proposal of the War Office to allocate to the expeditionary force any artillery production in excess of that already marked for A.A. defence. The information regarding the size of an expeditionary force that might be sent to France was to be conveyed to the French government, which was to be left in no doubt as to the extent of assistance on land it could expect from Britain.[1]

The provision of enough anti-aircraft artillery for the defence of Britain at an adequate level—and that planned for and achieved by early 1938 was far from adequate—delayed the modernizing of the field artillery of the Army. This deficiency could be accepted when imperial defence was the prime role of the Army, but after 12 March, when the absorption of Austria gave an indication of the possible trend of German policy, there was an ever-growing likelihood that Britain would eventually become engaged in warfare on the Continent. In such a case, the expeditionary force would be severely handicapped, for, although successive papers by the Chiefs of Staff and decisions by the C.I.D. had spoken of it as being for defensive purposes, it was, in fact, a counter-offensive force. Such a force, which was planned to consist of a mixture of

[1] Cab. 2/7, Minutes of the 313th meeting of the C.I.D., 17 March 1938. The discussion centred on Hore-Belisha's paper, 'The Organization of the Army for its Role in War', C.P. 26(38), Cab. 24/274. See above, chap. 5.

armour and infantry, needed a strong defensive capability, particularly in artillery. On the insistence of the Cabinet, however, artillery production was channelled into the A.A. defence of Britain, and while imperial defence was held to be the prime role of the Army, artillery, either field or A.A., was not as important as it became when continental warfare, even on a limited scale, was contemplated.

Liddell Hart, whose influence on Hore-Belisha was at its height in early 1938, consistently overlooked the necessity of strong artillery for Britain's expeditionary force. He tended to forget that, although in his view, a wholly armoured force was the best land contribution that Britain could make, the expeditionary force that Britain did have, or would be most likely to have, would operate as a counter-offensive force, in which the offensive capabilities of the tank would be qualified by the need to have a secure operational base, which only strong defensive equipment, i.e. dual-purpose (field and A.A.) artillery, could provide.

The limitations of the talks with the French were not settled for several weeks. On 6 April the Cabinet agreed 'in principle' that talks should involve all three services and 'should not be limited to the channels of Service Attachés'.[1] The Chiefs of Staff explained that once an initial land commitment to France was made, Britain would, in fact—as in 1914—find herself committed on a much greater scale: the question of reinforcements was the natural corollary which had to be faced.[2] Simon was anxious lest the scale of talks suggested by the Chiefs of Staff would lead the French to think that Britain was prepared to make a large commitment to the Continent. Chamberlain was equally determined that the French should be under no illusions regarding British intentions, and that they should realize the importance of air defence in both countries for 'safeguarding their brain centres and their wealth'. He also suggested that if the French were informed that they could expect little assistance on land from Britain, they might be pushed into completing work on the Maginot Line.[3]

The Cabinet therefore decided that the talks should be limited strictly to a discussion of war in which Germany was the sole

[1] Cab. 23/93, Minutes 18(38)7.
[2] C.O.S., 'Staff Conversations with France and Belgium', C.O.S. Paper no. 680, para. 17. C.P. 106(38), Cab. 24/276.
[3] Cab. 2/7, Minutes of the 318th meeting of the C.I.D., 7 April 1938.

aggressor, and that the British representatives should not enter into hypothetical situations involving other allies or enemies. Furthermore, the talks were to be centred around a war in which Britain was the victim of a sudden air attack by Germany, rather than a German offensive against the Maginot Line. In view of this assumption and the decision regarding the major duty of the Army, the French General Staff was to be advised 'to base their plans on the assumption that, in the early stages of a war at any rate, it . . . [would] probably not be practicable for . . . [Britain] to send a military Expeditionary Force to the Continent'. The Cabinet was anxious to remain clear of firm commitments without giving the French the impression that Britain would never at any stage be prepared or willing to send land forces to the Continent.[1]

Financial considerations imposed further restrictions on the military contribution Britain could discuss with France. The expeditionary force was to be equipped for the purpose of imperial defence rather than for a continental campaign, and this made possible a reduction in expenditure on tanks and ammunition reserves. Similarly, £13 million could be saved by changing the role of two Territorial divisions, previously earmarked for the expeditionary force four months after the outbreak of war, to imperial duties. Substantial as these savings were, they had the effect, as both Hore-Belisha and Inskip emphasized, of denying reinforcements to the first two contingents of the expeditionary force, i.e. the four Regular and one mobile division, for a period of up to one year, and possibly even longer.[2] Hore-Belisha was told to reduce Army expenditure by £70 million from his March estimates, and he proposed to achieve this by holding back on the Territorial Army, which would consequently not be able to take the field until a year after the outbreak of war. The adverse effect this would have on Territorial recruiting could be minimized— at least in the immediate future—by not announcing that this would, in fact, be the case. A.A. defence would also be restricted, with the number of guns reduced from the 1937 revised scheme total of 1,264 to a planned 928, and searchlight companies reduced from 196 to 152. Hore-Belisha was not unduly worried by these cuts—which affected the primary role of the Army as announced

---

[1] Cab. 23/93, Minutes 19(38), 13 April 1938.
[2] Inskip, 'Defence Expenditure in Future Years—the War Office Programme. Further Report by the Minister for Co-ordination of Defence', 22 April 1938. C.P. 99(38), Cab. 24/276.

by the Government—since the provision of adequate A.A. defence was a long-range project.[1]

Anglo-French conversations were held in London on 28 and 29 April.[2] The British were determined to avoid being talked into any military commitment, and to show the French that their assistance would best be rendered in ways other than by sending a large land force to the Continent.

The conversations centred around the roles of the Armies and Air Forces. It was quickly appreciated that air co-operation would be a vital factor in war, and the representatives decided to authorize air conversations at the attaché level. Disagreement arose over the role of the British Army. Halifax explained the Government's defence priorities, and said that in view of the heavy air and naval support Britain contemplated, the largest land force that could be sent to France—if one was sent at all—would be two divisions. Although these could arrive within fourteen days after the decision to send them had been made, they 'would not necessarily be completely equipped with material regarded as essential for modern war, and they might also be short in certain effectives'. Edouard Daladier, the French Premier, replied that while he was aware that Britain's resources were not unlimited, it would surely not be unreasonable to expect that the two divisions be motorized. The French also wanted contact between the Army staffs to co-ordinate plans.[3]

Chamberlain did not think that Army conversations would be very useful, since the scale of British military involvement would be too small to warrant formal talks. The decision to send even a two-division force was a 'difficult' one for the Government to make, and it was a decision in principle only: 'the Government of the day might decide to . . . [send a force] or they might not.' Later in the talks he further emphasized this point:

> The British public were . . . very nervous about land
> commitments, and His Majesty's Government were anxious
> to avoid being drawn unconsciously and against their will
> into any engagements regarding the assistance they could
> render on land in a continental war which might prevent
> them utilising British armed forces in a way considered most
> desirable in the national interest on the outbreak of war.

[1] Cab. 23/93, Minutes 21(38)5, 27 April 1938.
[2] The British record of the Anglo-French conversations is in *DBFP*, I, 198–233.
[3] *DBFP*, I, 201–3.

In view of these considerations, the Government was not prepared to equip two divisions for the specific purpose of fighting on the Continent.[1]

Daladier again pressed for staff talks, and added that although two divisions as such were of little military significance, they would have great 'moral' importance, and might even persuade Belgium to join an alliance with France and Britain. Chamberlain therefore agreed to military talks between the respective attachés if it was clearly understood that this was not interpreted as a definite British commitment to provide any assistance on land.[2] The military section of the talks ended on this vague, tentative note.

The results were disappointing for the French. Despite the British offer of a large measure of naval and air support, the French tended to evaluate the British contribution in terms of how many divisions they were prepared to dispatch to the Continent. To be told that 'perhaps' two divisions might be sent was far from reassuring, and did little to encourage them to pursue a firm line in Europe. Although Chamberlain succeeded in relaying to the French the decision on the role of the Army, and avoided entering into any military commitments, there were signs that the French were not satisfied with the British position or convinced by their reasoning. In their eyes, plans for the A.A. defence of London or Singapore, or for an increase in British naval strength, were incidental to the security of France, and did nothing to reassure them of British resolve. Military arguments aside, the French could—and increasingly did—claim that the morale factor was the most important: unless the French nation could see a large British land presence on the Continent, it would discount the value of an alliance— formal or informal—with Britain, and redirect its foreign policy accordingly.

The absorption of Austria into the Reich in March 1938 sharpened tensions in Czechoslovakia, which saw itself outflanked on two sides by a rabidly nationalistic regime which played upon the aspirations of the Sudetenland Germans in western Czechoslovakia. The British Military Attaché in Prague bluntly warned: 'Nothing short of incorporation in the German Reich will satisfy the majority of people.'[3] The Sudeten Germans, led by Konrad

[1] *DBFP*, I, 204, 208–9.
[2] *Ibid.*, 209–10.
[3] *Ibid.*, 121. Lt-Col. H. C. T. Stronge to Newton, 3 April 1938.

K

133

Henlein, himself under German control, pressed ever-widening demands for a greater degree of autonomy and, eventually, complete separation and incorporation into Germany.[1]

France had made an alliance with Czechoslovakia in 1925, and her obligation to assist if Czechoslovakia was attacked was clear. The presence of a strong, determined state on Germany's eastern frontier was clearly to France's advantage, especially when Czechoslovakia had a valuable armament industry, centred on the Skoda works near Prague. After the Anschluss, additional frontier fortifications were built to prevent any outflanking attack. Unfortunately for the Czechs, Léon Blum's government, which had assured Prague of support, fell early in April, and was replaced by a government headed by Edouard Daladier, with Georges Bonnet as Foreign Minister. Neither of them was willing to involve France in a war on Czechoslovakia's behalf, especially if the Czech government could be pressured into an accommodation with the Sudeten Germans. The Czechs' position was further weakened by the fact that their 1935 treaty with Russia, under which Russia promised military assistance, did not come into effect until France had first gone to Czechoslovakia's aid. In addition, there appeared to be no way that Russia could intervene in Czechoslovakia, since both Poland and Rumania had made it clear that they would not grant transit rights to Russian troops.

The British government was no friend of the existing order in Czechoslovakia. Chamberlain showed himself ready at Berchtesgaden to accept the principle of separation of the Sudeten Germans from Czechoslovakia, a solution that would remove one of the 'trouble spots' of Europe.[2] In March he had touched on the possibility of assisting Czechoslovakia through the League of Nations, but so hemmed in with qualifying clauses and conditions was his statement, that the net effect was to make it clear that—in his opinion—Czechoslovakia was 'an area where Britain's vital interests were not concerned in the same degree as they were in the case of France and Belgium.'[3] By September, Czechoslovakia had

---

[1] For a general survey of the Czechoslovakian crisis see John W. Wheeler-Bennett, *Munich: Prologue to Tragedy* (New York: Viking Press, 1964); Keith Eubank, *Munich* (Norman: University of Oklahoma Press, 1963); Martin Gilbert and Richard Gott, *The Appeasers* (London: Weidenfeld and Nicolson, 1963); Keith Robbins, *Munich 1938* (London: Cassell, 1968); and the memoirs of the various participants listed in the bibliography below.

[2] *DBFP*, I, 338–41. Notes by Chamberlain of his conversation with Hitler at Berchtesgaden, 15 Sept. 1938.

[3] 5 *Parl. Debs.* CCCXXXIII, 1403–7, 24 March 1938.

become a 'far-away country' with quarrels between 'people of whom we know nothing'.[1] The prime motive force behind Chamberlain's foreign policy was his desire to maintain peace by an amicable settlement of Europe's problems. Conversely, he was prepared to go to almost any lengths to avoid war, which to him involved a 'hateful and damnable' waste of resources needed for vital social works.[2] Again in September, he said that 'war is a fearful thing, and we must be very sure before we embark on it that it is really the great issues that are at stake.'[3] Polyglot Czechoslovakia, such an affront to the principle of self-determination, was clearly not one of the 'great issues'.

Military considerations were secondary in the development of British policy regarding Czechoslovakia. It was obvious to the Cabinet that Britain's forces could not offer any assistance to Czechoslovakia,[4] especially since the rearmament programme as it affected the Army had been based on a policy of avoiding a continental involvement. Hore-Belisha told the Cabinet on 30 August that Britain could send to the Continent a force of only two divisions inadequately equipped for offensive operations: 'We cannot at present put an army into the field large enough to have any decisive effect.'[5] But Britain's military weakness had little to do with Chamberlain's policy. 'Peace with honour' overrode the claims of a 'far-away' country. It was mainly an *ex post facto* argument that Britain had no other choice but to bow to Hitler's ultimatum.[6] Yet it was clear at the time, and Chamberlain realized and admitted it later, that the force of British foreign policy was greatly weakened by the common knowledge that it was not backed by a strong military arm.[7] The power of persuasion rested ultimately on the ability to threaten: *that* the British utterly lacked. For the moment, however, these considerations were subordinated to a policy that saw the Czech problem as the first

---

[1] Broadcast, 17 Sept. 1938. *The Times*, 18 Sept. 1938.
[2] Speech at Birmingham, 9 April 1938. *The Times*, 11 April 1938.
[3] *The Times*, 18 Sept. 1938.
[4] Feiling, *Neville Chamberlain*, pp. 347–8.
[5] Minney, *Hore-Belisha*, p. 138.
[6] Hoare later wrote: 'it would not be correct to say that our military weakness was the principal cause of the Munich Agreement. The over-riding consideration with Chamberlain and his colleagues was that the very complicated problems of Czechoslovakia ought not to lead to a world war, and must at almost any price be settled by peaceful means.' Templewood, *Nine Troubled Years*, p. 289.
[7] See below, p. 142.

of a series of disputes that had to be settled by peaceful, rational means—appeasement—before Europe could move into the 'golden age'.

On 24 April Henlein presented the demands of the Sudeten Germans, the eight points of the 'Karlsbad formula'. The negotiations that opened shortly afterwards were foredoomed to failure, for Henlein had decided, with Hitler's approval, that 'we must always demand so much that we can never be satisfied'.[1] In response to rumours of threatening German troop movements, the Czech forces were partially mobilized on 20–1 May. Although the French promised to honour their commitment to Czechoslovakia,[2] and Halifax warned that, in the event of a general war, Britain would be bound to intervene,[3] this support quickly waned. Bonnet cautioned the Czechs against further mobilization, and told Phipps that France would absolve herself of any obligation if the Czech government persisted in taking an unreasonable line over the Sudeten question.[4] His statement to Ribbentrop notwithstanding, Halifax made it clear to the French that they could not expect any assistance from Britain if they went to the aid of the Czechs.[5] The German government was not unaware of the lukewarm attitude of France and Britain towards Czechoslovakia, and this only further encouraged Hitler in his designs upon the Sudetenland.[6]

Tension increased as negotiations dragged on throughout the summer of 1938, and were brought to a climax on 7 September when President Beneš offered to concede all the Sudeten Germans' demands. Henlein quickly manufactured an incident to justify abandoning negotiations, riots broke out in the Sudetenland, and the Czech Army began to mobilize unofficially. Having fled into Germany, Henlein publicly called for the incorporation of the Sudeten Germans into the Reich.

Chamberlain then took it upon himself to fly to Germany and

[1] German Foreign Ministry, *Documents on German Foreign Policy, 1918–1945* (Series D, 1937–45; 12 vols; Washington: Government Printing Office, 1949–54), II, 197–8. Report of a conversation between Hitler and Henlein, 28 March 1938. Hereafter all references to *Documents on German Foreign Policy* are to Series D, cited as *DGFP*. References are to page numbers.
[2] *DBFP*, I, 340. Phipps to Halifax, 22 May 1938.
[3] *Ibid.*, 341. Halifax to Henderson, 22 May 1938.
[4] *Ibid.*, 357. Phipps to Halifax, 23 May 1938.
[5] *Ibid.*, 346–7. Halifax to Phipps, 22 May 1938.
[6] *DGFP*, II, 376–7 (minute by Weizsäker, State Secretary, 1 June 1938); 399–401 (Dirksen to Foreign Ministry, 9 June 1938).

talk with Hitler at Berchtesgaden on 15 September. In a three-hour meeting between the two leaders, at which the only other person present was Hitler's interpreter, Chamberlain told Hitler that although he could not speak either for his Cabinet colleagues or for the French, his personal opinion was that 'on principle I had nothing to say against the separation of the Sudeten Germans from the rest of Czechoslovakia, provided that the practical difficulties could be overcome.'[1] Having essentially capitulated to Hitler's demands, Chamberlain was faced with the prospect of convincing his colleagues and the French that they would have to accede.

When Daladier and Bonnet came to London on 18 September, they were reluctant to accept the course of action that Chamberlain thought necessary. They were not convinced that Hitler's aims were limited, but they were restricted by the knowledge that Britain was not prepared to assist Czechoslovakia militarily. Chamberlain insisted that only self-determination would prevent war, and under pressure from the British delegation, the French gave way, agreed that Prague should cede at least parts of the Sudetenland to Germany, and admitted that pressure would have to be put on Beneš if he showed signs of refusing to go along with this 'settlement'.[2]

Beneš initially tried to resist, but, in the face of French and British refusals to assist Czechoslovakia, was forced to agree to the Berchtesgaden terms on 21 September. Not to be robbed of his victory over Prague, Hitler used Polish and Hungarian demands against Czechoslovakia to raise his terms. When Chamberlain and Hitler met at Godesberg on 22 September, Hitler rejected Chamberlain's proposals, which were constructed along the line of their previous talk at Berchtesgaden, as 'no longer any use'. Chamberlain was naturally dismayed, and the talks that day ended in a deadlock. There was no progress on the 23rd, save for Hitler's indication that he was prepared to set back the date for German occupation of the Sudetenland from 26 September to 1 October.[3]

Chamberlain's initial shock and anger turned into acceptance by the time he reached London.[4] On this occasion, however, the

[1] DBFP, II, 338–41. Notes by Chamberlain of his conversation with Hitler at Berchtesgaden.
[2] Ibid., 373–400. Record of Anglo-French Conversations, 18 Sept. 1938.
[3] Ibid., 463–73, 499–508. Notes of conversations between Chamberlain and Hitler, 22, 23–4 Sept. 1938.
[4] Sir Alexander Cadogan, quoted in Earl of Birkenhead, Halifax: The Life of Lord Halifax (London: Hamish Hamilton, 1965), p. 399.

Cabinet was not so ready to go along with the new settlement. Duff Cooper urged rejection,[1] but Halifax, Simon, and Hoare agreed with Chamberlain that the terms should be accepted.[2] It was made clear to the Government that if Britain refused to comply with Hitler's demands, the Dominions might not give their whole-hearted support, especially when the dispute was now essentially one of timing rather than principle.[3]

The Czech government rejected the Godesberg plan, as they were bound to, for it was, as Chamberlain said, a 'Diktat' rather than a set of proposals to form the basis of discussion.[4] Chamberlain secretly assured Hitler that Prague's answer was not to be taken as 'the last word'.[5] One way or another, the Czech problem would be settled to the satisfaction of Germany, France, and Britain.

Further Anglo-French talks were held in London on 25–26 September. In marked contrast to the attitude of the British delegation, Daladier showed signs of appreciating the sacrifices the Czechs were being called upon to make, and he argued that there were 'moral' considerations to be taken into account. It was inconceivable that Czechoslovakia should be dismembered without giving the Czech government a chance to discuss the fate of their country: 'The Czechs were . . . human beings.' Daladier proposed that Britain and France insist on going back to the proposals of 18 September and that, if rejected by Hitler, France would stand by Czechoslovakia and 'do what was incumbent' upon her. Chamberlain and Simon thereupon pressed Daladier to clarify the military measures France would take, and suggested, none too gently, that the French Air Force was hardly in a condition to afford air protection to France.[6]

Despite the inability of Daladier to say much more than 'France would do her duty', Chamberlain did not have the consensus of

---

[1] A. Duff Cooper, *Old Men Forget: The Autobiography of Duff Cooper* (*Viscount Norwich*) (London: Rupert Hart-Davis, 1954), pp. 234–5.

[2] Cadogan, quoted in Birkenhead, *Halifax*, p. 399.

[3] D. C. Watt, *Personalities and Policies: Studies in the Formulation of British Foreign Policy in the Twentieth Century* (Notre Dame, Ind.: University of Notre Dame Press, 1965), p. 173; Vincent Massey, *What's Past is Prologue* (New York: St. Martin's Press, 1964), pp. 258–62.

[4] *DBFP*, II, 518–19. Masaryk to Halifax, 25 Sept. 1938.

[5] *DGFP*, II, 933. German Chargé d'Affaires (London) to German Foreign Ministry, 26 Sept. 1938.

[6] *DBFP*, II, 520–35. Record of Anglo-French Conversation in London, 25 Sept. 1938.

opinion he wanted. Halifax had studied the criticisms that Cadogan had given him, and on 25 September he told Chamberlain that the Godesberg plan should be rejected.[1] Under pressure from Halifax, Chamberlain told the French, on 26 September, that Britain would assist France if the latter decided to fulfil her treaty obligations to Czechoslovakia. At the same time, he proposed another attempt at conciliation, and it was finally agreed that Sir Horace Wilson, the Prime Minister's personal adviser, should appeal to Hitler for peace.[2]

Wilson's visit merely gave Hitler another opportunity to display his hatred of the Czechs, and on 26 September, in a savage denunciation of Beneš delivered at the Sportpalast, he demanded that the Czechs accept his terms within two days. Wilson's mention of British and French resolve to stand by Czechoslovakia had no effect upon Hitler's hysterical determination.[3]

War seemed imminent, but the British and French decision to stand by Czechoslovakia was steadily being pushed into the background. The sight of war preparations in London moved Chamberlain to broadcast in despair that Britain had to be very sure that the 'great issues' were at stake before taking the plunge into war. Desperate for a solution, he made it clear that the claims of Czechoslovakia were not sufficient reason for war.[4] The next morning, he replied to Hitler's suggestion for another meeting, that Britain and France would see that Germany was given 'all essentials without war and without delay'.[5] Unprecedented scenes of relief greeted Chamberlain's announcement to the House of Commons that Hitler had agreed to a meeting of the representatives of Germany, France, Britain, and Italy.[6] The exclusion of Czech delegates would ensure that there would be no delay in giving Hitler 'all essentials'.

The Munich conference gave Hitler all his demands with only minor efforts by Daladier and Chamberlain to adjust the details of the settlement.[7] War was avoided at the expense of Czechoslovakia, which lost 11,000 square miles of territory, and over 80

[1] Birkenhead, *Halifax*, pp. 400–1.
[2] *DBFP*, II, 536–41. Record of Anglo-French Conversation in London, 26 Sept. 1938.
[3] *Ibid.*, 554–7, 564–7. Notes of conversations between Wilson and Hitler, 26, 27 Sept. 1938.
[4] *The Times*, 28 Sept. 1938.
[5] *DBFP*, II, 587. Halifax to Henderson, 28 Sept. 1938.
[6] 5 *Parl. Debs.* CCCXXXVIII, 26, 28 Sept. 1938.
[7] *DGFP*, II, 1014–15. Text of Munich Agreement, 29 Sept. 1938.

per cent of its industrial capacity. More important, at least for the western allies, was the effective loss of between thirty-four and forty Czech divisions and the removal of a powerful military force on Germany's eastern frontier.

The difficulty facing Chamberlain after Munich was how to follow up this triumph of appeasement. He became more convinced than ever that he knew how to deal with foreign affairs, and that Hitler was basically an honourable man who could be trusted. There was, however, a recognition that Britain's military weakness had been such that the Munich settlement was probably the only realistic course open to Britain, apart from the moral considerations which had been the prime motive force behind Chamberlain's policy. If the flush of victory distorted reality for the moment, it increasingly became clear in the months that followed that appeasement itself could not succeed unless Britain could negotiate from a position of military as well as moral strength.

The destruction of Czechoslovakia as a formidable military power changed the balance of force in Europe. The loss of thirty-five Czech divisions enabled Hitler, if he chose, to add at least an equivalent number to his forces on Germany's western frontier. The French were under no illusions: they realized that the dismemberment of Czechoslovakia involved more than a loss of French prestige. In the months to come, they looked to Britain to make up for the Czech divisions. During the Czech negotiations, Chamberlain had consistently subordinated military considerations to the moral claims of appeasement. Having avoided military involvement on the Continent, he took it upon Britain to impose a political settlement on Czechoslovakia. Whatever the short-term gains of Munich, the military balance was radically changed. Chamberlain and his supporters, however, took another six months to realize what had happened. Having led the French to abandon their 'obligation of honour', Chamberlain himself eventually had to listen to 'a counsel of expediency'.

8 'Peace with honour' October–December 1938

The Munich crisis exposed the serious military weakness of the western allies, and therefore undermined the effectiveness of Chamberlain's diplomatic initiative. The defences of Britain, especially against air attack, were shown to be almost non-existent, and it was clear that, even had the Government been prepared to consider the use of armed force to bring about a settlement to the German-Czechoslovakian dispute, it could have done little more than it actually did—to mobilize the Royal Navy. At a time when Europe seemed to be poised on the brink of war, and the fear of aerial attack was at its height, Britain appeared ready to reap the whirlwind of years of neglect of air defence. The R.A.F. had at its disposal five squadrons of Hurricanes and one of Spitfires, and the lack of heating apparatus rendered the Hurricanes inoperable above 15,000 feet—the expected altitude of the German bomber formations. Against an estimated German first-line fighter and bomber strength of 3,200, the R.A.F. had only 1,606. The ground defence situation was even worse. There was no effective A.A. artillery, the 3.7 and 4.5 inch guns not yet having come into production, while searchlights and balloons were 60 per cent under strength.[1] The September crisis revealed these deficiencies, but it took another six months and a further crisis before remedial action of any great consequence was taken.

In the weeks following the Munich settlement, the Government made no attempt to conceal the seriousness of the defence situation. Inskip, Minister for Co-ordination of Defence and a staunch supporter of appeasement, was—for once—explicit in public: 'I can say quite frankly that nobody who has seen this most valuable test of our arrangements can be unaware of the fact that there have been gaps, serious gaps, and defects which must be remedied in our preparations.'[2] A similar admission came from C. W. G. Eady, Deputy Secretary of State at the Home Office,

[1] Templewood, *Nine Troubled Years*, pp. 332–3.
[2] 5 *Parl. Debs.* CCCXXXIX, 308, 4 Oct. 1938.

who, in a lecture at the R.U.S.I., said that the authorities had been under 'no illusions' about the lack of proper air defences: 'We were not prepared; we had hardly begun to prepare.'[1] Statements such as these were at least indicative of the Government's recognition of the deficiencies; the question remained, how far would it act to repair them?

Upon his return from Munich, Chamberlain was widely acclaimed throughout Europe as the great peacemaker. This was undoubtedly his finest hour, and the few dissenting voices that cried 'shame'[2] and 'betrayal'[3] were all but drowned in the roar of public approval. Munich, for Chamberlain, was only the first step in the appeasement policy. Hitler had ultimately bowed to reason, and he would do so again. Yet Chamberlain was sufficiently realistic to understand that, had Hitler chosen war, Britain and France would have been severely pressed to take any effective military action. When war had seemed imminent in September, the Joint Planning Committee advised the Chiefs of Staff that Germany would be able to attack Czechoslovakia and still deploy sufficient forces on its western frontier to 'match any French offensive which—if it were to materialise—would be a costly and probably ineffective operation.'[4] Chamberlain had always been an advocate, if only a half-hearted one, of diplomacy backed by armed force. Munich showed Britain's military strength in its true light, and on his return to London, Chamberlain announced his intention to put greater emphasis on rearmament:[5]

> Our past experience has shown us only too clearly that weakness in armed strength means weakness in diplomacy, and if we want to secure a lasting peace, I realise that diplomacy cannot be effective unless the consciousness exists, not here alone, but elsewhere, that behind the diplomacy is the strength to give effect to it.

In Chamberlain's mind appeasement and rearmament were not incompatible, and appeasement was not a temporary policy to be

---

[1] C. W. G. Eady, 'The Progress of Air Raid Precautions' (lecture, 26 Oct. 1938), *JRUSI*, LXXXIV (Feb. 1939, no. 533), 1–23.

[2] See Duff Cooper's resignation speech: 5 *Parl. Debs.* CCCXXXIX, 29–40, 3 Oct. 1938.

[3] See Attlee's speech denouncing the government's policy that had led to Munich: 5 *Parl. Debs.* CCCXXXIX, 50–60, 3 Oct. 1938.

[4] Sir John Slessor, *The Central Blue: The Autobiography of Sir John Slessor, Marshal of the R.A.F.* (London: Cassell, 1956), p. 147.

[5] 5 *Parl. Debs.* CCCXXXIX, 551, 6 Oct. 1938.

pursued until, and only until, Britain had rearmed. The glow of success that Munich had brought was still new, and he said that 'with an equal sense of reality ... I ... see fresh opportunities of approaching this subject of disarmament opening up before us, and I believe they are at least as hopeful today as they have been at any previous time'.[1] Since, in his eyes, Munich was a triumph for reasoned diplomacy, he had none of the sense of urgency that the opponents of Munich spoke of in condemning his handling of the crisis. Even Baldwin had written to urge him to action: 'you have everything in your hands now,—for a time—and you can do anything you like. Use that time well, for it won't last.'[2] But Chamberlain saw no need for drastic action, least of all in rearmament. He told the Cabinet that for years he had been worried by the possibility that a heavy rearmament programme might bring financial ruin to the country. While in the existing circumstances Britain could not unilaterally undertake to stop rearming, 'that, however, was not the same thing as to say that as a thank offering for the present *detente*, we should at once embark on a great increase in our armaments programme.'[3] Similarly Chamberlain made it clear in Parliament that military alliances had no place in his policy. He had no intention of arming Britain to the teeth and then signing mutual defence agreements with other powers in the hope of forestalling war. That, to his mind, was a 'policy of utter despair'.[4] This was probably intended, at least in part, as an answer to the criticism from the Opposition, which continually pressed for the inclusion of the Soviet Union in any European agreements.[5] But it was also a reflection of his long-standing antipathy—shared by many of his Cabinet colleagues and the Chiefs of Staff—to alliances or informal understandings that might involve Britain in a military commitment in unforeseen circumstances.

The Cabinet had to decide how best to marshal the country's resources to achieve a reasonable degree of preparedness without imposing restrictions on private enterprise and individual liberties, and without antagonizing Hitler and giving him the pretext for abandoning the peaceful formula agreed upon at Munich.

[1] 5 *Parl. Debs.* CCCXXXIX, 50, 3 Oct. 1938.
[2] Feiling, *Neville Chamberlain*, p. 382. 30 Sept. 1938.
[3] Cab. 23/95, Minutes 48(38)5, 3 Oct. 1938.
[4] 5 *Parl. Debs.* CCCXXXIX, 236, 4 Oct. 1938.
[5] See the statements of Sinclair (Liberal) and Dalton (Labour) in 5 *Parl. Debs.* CCCXXXIX, 74, 142, 3 Oct. 1938.

Diplomacy was not to be given an effective military backing at the expense of the 'business as usual' policy. On two specific matters which were being increasingly discussed in the post-Munich period, Chamberlain made categorical statements. He repeated his pledge that the Government would not introduce conscription in peacetime,[1] and he refused to establish a Ministry of Supply: 'It must be remembered that we are not today in the same position as we were in 1914, in this respect: that we are not now contemplating the equipment of an army on a continental scale.'[2]

Hore-Belisha, however, had reached the conclusion that the Government would have to take some compulsory powers if there was to be a marked improvement in the defence position. Under the existing scheme, production for anti-aircraft defence could only be increased at the expense of some other requirement of the field army; if all-round production was to be increased the Government would have to secure an adequate supply of skilled labour and force factories to give priority to government orders over private contracts. He recorded in his diary: 'If we are to have any material improvement in the near future these powers should be taken immediately, and we must face the political and economic consequences involved.'[3] Inskip agreed with this proposal, and advised the Cabinet that 'the only way of obtaining more equipment by the 1st August 1939, would be by a somewhat drastic use of compulsory powers'.[4] Chamberlain re-emphasized the importance of Britain's financial staying power, and warned that confidence in the financial position had recently shown signs of weakening'. In considering increases in the rearmament programme, total expenditure had to be related to Britain's financial capability, so that short-term improvements were not made at the expense of long-term staying power.[5] For this reason Chamberlain opposed the establishment of a Ministry of Supply, even though such a move would have given Parliament, as Hore-Belisha suggested,[6] some reassurance that the Government was making serious attempts to remedy the shortcomings revealed during the Munich crisis.

There were several other proposals being made at this time. Hoare advised Chamberlain to hold a general election. The basis of

[1] 5 *Parl. Debs.* CCCXXXIX, 474, 6 Oct. 1938.
[2] *Ibid.*, CCCXL, 86, 1 Nov. 1938.
[3] Minney, *Hore-Belisha*, p. 158. Diary entry, 6 Oct. 1938.
[4] Cab. 23/96, Minutes 49(38)11, 19 Oct. 1938.
[5] Cab. 23/96, Minutes 50(38)4, 26 Oct. 1938.
[6] Minney, *Hore-Belisha*, pp. 159–60.

the Government could be broadened by including new blood, and the return of Anthony Eden, 'if and when' he would agree, would be widely welcomed. However, there was little or no common ground between the Government and the Labour party and Churchill, and rather than attempt to form any sort of 'national' government, Chamberlain should seize the opportunity to strengthen the Government's support in the Commons.[1] But Halifax warned Chamberlain against the temptation to make party capital out of his post-Munich popularity, and urged him instead to work for national unity. Efforts should be made to bring Labour and Eden into the government as a sign to Europe that Britain supported appeasement.[2] This was a forlorn hope, however, for Attlee had told Amery that Labour would never consider any form of co-operation with the Government as long as Chamberlain, whom they thought only too ready to 'truckle to the dictators', was Prime Minister.[3] Chamberlain himself felt that Eden misunderstood his policy, and put too much stress on the need for greater rearmament at the expense of attempts to settle disputes with Germany peacefully.[4]

The other suggestion was on the subject of 'national service'. Upon Chamberlain's return from Munich, there was widespread discussion of the various forms of organizing the nation's man-power to face a possible crisis. Following the tensions of September there had been a great upsurge of interest in the Territorial Army, and recruiting received such a boost that, by 1 December, the War Office was able to announce that the Territorials had reached a strength of 200,190, only a few hundred below its establishment which was fixed on 1 November, and the highest figure achieved since the Territorials were reconstituted from the old militia and yeomanry units in 1921.[5] The danger was that in time of mobilization, the call-up of forces that had been indiscriminately recruited might deprive industry of vital skilled labour. The problem, therefore, was how far, if at all, the Government should regulate or organize voluntary service for national defence. Even more basic was the question of whether the Government should

[1] Hoare to Chamberlain, 5 Oct. 1938. Templewood Papers, X(3).
[2] Halifax to Chamberlain, 11 Oct. 1938. Feiling, *Neville Chamberlain*, p. 385. Also Amery to Hoare, 12 Oct. 1938. Templewood Papers, X(3).
[3] L. S. Amery, *My Political Life*, vol. III, *The Unforgiving Years, 1929–1940* (London: Hutchinson, 1955), pp. 298–9. Diary entry, 21 Oct. 1938.
[4] Feiling, *Neville Chamberlain*, pp. 385–6. Diary entry, 16 Oct. 1938.
[5] *The Times*, 9 Dec. 1938.

give a lead to the public enthusiasm that was apparent during and after the Munich crisis.

Once the question of government organization had been raised, the further question of compulsion arose. Chamberlain had already repeated his pledge that the Government would not introduce conscription in peacetime, but this did not quell public discussion. Those who were opposed to compulsion had seen this trend soon after the Anschluss in March. Liddell Hart had written to *The Times* to point out that conscription was not the panacea that it was often imagined to be,[1] and he had received strong support from Sir Auckland Geddes and Archibald Sinclair. Geddes, Director of National Service, 1917–19, upheld Liddell Hart's 'quaint superstition' that volunteer troops were best able to defend democracy, and suggested that they would soon have to 'defend with vigour' their anti-conscription views.[2] Sinclair was prepared to concede that conscription might be necessary in time of war, but he considered peacetime conscription, especially before the voluntary principle had been fully tested, to be a 'preposterous suggestion'.[3]

Geddes amplified his views in an article in the *Daily Mail* in October. He was completely opposed to conscription for overseas service, although he admitted that compulsory powers might have to be given to a Ministry of National Service—the most important requirement—which should be set up to register manpower numbers and skills, and perhaps even enrol eligible men in home defence units. Only if such a register existed prior to an emergency could the country avoid the chaos that had occurred in 1914–15.[4] Even if conscription were to be introduced, a national register would be a vital preliminary step.[5]

There was considerable support in the press for this proposal. The *Spectator* urged the Government to establish a voluntary national register immediately, and argued that it was doubtful that there would ever be a need for any form of compulsion. However, it was not willing to see the Government compel citizens to register;[6] yet, without this obligatory registration of 'every citizen's experience and capacity', the scheme would at

---

[1] *The Times*, 14 March 1938.
[2] Geddes to Liddell Hart, 29 March 1938. Liddell Hart Papers, K2.
[3] Sinclair to Liddell Hart, 16 March 1938. Liddell Hart Papers, K2.
[4] 'I Want a Ministry of National Service Again', *Daily Mail*, 18 Oct. 1938.
[5] Geddes, letter to *The Times*, 13 Oct. 1938.
[6] 'Organize or Compel?', *Spectator*, CLXI (21 Oct. 1938), 640–1.

best be a half measure. In time of war—which was the critical period towards which a register was directed—questions of the readiness of the individual to 'employ [his expertise] in the public service' would become irrelevant. Since 1922 the Man-Power Sub-Committee had based its proposals upon the premise that, in time of war, the Government would assume powers of compulsion to regulate the distribution of manpower. *The Times* agreed that British diplomacy required a strong backing of armed force, but even more did it need 'the self-confidence of a people voluntarily organized and prepared'. It was the Government's duty to include in its overhaul of the defence system 'the right outlets . . . for the great surge of public spirit' shown during September.[1]

Whilst disclaiming any partiality, the *Daily Mail* sponsored a readers' poll on the question, 'Are you in favour of VOLUNTARY/COMPULSORY National Service?' It was careful to distinguish national service and military conscription—a distinction that became less and less clear as the months passed. The former included 'not only military service but A[ir] R[aid] P[recautions] duties, work on munitions and in special industries, distribution of food, and other national defence activities.' As a guideline for voters, the *Daily Mail* summarized the arguments used by proponents of each case. Those who favoured compulsion pointed to the chaos that had resulted from the voluntary system in 1914 and in the war scares of the previous September. Conscription would be 'proof to the world that Britain cannot be bluffed'.[2] The arguments against conscription were most forcefully put forward in a series of letters. Major-General J. F. C. Fuller warned those who believed in freedom of conscience that 'the scare-mongers and sabre-rattling disciplinarians are screaming now for conscription', which, however, was 'completely at variance with the national spirit'.[3] Another correspondent, and a former M.P., Commander Carlyon Bellairs R.N. (retd), suggested that compulsory national service would be used to provide troops for the Army—a policy that 'went well on the road to bankrupt the country in the last war'. Its introduction might well lead to 'expectations on the Continent that great British expeditionary forces will be landed there'.[4]

[1] *The Times*, 7 Oct. 1938.
[2] *Daily Mail*, 2 Oct. 1938.
[3] *Ibid.*, 5 Oct. 1938. Fuller was an outspoken advocate of armoured warfare, and a trenchant critic of British generalship on the western front during the Great War.
[4] *Ibid.*, 17 Oct. 1938.

Liddell Hart was becoming increasingly vocal on the subject of conscription. In an address to the Youth Peace Conference in London, he argued that the Munich crisis had shown that Britain 'needed brains, efficiency, and machines rather than numbers of men', and that 'the spiritual folly of going totalitarian in an effort to stand against totalitarianism' was not to be dismissed lightly.[1] Conscription would have little deterrent effect on Germany, and might even provoke Hitler into an early war before Britain could significantly expand its Army. It was 'the wrong treatment for the present conditions'.[2]

One of the most outspoken advocates of 'national service' was L. S. Amery. Speaking at Birmingham on 30 September, he called for 'some form of national service which will permit our manpower and national resources to be organized for our national safety'.[3] Both here and subsequently in the House of Commons[4] he took pains to make it clear that he was not arguing for compulsory military service for all eligible men; the need was rather for a rational distribution of skills before a crisis arose. The best way of resolving the national service issue, he suggested to Hoare, was for the Government to follow the precedent of 1931, when a bipartisan inquiry was set up to examine the question of protection. Once the three parties had agreed on the form of national service to be introduced, it did not matter whether the proposals were adopted by a National government, on the lines of 1931, or whether the present government implemented them with the agreement of the Opposition parties to cast aside previous government statements on compulsion.[5]

That conscription, national service, and registration were being discussed—widely discussed—at this time cannot be denied, but whether these questions had become 'issues' is another matter. Certainly there was never any possibility that Labour would collaborate with the Chamberlain government—as Amery himself had been told—particularly on a question such as compulsory national service, for, no matter how much he tried to cloud

---

[1] *The Times*, 17 Oct. 1938.
[2] 'Reflections on the situation, its future and our policy', 12 Oct. 1938. Liddell Hart Papers, K2. The speech delivered at the Youth Peace Conference follows closely the points in this note, which appears to be the draft for that speech.
[3] *The Times*, 1 Oct. 1938.
[4] 5 *Parl. Debs.* CCCXXXIX, 205, 4 Oct. 1938.
[5] Amery to Hoare, 12 Oct. 1938. Templewood Papers, X(3).

the issue by talking of organizing the whole national manpower in all areas of defence activity, Amery was basically talking about military conscription and industrial conscription, both of which would infringe on trade-union rights. Given the position of the Opposition parties, especially Labour, and of the Government, with its categorical statements denying any intent to introduce conscription, Amery's talk of inter-party co-operation was unrealistic, to say the least.

A sub-committee of the Cabinet came to the conclusion that there would be no value in establishing a compulsory national register unless it was a precursor to compulsory national service.[1] Halifax, however, who had urged Chamberlain on his return from Munich to introduce conscription, thought that there was a good case for establishing a compulsory register that would tabulate the nation's resources, but which could still be linked to a voluntary system. Colville, Secretary of State for Scotland, agreed, since the automatic adoption of compulsory service in wartime would be most efficiently carried out if preceded by a national register. Public opinion and the interest expressed in participation in national defence would not be satisfied with a token measure such as the publication of a handbook outlining the avenues open to interested citizens.[2] The *Daily Mail* reported on 15 October that the Government was about to establish a Ministry of National Service under Sir John Anderson, who would be responsible for drawing up a register of manpower resources.[3] On 26 October it published the results of its poll. Of the 52,000 readers who returned coupons, 50.2 per cent supported voluntary national service, and 49.8 per cent thought that compulsion should be applied.[4]

Chamberlain, however, was unmoved by this talk. He told the Commons on 1 November that since the Government was not 'contemplating the equipment of an army on a continental scale', there was no need for a Ministry of Supply. What the country did need were 'certain classes of specially skilled labour', and these could be obtained without the resort to compulsory powers. As the *Daily Mail* had predicted, he announced that Sir John

[1] See Cab. 23/96, Minutes 50(38)5, 26 Oct. 1938. Discussion centred on C.P. 235(38), Cab. 24/281.
[2] *Ibid.*
[3] *Daily Mail*, 15 Oct. 1938.
[4] The exact figures were:
  Voluntary   51,511 (50.184 per cent)
  Compulsory 51,133 (49.816 per cent)

L

Anderson, a former distinguished civil servant, had been appointed Minister of Civilian Defence, with special responsibility for air-raid precautions.[1] The *Daily Mail*'s response was to congratulate the Government on its 'thoroughly wise decision' to avoid a continental land commitment. 'Everyone understands', it wrote, 'that what matters above all for our security is a great and powerful force in the air.'[2] Nevertheless there were some doubts voiced: Sinclair pressed for an assurance that, notwithstanding his previous conviction that Britain should not assume a continental land role, Britain would, in the opinion of the Government's military advisers be able to fulfil its obligations without a continental army.[3] Despite the *Daily Mail*'s assertion, it was not at all clear to some critics that Britain could play her full part in the defence of Europe without a continental army, especially since the western allies had lost the benefit of thirty-five strong Czech divisions, which freed (at least) a corresponding number of German divisions for possible use in the west.

The renewed British defence efforts came under close scrutiny in France. Being a continental nation with long land frontiers, the French were much more inclined to think of defence in terms of land troops. The French Air Force was poorly equipped, and there had long been anxiety in the British government over the inadequate plans the French put forward to increase their aircraft production.[4] The Chief of the Air Staff, Sir Cyril Newall, reported that far from taking drastic steps to remedy the situation, the French did not even appreciate what the real problem—the organization of production—was: their outlook was 'hopelessly optimistic'. Halifax suggested that this would provide Chamberlain with a convenient counter to any move by the French to pressure Britain into increasing its land commitment to Europe.[5]

Phipps reported to the Foreign Office that French government circles had generally been favourable to Chamberlain's statement that peace through negotiation had to be preceded by a strengthening of national defences and the obtaining of the 'necessary guarantees which the safety of each nation requires'.

[1] 5 *Parl. Debs.* CCCXL, 83–6, 1 Nov. 1938.
[2] *Daily Mail*, 2 Nov. 1938.
[3] 5 *Parl. Debs.* CCCXL, 94, 1 Nov. 1938.
[4] See the reports in F.O. 371/21694.
[5] Halifax to Phipps, 25 Oct. 1938. F.O. 371/21592. C 13347/13/17.

This latter step would be difficult for Britain, *Le Temps* had suggested, because the British people disliked any form of military conscription. The clear inference was that France might not think it in her interest to conclude a mutual guarantee with Britain unless in return Britain was prepared to make a substantial land contribution to the defence of western Europe. In French eyes such a contribution involved the introduction of compulsory military service. Bonnet told Phipps that he had 'partially inspired' the article.[1] The Foreign Office commented: 'The French cannot altogether understand the feeling in this country against any form of conscription in peace time.'[2] It was apparent that there would be increasing pressure from the French for Britain to reverse its policy against a continental commitment.

The Foreign Office, in fact, was informed that this was indeed the case. According to a report it had received, Daladier had requested that a brief be prepared for use in the forthcoming talks with Chamberlain and Halifax in Paris. The resultant paper recommended that the French should make defence the central question of the talks, and that they should point out that in view of the loss of the Czech divisions and the increased German ability to concentrate on the French frontier, France would require even more urgently the assistance of a British Expeditionary Force. The French ministers at the talks were advised to press the British strongly on this point in the 'reasonable hope' that they would agree to enlarge their commitment to the Continent.[3] Cadogan suggested that Britain could reply to a request for a large expeditionary force by pointing to the Navy, which was vital to French maritime security, and to the Royal Air Force, which was probably more efficient than its French counterpart. If Britain were to make clear the extent of its considerable contribution, it might well take the opportunity to ask France what it would do if Germany launched an unprovoked attack on Britain without directly attacking France.[4]

Anglo-French talks were held in Paris on 24 November. Chamberlain and Halifax soon found themselves pressed by Daladier to make a definite and, in the French view, a realistic commitment. Daladier conceded that France had to make greater

---

[1] Phipps to Halifax, 2 Nov. 1938. F.O. 371/21613. C 13320/1083/17.
[2] Barclay, note, 3 Nov. 1938. F.O. 371/21613. C 13320/1083/17.
[3] Peake, minute to Strang, 17 Nov. 1938. F.O. 371/21592. C 14137/13/17.
[4] Cadogan, note, 17 Nov. 1938. F.O. 371/21592. C 14137/13/17.

efforts to improve her air force, but plans were in hand, he announced, to increase production fivefold to 400 a month, so that by the end of the year France would have 4,000 aircraft. When questioned by Chamberlain about this marked increase in production rate—it no doubt seemed another example of the 'hopelessly optimistic' outlook of the French regarding air defence—Daladier reaffirmed his belief that the figure was attainable.

In return for this greater air effort, Daladier suggested that Britain do more on land. If war broke out, the French Army could mobilize 100 divisions, 15 of which would be stationed in fixed fortifications, and the rest placed where needed. On top of this, France had 2,000 tanks in hand, and hoped to double this figure by 1940. As against this, the British promise of two divisions and 150 aircraft within three weeks of the outbreak of war was paltry: far greater land support from Britain was needed.

The French demand presented Chamberlain with a double-edged problem. As he explained to the French delegation, Britain was faced with a conflict of priorities. The development of aviation had changed the strategic situation in Europe to Britain's disadvantage. Whereas previously the Channel had provided a barrier against attack, Britain was now exposed to aerial bombardment. Since her principal armament and communication centres were within range of enemy aircraft, it was clearly the Government's first duty 'to make Great Britain as safe as possible. . . . The result of their consideration had been that they had decided to give priority to anti-aircraft defences over the demands of the land forces, whenever they competed.' Anti-aircraft artillery would have first call on industrial production over the Army's requirements for field artillery. Chamberlain admitted that much of the Army's equipment was 'obsolescent, if not obsolete', and said that consequently 'it seemed to be of no use to increase the number of troops which would be ready to be sent abroad, if it were not possible to equip them properly'. What Chamberlain did not say was that a large increase in the size of the expeditionary force could only be achieved if conscription was introduced. Apart from his own pledges not to take that step in peacetime, he was aware that any attempt to use compulsion in military or industrial defence areas would spark off widespread industrial unrest that would adversely affect the whole programme of war production. Equipment—not men—was the first need, and any attempt to increase the land commitment to France through conscription would not only unbalance the rearmament programme in general, but would in all likelihood jeopardize the re-equipment of the proposed two divisions, which the French thought inadequate. Two divisions, well-equipped and backed by the strength of British naval and air-power, were, in Chamberlain's eyes, of more value than a large number of poorly armed and ill-prepared divisions.

In the face of this logic there was little Daladier could say. He admitted the force of Chamberlain's arguments, but hoped that discussions could continue 'without unnecessary publicity' so that an agreement might be reached whereby Britain would be able to dispatch to France two divisions 'at least as early as the eighth day after the outbreak of hostilities'. Chamberlain agreed that further talks were desirable,[1] and Strang in the Foreign Office concluded that 'the possibility of such an acceleration [of Britain's land commitment] should now become the subject of conversations between the two Military Staffs'.[2]

The British Chiefs of Staff, however, continued to advise against detailed talks with the French. Conversations, they said, had dealt with the assembly of a British Expeditionary Force on the Continent, but any widening of the discussions to include the 'subsequent employment' of those troops would be militarily 'undesirable', because it would tend to commit the British to a French plan over which they would have insufficient control.[3] Memories of 1914 had not dimmed. On this point there was a divergence between the Chiefs of Staff and the Foreign Office, which could not understand the military objection to broadening the scope of the talks to include the deployment of the expeditionary force.[4]

Increasing pressure from the French was not unexpected. There had been indications since October that Britain's commitment was considered unsatisfactory. In October the British Military Attaché in Paris, Colonel Fraser, had talked with senior French officials, who had made clear to him the uneasiness with which the French regarded the proposed British contribution. General Dentz, the Deputy Chief of the French General Staff, had told Fraser that

---

[1] DBFP, III, 285–94. Record of Anglo-French Conversations held at the Quai d'Orsay on 24 November 1938.
[2] Strang, minute, 29 Nov. 1938. F.O. 371/21592. C 14287/13/17.
[3] C.O.S., 'Staff Conversations with France', 18 Nov. 1938. C.O.S. Paper No. 795. F.O. 371/21592. C 14287/13/17.
[4] Strang, minute, 29 Nov. 1938. F.O. 371/21592. C 14287/13/17.

there was a possibility that Hitler might try to separate the western allies by extending a guarantee to France in order to move against Britain. The danger was that if the impression were gained that Britain was willing to fight only to the last French soldier, the elements in France that were seeking an accommodation with Germany would be considerably strengthened. A strong German propaganda campaign was already playing on these sentiments in France.[1]

Fraser had also met with Colonel Petibon, of General Gamelin's Staff, who had argued that, given the existing state of tension in Europe, Britain could not avoid introducing conscription. Petibon admitted that Britain carried an enormous financial burden in maintaining a strong navy and air force, but added that what was needed was an *effort du sang*. France could not contemplate a repetition of the last war, when she had borne the brunt of the German attack while Britain trained an army—a process that had taken almost a year. Britain had to be capable of putting a large force into the field within three or four months of the outbreak of war, and preferably sooner: Britain 'must be in a position to develop [its] effort on a really effective scale early, and that could only be done if we introduced some form of military training on a large scale in peace.' Militarily and psychologically, France demanded a substantial land commitment—substantial in numbers of men—from Britain.[2]

This report did not reach the Foreign Office until the middle of November, only a week before the Paris meetings. Roberts wrote that 'only some spectacular decision involving national service will convince the world that we really mean business', and Makins suggested that Britain needed to introduce some measure that would be an 'outward and visible sign of an inward determination and a resolute spirit'. Sargent and Cadogan were worried by Dentz's reference to the possibility of certain elements in France coming to an agreement with Germany, and both advised that the British government should press Daladier to make a public statement guaranteeing French assistance in the event of a German attack on Britain that did not directly involve France.[3]

[1] Fraser to Col. W. E. van Cutson (War Office), 18 Oct. 1938. F.O. 371/21592. C 14067/13/17.
[2] *Ibid.*
[3] Notes by Roberts, Makins, Sargent, Cadogan, 19 Nov. 1938. F.O. 371/21592. C 14067/13/17. F. K. Roberts became Deputy Under-Secretary of State for

Pressure from the French continued after the Paris talks. Fraser reported that he was constantly asked, 'Is public opinion in Great Britain beginning to recognize the necessity for conscription?' In the afterlight of the Munich settlement the weakness of the French strategic position was clear, and the arguments that had been long put forward against a strong British land commitment no longer carried much weight. The Maginot Line— assuming that it was not breached—could not hold off a German attack indefinitely, and now the French General Staff were by no means sure of its impregnability. Besides these military considerations, there was the question of morale, and Fraser put it in terms that were heard more and more frequently in the months to follow:

> I think we must recognise that there is always latent in
> France the idea that Great Britain is very willing to fight
> her battles in Europe with French soldiers, and if this idea
> gains ground and she realises that British help on land is
> to be so limited that it can have no decisive effect, she may
> lose heart, with results which might eventually be disastrous
> to ourselves.

Whereas Daladier had put the emphasis on the early dispatch of the British Expeditionary Force to France, Fraser's military contacts, especially Colonel Petibon, stressed that size was the important factor. Fraser thought that the French would not be satisfied with less than twenty divisions within three months. This could not be done unless the 'necessary steps' had been taken before the outbreak of war.[1] In the eyes of the French, that meant conscription.

Phipps agreed with Fraser's interpretation of the French state of mind. M. Berenger, President of the Senate Commission for Foreign Affairs, had emphasized the size of Britain's land forces. While admitting that Britain was making a large contribution on the sea and in the air, and was carrying a huge financial burden, he pointed out that the French public computed British assistance in terms of numbers of soldiers sent to France. The psychological aspect could not be dismissed, and there was a danger that Britain's

---

Foreign Affairs in 1951. R. M. Makins served as Assistant Under-Secretary of State for Foreign Affairs, 1947–8.

[1] Fraser to Phipps, 5 Dec. 1938. F.O. 371/21597. C 15175/36/17.

failure to increase significantly her land commitment would weaken French morale. Phipps wrote that the problem of size 'will present itself in the guise of an antithesis between blood and sweat in constant danger on the one side and treasure and sweat in comparative security on the other'.[1]

The Foreign Office was quick to appreciate the strength of fears in France, but, as Roberts wrote, any decision to send land forces to France on the scale suggested by Fraser would entail a complete reversal of government policy. Fraser had mentioned that considerable dismay had been caused in France by the appearance in *The Times* of letters from such authorities as General Sir John Burnett-Stuart, Sir Auckland Geddes, and Liddell Hart in support of a policy of limited liability on land for Britain,[2] but Roberts pointed out that they undoubtedly represented British public opinion. At the same time he recognized that some gesture was needed to boost French morale, and the introduction of 'some form of national service' was one possibility.[3] Cadogan agreed, but added that there were serious obstacles to be surmounted before Britain could effectively equip a conscript army.[4] Vansittart, out of office but no less vocal because of that, lashed out against the British game of 'playing ostrich', and warned that unless Britain faced the fact immediately that it would have to send large land forces to France, French support could not be counted upon and Britain would lose the war.[5] Halifax passed Fraser's paper to Chamberlain for consideration.[6]

Later in December Fraser again put forward the French case for greater British assistance on land. He stressed that the correspondence in *The Times* had afforded some proof to those in France who thought that Britain was ready to fight to the last French soldier. The French appreciated the burden Britain was carrying in maintaining a large navy and air force, and did not expect that she should simultaneously build up a large professional army. A conscript army, however, *was* within Britain's financial means, and only with a conscript army could Britain make up the weight of the Czech divisions lost after Munich. Questions of

[1] Phipps to Halifax, 8 Dec. 1938. F.O. 371/21597. C 15175/36/17. These reports by Phipps and Fraser are also to be found in Cab. 21/510.
[2] See *The Times,* letters, 8, 16, 19, 22, 28 Nov. 1938.
[3] Roberts, minute, 12 Dec. 1938. F.O. 371/21597. C 15175/36/17.
[4] Cadogan, note, 20 Dec. 1938. F.O. 371/21597. C 15175/36/17.
[5] Vansittart, note, 21 Dec. 1938. F..O 371/21597. C 15175/36/17.
[6] Halifax, note, 22 Dec. 1938. F.O. 371/21597. C 15175/36/17.

financial stability were peripheral in times of serious danger: what France demanded was—to use Petibon's phrase—an *effort du sang*.[1]

German propaganda was not slow to touch on the disharmony within Britain and between the western allies. Chamberlain himself was in a difficult position, for his self-proclaimed double goal of a continuation of appeasement and a greater emphasis on rearmament required him to maintain a delicate balance between giving a lead to the nation in the rearmament and civil defence programmes without unduly provoking Hitler on the one hand or justifying, on the other, the charges of his domestic critics that he failed to appreciate the gravity of the situation. No sooner had he announced an increased effort in rearmament—all the time stressing its defensive nature—than the German press unleashed a savage attack. Newspapers throughout Germany, especially the *Frankfurter Zeitung* and the *Kölnische Zeitung*, railed against the military build-up as being contrary to the spirit of the Munich agreement, and an indication that the British government had no faith in Hitler's good intentions as expressed in the Anglo-German agreement which had been triumphantly brandished by Chamberlain upon his return from Munich. The press campaign was instigated on the direct order of Joachim von Ribbentrop, the German Foreign Minister, and its object was

> to achieve a breach between those who on no account would want a war with Germany, and those who held the view that, at Munich, England had recoiled before Germany and demanded an increase and acceleration in order to face up squarely to Germany 'next time', regardless of the consequences.[2]

Herbert von Dirksen, the German Ambassador in London, was ordered to arrange for German journalists in England to write articles along the lines of those appearing in domestic German newspapers.[3]

---

[1] Fraser to Phipps, 22 Dec. 1938. Cab. 21/555, Enclosure No. 1. Fraser sent Phipps similar reports on meetings with Petibon, who constantly referred to the French General Staff's and the French public's anxiety over Britain's failure to increase her land forces by introducing some form of conscription. See Fraser to Phipps, 23 Dec. 1938; 4 Jan. 1939. Cab. 21/555.

[2] *DGFP*, IV, 311–12. Weizäcker to Dirksen, 17 Oct. 1938.

[3] *DGFP*, IV, 313. Gottfried Aschmann (Director of Information and Press Dept., Foreign Ministry) to Dirksen, 17 Oct. 1938.

From London, Dirksen regularly sent political reports to the German Foreign Office that were remarkably accurate in outlining the shifts in British policy. He noted that, since Munich, relations with the French had by no means been free of friction and disappointment. To some extent it appeared that France was urging Britain to adopt a far more determined policy towards the dictators.[1] On the question of the British attitude towards possible German expansion eastward into Poland and the Soviet Union, Dirksen advised that although there seemed to be no firmly defined views in the upper ranks of the Government, 'it can be assumed that, in accordance with the basic trend of Chamberlain's policy, they will accept a German expansionist policy in eastern Europe.'[2] In fact, Halifax had expressed precisely this opinion when he wrote to Phipps in Paris that German expansion eastward was a 'normal and a natural thing.'[3]

> Henceforward we must count with German predominance in Central Europe. Incidentally I have always felt myself that, once Germany recovered her normal strength, this predominance was inevitable for geographical and economic reasons . . . .
> The greatest lesson of the crisis has been the unwisdom of basing a foreign policy on insufficient armed strength. . . . It would be fatal for us to be caught again with insufficient strength.

Five months later, the threat of that 'normal' expansion was to result in a guarantee to Poland that was without parallel in the history of British foreign policy.

The central issue in Franco-British relations was changing. The military arguments for and against a large British commitment on land in Europe had long been debated, and even the loss of the Czech divisions had not vitiated the arguments against unlimited liability: increased air-power could neutralize the additional German strength on the French frontier. The question had now

[1] Henderson reported that one German newspaper, *Völkischer Beobachter*, saw the Anglo-French alliance as the reason for Britain's decision to strengthen her continental expeditionary force. Henderson to Halifax, 13 Oct. 1938. *DBFP*, III, 171–2.
[2] *DGFP*, IV, 364–7. Dirksen to Foreign Ministry, 'Political Report: Britain's attitude towards eastern European questions'.
[3] *DBFP*, III, 251–3. Halifax to Phipps, 1 Nov. 1938.

become one of morale, and military reasoning—sound or otherwise—could not convince public opinion in France that its fears were groundless. If the French thought of British assistance in terms of the number of soldiers in Europe—and indications from military and political circles suggested this was the case—then it was of no use pointing to the size of the British Navy or Air Force, or talking of Britain's financial stability as the fourth arm of her defence. Rightly or wrongly, French public opinion wanted large numbers of British troops in Europe, and rational military arguments could not prevail over desires that had deep psychological and historical roots.

Chamberlain showed few signs of being aware of the discontent in France. Speaking to the Foreign Press Association in December, he asserted that, although he had suffered 'setbacks and disappointments—perhaps in greater measure than he had anticipated', they were merely 'passing phases' that could not destroy his basic optimism that peace would be preserved. Rumours of a deterioration in relations with France were unfounded: 'In fact, our relations with France are so close as to pass beyond mere legal obligations, since they are founded on identity of interest.'[1] Assurances such as this, however, could not begin to assuage French fears that Britain was ready to fight to the last French soldier. Indications were that something more was needed to steady French opinion, and that was conscription. It seemed that nothing less would satisfy the French.

[1] *The Times*, 14 Dec. 1938.

9 The call for volunteers January–March 1939

Under continuing pressure from the French and in the face of threats of further German expansion in eastern Europe during January 1939, the British government moved haltingly towards organizing the nation and its resources for possible war. The steps that it did take were an attempt to pacify public opinion rather than to formulate a coherent policy that would enable Britain to face a critical situation. Although Chamberlain remained firmly wedded to the idea that international problems could be settled peacefully and reasonably, as they had been at Munich, some of his Cabinet colleagues were becoming convinced that measures that were drastic in the light of hitherto accepted policy were required to improve significantly Britain's military and diplomatic strength.

Upon receipt of Fraser's reports from Paris, the Foreign Office decided that it was time to insist that, despite the long-standing objections of the Chiefs of Staff, Britain should hold staff conversations with France on the question of military co-operation. Cadogan added that the French General Staff would use such talks to press the British for a guarantee to provide sufficient land forces to replace the lost Czech divisions. One answer the British representatives could give was a promise to introduce conscription, but that would be an 'empty gesture', for equipment deficiencies would render the additional troops useless for some time. On the other hand, Britain's industrial and financial resources, which were constantly mentioned as important factors in Britain's defences, could be geared more closely and obviously to the needs of defence.[1] Without some such measures, Strang suggested, it would be difficult to answer the French case that Britain was responsible for making up the land forces France had lost after Munich.[2]

Information received from British embassies continued to point to some new venture by Hitler. Notwithstanding Chamber-

[1] Cadogan, minute, 6 Jan. 1939. F.O. 371/21597. C 16018/36/17.
[2] Strang, minute, 5 Jan. 1939. F.O. 371/21597. C 16018/36/17.

lain's myopic view of the international scene, Hitler's image had been considerably tarnished by the savage pogroms unleashed after a young Jew killed a German diplomat in Paris. From Berlin, Ogilvie-Forbes reported rumours of German moves against the Ukraine in collaboration with Poland, or, lacking Polish support, against Poland as well. Hitler's previous spectacular successes had set a pattern for expansion, and this desire for further cheap victories was reinforced by the need to gain access to vital raw materials to give a much-needed boost to the straining German economy.[1]

Halifax thought that there were four courses open to Germany. Hitler might encourage Italy to press its claims against France, and use the French refusal as a pretext for war; he might make impossible colonial demands that he knew would be rejected (this seemed the least likely); he might attack Holland; or he might suddenly launch an air strike against Britain, followed by a land and air offensive against the western powers. The Foreign Office had 'definite information from a highly placed German that preparations for such a *coup* . . . [were] being made'.[2] At the end of January, the British Military Attaché in Berlin reported that it was generally accepted that a major military action was being planned, possibly against the Maginot Line.[3]

Yet the whole thrust of German policy since 1919 had been eastwards, and Halifax himself had admitted that German expansion to the east was 'a natural thing'.[4] Despite this trend, which was supported by evidence of growing tension over the position of Danzig, and by reports from Ogilvie-Forbes, Halifax believed that Hitler's priorities lay in the west: potential German gains in the east did not enter into Halifax's appreciation of the situation. Likewise, the Military Attaché's reports on German military priorities were remarkably inaccurate, and not at all in keeping with German policy.

The French renewed their pressure on the British for a firm commitment of larger land forces,[5] and underlined the seriousness of the situation by announcing, on 17 January, that the two-years military service law, which had been in force since March 1936

---

[1] *DBFP*, III, 544–51. Col. F. N. Mason-MacFarlane, 'Memorandum respecting the military possibilities in 1939', 26 Dec. 1938; 561–4. Ogilvie-Forbes to Halifax, 3 Jan. 1939.

[2] *Ibid.*, IV, 4–6. Halifax to Mallet (Washington), 24 Jan. 1939.

[3] *Ibid.*, 30. Ogilvie-Forbes to Halifax, 27 Jan. 1939.

[4] See above, p. 158.

[5] *DBFP*, IV, 569–71. Fraser to Phipps, 4 Jan. 1939.

(when Hitler reoccupied the demilitarized zone of the Rhineland), and which was due to expire in October 1939, would be renewed: the international situation did not allow a return to the one-year period, which would have entailed a decrease of 100,000 in the strength of the armed forces.[1]

Once the September crisis had shown the weakness of Britain's defences, particularly against air attack, there was increasing criticism of the Government for having allowed the defence situation to become so serious. This criticism was especially directed against Hore-Belisha and Inskip, and Anderson's appointment as Minister of Civilian Defence was a sign that the Government was aware of the public unease over anti-aircraft protection. Such was the strength of this feeling that Chamberlain came under pressure to make changes within his Cabinet.

Hore-Belisha was attacked for inadequacies of A.A. defence. Three junior ministers, Robert Hudson (Secretary of the Department of Overseas Trade), the Marquis of Dufferin and Ava (Parliamentary Under-Secretary for the Colonies), and Lord Strathcona and Mount Royal (Parliamentary Under-Secretary of State for War) expressed to Chamberlain their lack of confidence in Hore-Belisha, and threatened resignation if he was not replaced. Press reports that the 'revolt' had been partially inspired from within the War Office—i.e. among the military members—caused Hore-Belisha to defend vigorously his record in office.[2] Speaking in his constituency on 6 January, he asserted that in carrying out his task of modernizing the Army—without which no re-equipment scheme could be effective—he was fully aware of the obstacles he would have to surmount, but: 'My knowledge that the Prime Minister was equally acquainted with the character of the task and of the repercussions which must follow from the forthright measures to be taken has throughout sustained me.'[3] The *Spectator* thought the accusations made against Hore-Belisha were not without foundation; indeed, the inadequacies revealed by the September crisis and Hore-Belisha's 'tactlessness' and 'lack of the simple virtues of kindliness and sympathy' raised the question of the justification for continued public confidence in him. However, it added, his record had otherwise been good:

[1] *The Times*, 18 Jan. 1939.
[2] Minney, *Hore-Belisha*, 161–6.
[3] *The Times*, 7 Jan. 1939.

'It is best to hope that he will have another chance, that he has learnt a lesson, and that he will not forget.'[1]

Although there was a growing divergence between Chamberlain and Hore-Belisha over such questions as a continental role for the Army, the establishment of a Ministry of Supply, and the introduction of conscription—all of which Hore-Belisha supported,[2] Chamberlain did not see fit to remove him from the War Office. Instead, he shifted Inskip to the Dominions Office, and replaced him by Lord Chatfield, formerly First Sea Lord (1933–8). William Morrison, previously Minister of Agriculture, was appointed Chatfield's deputy in the House of Commons. Commented the Labour *Daily Herald*: 'this is hardly likely to be a satisfactory arrangement.'[3]

By the middle of January the Government was moving towards the establishment of a national register. The question was: should it be compulsory or voluntary? At the first meeting of the Citizen Service League (the renamed Army and Home and Empire Defence League), Amery called for a system of compulsory national service training, not simply military conscription but enrolment by all age levels in the most suitable sphere of national defence.[4] This presupposed the establishment of a compulsory national register, for without it there could be no government control to ensure that manpower skills and resources were most effectively allotted. Sir John Anderson firmly rejected the use of compulsion, however, when he said that a compulsory national register was of no use in peacetime except for statistical purposes.[5]

The Government's plans were unveiled on 23 January, when Chamberlain broadcast a National Service Appeal to the nation. He called on able citizens to enrol in the special forces for which they were best fitted, but stressed that their decision was to be a voluntary one—and all the firmer because of it:

> Compulsion is not in accordance with the democratic system under which we live, or consistent with the tradition of freedom which we have always striven to maintain. We are confident that we shall get all the volunteers we want without recourse to compulsion.

[1] 'Mr. Hore-Belisha's record', *Spectator*, CLXII (13 Jan. 1939), 41–2.
[2] As he told Strathcona. Minney, *Hore-Belisha*, p. 162.
[3] *Daily Herald*, 30 Jan. 1939.
[4] *Daily Telegraph*, 18 Jan. 1939.
[5] *The Times*, 10 Jan. 1939.

A compulsory register, he asserted, would get little public support and was, in any case, unnecessary, since a comprehensive register could be drawn up within three or four weeks of the outbreak of war.[1] This seemed to ignore the critics' point that it was the question of timing that was the essence of the whole problem. In the last war it had taken many months before manpower was distributed on anything approaching rational lines, but since then technological changes had immensely speeded up the mobilization time, and the country might not be able to afford the luxury of even as little as three weeks of unpreparedness and confusion.

The broadcast was followed by an all-party rally in Albert Hall, at which the Labour party promised its full support for the campaign which would show that conscription was unnecessary.[2] To coincide with this public launching the Government published twenty million National Service Appeal Handbooks. These listed the various fields of service open to men and women, but, to the disappointment of the French government, the requirements of the Regular Army were dealt with only briefly and given little prominence. As a guideline to service the Government also released a schedule of 'reserved occupations', which were considered important in their own right. Those who were listed in the 'reserved' category were not free to volunteer for duties—e.g. the armed forces—that would interfere with the performance of their primary jobs. The Government made it clear that the scheme would be watched closely, and the results studied after two months to see if they were likely to fulfil the country's needs.[3]

The reaction was generally favourable. The press interpreted the campaign as a sign that the Government was at last cognizant of the mood of restlessness in the country,[4] and the *Daily Mail* welcomed it as a chance to 'see some real action'.[5] At the same time there was some disquiet over some features of the scheme, especially the wide range of occupations included in the 'reserved'

[1] *The Times*, 24 Jan. 1939.
[2] *Ibid.*, 25 Jan. 1939.
[3] *Ibid.*, 26 Jan. 1939.
[4] See *The Times, Birmingham Post, Daily Telegraph*, 26 Jan. 1939. The *Manchester Guardian*, however, reported (23 Jan.) the formation of a 'No Conscription League', supported by branches of the Co-operative Movement, the Independent Labour Party, the Peace Pledge Union, and various trades unions and local Labour party committees. The League argued that the National Service campaign was merely the first step in the government's plan to introduce military and industrial conscription.
[5] *Daily Mail*, 24 Jan. 1939.

schedule. Why, asked the *Daily Mail*, when the Government was appealing for volunteers to assist in time of possible crisis, were such occupations as *chef de cuisine* or sleeve link maker held to be vital?[1] The *Daily Mail*'s preferences were made clear on 26 January when it advised young men:

> If you are fit and near the twenties:
> Remember: THE AIR COMES FIRST!

Sir John Simon, however, spoke in a different vein. He decried attempts to make armed strength the sole measure of Britain's influence and, echoing Chamberlain's longstanding views, said: 'There is our financial strength, which in the past has so often been the decisive influence and which remains as important a weapon of defence as ever before'.[2] Comments such as this, combined with an apparently half-hearted approach by the Government, did little to help convince the public that its services were urgently needed: many of the handbooks were not delivered until several days after the opening broadcast, and thereby lost much of their impact, and the book itself was criticized for uninspiring design and poor order of priorities. The results reflected the Government's failure to present its case in a forthright manner: enrolments were relatively slow, and did not match expectations.[3]

The second measure that was discussed was the establishment of a Ministry of Supply. If a national register was introduced to rationalize the future distribution of manpower, it seemed natural to many observers that the Government should make all the provisions necessary to ensure the efficient use of industrial resources for defence purposes. Early in January Hore-Belisha had admitted that he lacked the necessary power to effect his plans with a minimum of delay.[4] The *Daily Telegraph* wrote that this 'significant confession' was proof of 'the soundness of the demand for a Ministry of Supply'.[5] According to Anthony Eden, the British public was aware that Britain's strategic position had been weakened by the outcome of the September crisis, and would therefore welcome government steps to organize the whole nation for defence—perhaps on a wartime basis.[6] In fact, in view of

[1] *Daily Mail*, 25 Jan. 1939.
[2] *Daily Telegraph*, 28 Jan. 1939.
[3] Amery, *The Unforgiving Years*, p. 302.
[4] *The Times*, 9 Jan. 1939.
[5] *Daily Telegraph*, 9 Jan. 1939.
[6] *Ibid.*, 13 Jan. 1939.

the Government's insistence on the provision of adequate A.A. defence, a provision that had to be completed before Britain would countenance increased support on land for France, a Ministry of Supply was more important than a mobilization— voluntary or otherwise—of the nation's manpower.

Within the ranks of the Government there was growing support for the establishment of a Ministry of Supply. On 26 January, Hore-Belisha stated flatly that the strategic considerations upon which British policy was based had been changed by Hitler's occupation of Austria and subsequent expansion into the Sudetenland. In a future war Britain could not fight on the basis of 'limited liability', and the great expansion of the Army which this reversal of policy involved forcefully argued for a Ministry of Supply to co-ordinate production and equipment. Unless this vital step was taken in peacetime, Britain might not be given a breathing space once war had broken out. It was significant that Hore-Belisha's case was supported by Halifax and Ernest Brown, Minister of Labour.[1] Despite his close ties with Chamberlain and his firm support of the general trend of appeasement, Halifax had begun to diverge from Chamberlain since Munich with suggestions of a widening of the Cabinet membership and the introduction of conscription. Brown had long tangled with the War Office over any suggestion that the Ministry of Labour become even tangentially involved with service recruiting, since such an association would leave the Ministry open to charges from Labour supporters that the Government was planning to conscript workers for military and industrial purposes. The establishment of a Ministry of Supply, however, implied government powers over labour, for without the ability to direct labour, the Government could not channel production into the desired areas.

Hore-Belisha was also supported by Inskip, who submitted a paper to the Cabinet just before he was replaced by Chatfield. Inskip suggested that there were sound political reasons for establishing a Ministry of Supply, in that such a step would 'be acceptable to some strong currents of opinion in the House of Commons' and it would have a 'steadying effect' on public opinion both in Britain and abroad. If the Government decided to take that step, it would need some compulsory powers. Inskip thought

[1] Cab. 2/8, Minutes of the 345th meeting of the C.I.D.; Minney, *Hore-Belisha*, pp. 170–2. Diary entries, 19, 26 Jan. 1939.

that compulsory military service would be 'wholly impracticable' and that the Government would have to limit its compulsory powers to industry. This, however, would not harm Britain's defence preparations, since conscription in the last war had only been introduced because of the decision to send large land forces to France. Although he realized that many of those who supported a Ministry of Supply did so because they saw it as the necessary first step in the creation of large land forces, he did not believe that anyone now favoured a land effort on the same scale that Britain had made in 1914–18. This, however, was precisely the view towards which Hore-Belisha was moving. But in Inskip's mind the political objections to conscription were overwhelming: the experiences of 1914–18 and subsequent political developments had shown that labour's services would have to be won by persuasion and not by compulsion.[1] The difficulty was—and this was at the heart of Chamberlain's unwillingness to agree to a Ministry of Supply—that a Ministry of Supply could not be established on a limited basis, because labour would interpret compulsory powers over industry as the precursor of similar powers over manpower for military purposes. For this reason the matter was deferred for further consideration. Chamberlain was not yet ready to undertake such a potentially disruptive step which might well endanger the entire rearmament programme through a breakdown in labour relations. This fear was to carry increasing weight in the months to come.

Hore-Belisha's urging of a Ministry of Supply was all the stronger because of Army changes he recommended to the Cabinet in January. The situation in Europe had changed drastically since the Cabinet had approved a scale of Army preparation in March 1938, and the new circumstances forced a review of previously accepted standards. He proposed that the first two Regular divisions of the expeditionary force be equipped for offensive warfare rather than be restricted to defensive operations. The third and fourth divisions had only half the scale of reserves and ammunition required for defensive warfare, and he recommended that these be expanded to the full level required for an offensive role. Thirdly he suggested that special colonial units be established so that in time of war, comparatively minor operations—such as

[1] Inskip, 'The Establishment of a Ministry of Supply in Peace', 28 Jan. 1939. C.P. 33(39), Cab. 24/283.

those in Palestine—would not have to draw on the limited strength of the Regular Army which would be largely committed to the expeditionary force. Since the Territorial Army would provide the bulk of the third and subsequent contingents of the expeditionary force, he requested that the Cabinet approve the provision of war reserves and equipment for four Territorial infantry divisions and realistic training equipment for the remainder of the Territorial units. These changes would cost approximately £81 million. Despite his disclaimer that he was not proposing any change in the role of the Army,[1] it was clear that he thought it necessary for the Army to be prepared to play a greater part in operations on the Continent.

The Chiefs of Staff gave further proof of this increasing emphasis In stressing the dangerous delay that Britain would experience between the outbreak of war and the employment of her forces in the field if steps were not taken in peacetime to speed up the provision of equipment and reserves, the Chiefs of Staff argued that such considerations raised the general question of the best distribution of Britain's total resources. They were careful to point out that they did not wish to enter into the question of whether Britain should have a commitment or the ability to put into the field an army on the scale of that raised in 1914–18, but they noted that after the needs of industry and the other services had been satisfied, there would be a sizeable pool of manpower which could be used to satisfy any needs of the Army. What Britain needed was the ability to employ a flexible response, and this would be denied her if the Government persisted with its policy of planning on the basis of having only four infantry divisions and one mobile division available in the first year of war:

> If we were so limited, this might well mean that this
> country would not be in a position to make the best use
> of its available resources, or to put its whole strength into
> the war during what might prove to be the critical period.

The first requirement, therefore, was for industry to be so organized in peacetime that it could handle defence orders, and thus avoid a critical situation in the immediate post-mobilization period.

These changes implied a greater role for the Army, and the

---

[1] Hore-Belisha, 'The State of Preparedness of the Army in Relation to its Role', 13 Dec. 1938 (submitted to Cabinet, 27 Jan. 1939). C.P. 27(39), Cab. 24/282.

Chiefs of Staff explained that the unstable international situation might well demand the use of British land forces in the Far East, the Middle East, or the Mediterranean. To that extent, then, consideration of the Army's role had to be made on a wider basis than simply thinking of 'national armies engaged in trench warfare on the Continent'. However, the Chiefs of Staff then went on to argue that Britain now had to face the fact that in all probability she would be required to place large land forces in Europe. Halifax had told them that the French were worried lest Britain leave them to bear the greater part of the burden of the fighting on land, and might even prefer to make a separate peace with Germany rather than risk war against the combined strength of Germany and Italy without a sizeable commitment from Britain. Said the Chiefs of Staff: 'It is difficult to avoid the conclusion that such assistance may have to include support by land forces if only for the moral effect which would thereby be produced on the French nation.' The consequences of the fall of France would be so grave that the steps required to prevent such a situation arising should be included among Britain's top defence priorities. For these reasons the Chiefs of Staff supported Hore-Belisha's recommendations regarding the increases in equipment and reserves for the Regular and Territorial units of the expeditionary force.[1]

These proposals were sent to a committee of Cabinet ministers consisting of Chamberlain, Simon, Hore-Belisha, Chatfield, and Morrison. Chamberlain appreciated that the War Office was not asking for the creation of an Army on the scale of 1914–18, but the view was held in 'certain quarters' that once Britain had committed herself to a land war on the Continent, she could not avoid being involved on a basis of unlimited liability. The only way to forestall such a predicament would be to make it unmistakably clear to the French that Britain was not prepared to send more than a certain number of troops, and that consequently French plans should in no way be dependent on false expectations. Once that had been done, the French and British staffs could hold talks on the best use to be made of Britain's limited commitment.[2] In keeping with this wary approach, the committee recommended that Hore-Belisha's proposals that the second contingent of the

[1] C.O.S., 'The State of Preparedness of the Army in Relation to its Role', 25 Jan. 1939. C.P. 28(39), Cab. 24/283.
Cab. 21/511. Minutes of a meeting of Ministers, 10 Feb. 1939.

expeditionary force be so equipped that it could embark for the Continent within forty days of the outbreak of war be modified to sixty days.[1]

When these recommendations were presented to the Cabinet, Chamberlain explained that it was with reluctance that he had agreed to this change from an Army equipped for general purposes to one specifically equipped for a continental role. The extra equipment imposed serious additional burdens on Britain, but this was unavoidable in view of the deterioration of the strategic position of the western allies since September, and the feeling prevalent in France that Britain should make a significant land contribution. Not only did the French want a large British land commitment, they wanted it in France as soon as possible after the outbreak of war. The Chiefs of Staff were therefore studying possible means of speeding up the embarkation plans for the first contingent. On the other hand, however, the committee felt that the second contingent need not be sent as early as had originally been planned: financial considerations were still important, and the decision to send the second contingent after sixty rather than forty days would allow the Army to keep smaller reserves, and thereby save £1.4 million. The new strategic situation did not mean that Britain would commit unlimited numbers of troops, and Chamberlain stressed that in the proposed staff conversations with the French, the British representatives would not give any definite undertaking in regard to the employment of the Territorial Army. Nevertheless, Britain should be in a position to send some Territorial divisions to the Continent within the first year of war, and the committee recommended that four divisions within six months of the outbreak of war was the desirable target.

Simon agreed that the increases were necessary, but added that the financial aspect was serious and had to be constantly borne in mind. Halifax drew attention to the French failure to respond to Britain's request for staff talks, and suggested that the French government might be working on further proposals that Britain introduce conscription. Perhaps the accelerated timetable for the dispatch of the first contingent would counter undue pressure from the French. Hore-Belisha added that the changes would do something to satisfy growing demands in Parliament which argued

[1] Chamberlain, 'The State of Preparedness of the Army in Relation to its Role: Memorandum by the Prime Minister', 18 Feb. 1939. C.P. 49(39), Cab. 24/283.

that Britain's ties with France had to be cemented by the promise of substantial forces to the Continent.

The proposals put forward by the Ministerial committee were accepted by the Cabinet with the proviso that they did not interfere with the increased A.D.G.B. (Air Defence of Great Britain) programme and did not involve expenditure above that submitted as estimates by the War Office.[1] The Government was slowly moving towards a real increase in the rearmament programme, but the direction and nature of that increase seemed dictated by public opinion as much as by strategic considerations. The Munich settlement—in which Britain's unwillingness to stand with France had caused the French to renege on their promises to the Czechs—was coming home to roost. A French commitment to Czechoslovakia was replaced by a British commitment to France, and French morale, which could not be allowed to sink to a dangerous level, was soon to demand from Britain an unlimited liability in support of France.

If in private the Government was taking important steps to increase Britain's armed strength, its sense of the gravity of the situation was not conveyed to the nation at large. In the press and in Parliament criticism grew over what appeared to be its half-hearted, muddling ways. As early as mid-January, the *Manchester Guardian* spoke in support of those who questioned whether the government had any policy or overall plan to face the obvious threat which Germany posed.[2] Several days later it asserted that there was no need for Britain to contemplate sending land forces to France to help defend its eastern frontier; best they be used in connection with British sea-power to defend Anglo-French interests elsewhere.[3] Support for this argument came from Liddell Hart, writing in *The Times*. He maintained that Britain's traditional strategy had always been to rely on the Navy and to avoid committing large ground forces to Europe. When the latter had been done, as in 1914–18, the result had been a prolonged and useless bloodletting.[4] He was answered by several letters, all in disagreement, and was taken to task in Parliament by one Conservative M.P., who reminded the House that the B.E.F. had saved the situation in the first weeks of the war, both at the

[1] Cab. 23/97. Minutes 8(39)6, 22 Feb. 1939.
[2] *Manchester Guardian*, 26 Jan. 1939.
[3] *Ibid.*, 31 Jan. 1939.
[4] Liddell Hart, 'An Army Across The Channel?', *The Times*, 7, 8 Feb. 1939.

Marne and at Ypres. The 'mere existence' of such a force had had a salutary effect on French morale, and would do so again if war came.[1]

The *Daily Mirror* reported (9 January)—even before the National Service Appeal was launched—that the trial would not succeed, because without compulsion men would volunteer their services only for the easier jobs, and it alleged that the Government was already thinking about a compulsory scheme in March. However, the *Daily Mirror* thought that the voluntary system was the 'fairest symbol of democracy',[2] and it commended the Government for learning at least one lesson from 1914–18 by taking steps to protect the labour needs of industry:[3]

> Essential workers in important war industries must not be sacrificed to the 'more men' howls of cormorant generals, whose one idea is to conscript the whole manhood of the country indiscriminately, in order to get it indiscriminately massacred and then howl again for 'more men'.

But a closer examination of the schedule of reserved occupations prompted the *Mirror* to ask: 'Either it's all got something to do with mystery armaments, or else the authorities want "business as usual"—as they did last time; though they didn't get it.'[4]

By mid-February the National Service Appeal was showing signs of slowing down. The *Daily Telegraph* (13 February) criticized the Government for failing to give a proper lead, saying that apart from the opening rally and a subsequent speech by Ernest Brown, there had been few signs of official support and encouragement for the campaign. On the infrequent occasions that the appeal did rate a mention in the press, it was to report a brawl at a speech by Anderson in Glasgow,[5] or a breakdown in the administration of the campaign, which had caused many volunteers to be turned away with the comment that their services were not needed at the moment.[6]

The Labour *Daily Herald* repeatedly emphasized that Labour's whole-hearted participation in the scheme was a sign that they trusted the Government to stand by the voluntary system. The

[1] Captain Heilgers in 5 *Parl. Debs.* CCCXL, 149–50, 20 Feb. 1939.
[2] *Daily Mirror*, 23 Jan. 1939.
[3] *Ibid.*, 25 Jan. 1939.
[4] *Ibid* 26 Jan. 1939.
[5] *News Chronicle*, 15 Feb. 1939.
[6] *Daily Telegraph*, 17 Feb. 1939.

disappointing results of the first month would simply push the country into the hands of those who had always wanted to have conscription in the first place.[1] This was echoed by Ernest Bevin, Secretary of the Transport and General Workers' Union, who warned that 'if unions took a negative attitude they might easily slip into some form of compulsion on the ground that it was necessary for preparedness',[2] and G. D. H. Cole, the Labour academic, recalled how in the last war, Labour had been tricked into supporting the Government by means of an appeal for voluntary service, only to find it preparing the way for the introduction of conscription.[3] The *Daily Herald* (20 February) demanded that appeals for service—which might well turn into compulsory schemes—be accompanied by controls of profits, especially in the armament industry. 'Conscription of wealth' was soon to become a rallying cry of the Labour party against the Conservatives' 'conscription of man-power'.

The role of the Army and the nature of Britain's commitment to Europe were discussed at length in Parliament during February, when it appeared that the Government was preparing to make extensive changes. Simon introduced a bill to empower the Government to amend the 1937 Defence Loans Act and increase to £180 million the limit on the aggregate amount of money that could be drawn from the Consolidated Fund. Defence expenditure was to be extended to cover air-raid precautions and the stockpiling of essential commodities, especially food. On 6 February,[4] Chamberlain announced that Britain and France stood together, and he reaffirmed his statement of the previous December:

> It is impossible to examine in detail all the hypothetical cases which may arise, but I feel bound to make plain that the solidarity of interest, by which France and this country are united, is such that any threat to the vital interests of France from whatever quarter it came must evoke the immediate co-operation of this country.

This declaration was greeted with 'general cheers'.[5] Fine words, however, were not likely to satisfy the French, who had continued

[1] *Daily Herald*, 14 Feb. 1939.
[2] *Ibid.*, 15 Feb. 1939.
[3] *Ibid.*, 14 Feb. 1939.
[4] 5 *Parl. Debs.* CCCXLIII, 623.
[5] *The Times*, 7 Feb. 1939.

to apply pressure through diplomatic and military channels to convince the British that conscription was necessary to cement Anglo-French relations on a basis of confidence. Having rejected for so long the suggestion that staff talks include a discussion of the employment of forces after disembarkation on the Continent, the Government found it could not necessarily call the tune at its own convenience. The French did not immediately respond to Halifax's request for staff talks, and he warned the Cabinet that the French were undoubtedly holding off in the hope that the pressure of events and public opinion—especially in Britain—would force the Government to consider possible forms of aid it had hitherto ruled out as impracticable.[1]

Within Parliament the subject of greater British support for France was discussed during the Defence Loans debate. Conservative M.P.s questioned France's ability to defend three long land frontiers without substantial assistance from Britain,[2] and Sir Edward Grigg, an active member of Amery's National Service group, gave evidence that the Government's unwillingness to take drastic steps was undermining French confidence and encouraging an aggressive policy on the part of Germany.[3]

Amery and Robert Boothby (Conservative) pressed the Government to institute compulsory national service, although both insisted that this should not be limited to military training.[4] Boothby, however, stressed the importance of building up a trained cadre in peacetime so that the Territorial Army could be expanded rapidly if war broke out.[5] Unrest in France, and the growing awareness in Britain that France had suffered a military setback at Munich, led proponents of conscription to push more openly for its introduction. Despite their disclaimers, it was no coincidence that Chamberlain's declaration of solidarity of interest between Britain and France sparked off further demands for compulsory national service training, demands which increasingly centred on the military potential of the school-leaving and university age group.

The trend of a large and growing segment of Parliamentary opinion was epitomized by Archibald Sinclair, who admitted that only a year before he had vigorously denounced any proposal

[1] Cab. 23/97, Minutes 8(39)6, 22 Feb. 1939.
[2] 5 *Parl. Debs.* CCCXLIII, 73–4, 20 Feb. 1939.
[3] *Ibid.*, 318–19, 21 Feb. 1939.
[4] *Ibid.*, CCCXLIV, 1035, 27 Feb. 1939.
[5] *Ibid.*, 77, 20 Feb. 1939.

to send an expeditionary force to the Continent. The international situation had changed, however, and the outcome of the Munich Conference and Britain's pledges to assist France meant that 'the necessity of sending an army to France is one which we cannot refuse to contemplate'.[1] Limited liability no longer necessarily seemed the most efficacious formula on which to base British policy.

Chamberlain's reluctance to countenance additional defence expenditure was made clear to the House of Commons in February. At a time when press and Parliamentary opinion indicated a degree of misgiving over Britain's ability to assist France—even if there was not yet a strong consensus as to the nature that further support should take—he confessed that he was appalled by the projected expenditure, and that he thought there was 'a good deal of truth' in the belief that 'we are all piling up these ruinous armaments under a misunderstanding.'[2] Nevertheless, although Britain maintained a policy of 'friendliness' towards all countries, her military strength was such that

> when we reflect that what we are now considering is the
> effect of this country alone, without taking any account
> of the contribution that could be made, if need arose, by
> the great Dominions or by our allies and friends outside
> the British Empire, we may well feel that, to quote our
> own Shakespeare,
> > 'Come the three corners of the world in arms
> > And we shall shock them.'[3]

When pressed, however, to make a statement on the Government's intentions regarding an expeditionary force for the Continent, he stalled with the answer that the Army estimates debate would answer the Member's queries.[4]

Soothing reports to the Foreign Office continued to flow from Nevile Henderson in Berlin. He told Halifax, on the basis of talks with Göring, that unless Hitler was forced to it, he would not undertake any further foreign ventures. The German people wanted peace, and Hitler was not going to deny them this. The British government could help Hitler return to the 'fold of

---

[1] 5 *Parl. Debs.* CCCXLIV, 953–4, 27 Feb. 1939.
[2] *Ibid.*, 234–5, 21 Feb. 1939.
[3] *The Times*, 23 Feb. 1939. Speech at Blackburn.
[4] 5 *Parl. Debs.* CCCXLIII, 1115, 9 Feb. 1939.

comparative respectability' by publicly emphasizing their complete reliance on his peaceful intentions. At the same time Chamberlain could continue with his rearmament programme as a strictly defensive build-up.[1] Partly on the basis of this report, Halifax sent a reassuring appraisal of the situation to the British Ambassador in Washington, in which he noted that it seemed Hitler had 'abandoned the idea of precipitating an immediate crisis', so impressed was he with British rearmament and Chamberlain's statement on the Anglo-French solidarity of interests.[2]

The wonder is not that Henderson could send such reports— he had consistently been favourably disposed towards the Nazi regime, and was not especially noted for his reliable judgment[3]— but that Halifax would pass them on. Halifax, perhaps more than any other Minister, was aware of the French unrest over the British government's failure to respond to their requests for conscription, and he had already expressed concern lest French pressure on that point should prove embarrassing to the Government, and cause a rift between Britain and France.

As Chamberlain had promised, the question of Britain's contribution to the land defence of France and Belgium was central to the Army estimates debate in March. In presenting his second Army estimates on 8 March 1939, Hore-Belisha admitted the growing concern over the nature of Britain's military commitment should war break out:

> I recognize that this year the question uppermost in the mind of the House is to what extent we should be prepared, in the event of war, to intervene with land forces on the Continent of Europe. The question is a searching one, and can be adequately discussed only within the context of our strategic problems.

He went on to outline the development of British strategic thinking, beginning with Balfour who, in 1905, had shown that the security of Britain depended on the Royal Navy. The Secretary for War at that time, Arnold-Forster, had said in reference to the Army: 'The principal duty of the British Army is to fight

[1] *DBFP*, IV, 120–2, 18 Feb. 1939.
[2] *Ibid.*, 159–61. Halifax to Lindsay, 27 Feb. 1939.
[3] Duff Cooper thought that Henderson was 'hysterical': *Old Men Forget*, p. 227. Hoare put it more charitably: 'his sensitive nerves had been stretched almost to breaking point.... What he lacked was a very necessary measure of British phlegm.' *Nine Troubled Years*, p. 299.

the battles of this country across the sea.' The great military reformer, Haldane (Secretary of State for War, 1905–12), accepted this hypothesis as the basis for his reforms, and he set about rationalizing home defences.

> He dismantled the defences of London. 'I suppose,' he exclaimed, 'there are even plans for the protection of Birmingham.' Guns—300 of them—stores, ammunition, explosives, buildings, assembled on the now discarded assumption of a threat to our security, he scrapped them all or consigned them to other uses.

The wheel had turned full circle, Hore-Belisha claimed, for the greatest danger now facing Britain was the threat of air attack. He therefore planned to increase the number of anti-aircraft divisions to seven, and in the new financial year to increase the number of anti-aircraft guns by between 50 and 100 per cent.[1]

In discussing the nature of the expeditionary force, Hore-Belisha pointed to the development and strengthening of imperial defences, beginning with the establishment of a Middle East strategic reserve stationed in Palestine, which would leave the central strategic reserve free for other purposes. It was here that Hore-Belisha announced a fundamental change in government policy. Whereas in 1905 Haldane had projected an expeditionary force of one Regular cavalry division and six Regular infantry divisions, the Government now proposed to plan on the basis of four Regular infantry and two Regular armoured divisions, *and* nine Territorial infantry divisions, three Territorial motorized divisions, and one Territorial armoured division, supported by two Territorial cavalry brigades and a number of unbrigaded Regular and Territorial units, making a force of more than nineteen divisions. As if to underline the extent of this change, which was in marked contrast to the policy he had announced a year before, he said:

> Conversations between ourselves and the French have not committed us in this respect [an expeditionary force], but prudent minds should be ready for any eventuality. If we are involved in war, our contribution and the ways in which we can best make it will not be half-hearted nor upon any theory of limited liability.

[1] 5 *Parl.,Debs.* CCCXLIV, 2161–5.

Even now, when the Government was planning this huge increase in the size of the expeditionary force, Hore-Belisha appeared to all but close the door against conscription:

> While the case for national service in peacetime, providing a larger army now, may be argued on grounds of physical and moral well being, it would not necessarily affect in the degree sometimes imagined the dimensions of our initial military contribution.

He made it clear that this change in government policy was the natural result of Chamberlain's declaration of Anglo-French solidarity of interests,[1] but in fact there was little in the speech to reassure the French, who had consistently urged that only the introduction of peacetime conscription would enable Britain to make a useful land contribution in the critical early period of a German offensive against France or Belgium.[2] It was common knowledge that the Territorials, starved of modern equipment for so many years, were in no condition to take the field without several months of training after the outbreak of war. Despite the announcement that the British were planning on sending an expeditionary force of nineteen divisions, nothing was done to show the French that the initial commitment—to which they attached the greatest value—would in fact be significantly stronger than that already mentioned in staff talks. The British had offered no alternative to conscription to minimize the time-lapse between the declaration of war and the disembarkation of British troops on the Continent, yet the French insistence had been based on the need to defend the frontiers, a strategy that demanded the employment of the greatest number of troops in the opening stages of a war.

Except for a few dissenting speakers, the majority of the Members who participated in the debate agreed with Mr Adams (Conservative), who said that the arguments in favour of a larger Army were 'overwhelming', for 'it would make war itself

[1] 5 *Parl. Debs.* CCCXLIV, 2173–82.
[2] The News Department of the Foreign Office produced a paper, 'The French Government and Conscription in England', which argued that although Britain's failure to promise substantial assistance on land to France might seriously weaken French diplomatic resolve, the introduction of conscription could only be justified as a precautionary measure against a distant, rather than an immediate, threat. This opinion had the support of the Director of Military Operations. 4 Feb. 1939. F.O. 371/22932. C 5575/682/17.

less likely [and] if war came it would make victory certain'.[1] One by one, a series of Conservatives attacked the assumptions upon which the Cabinet, led by Chamberlain, had based its 'limited liability' policy. Lt-Cmdr Fletcher emphasized that the French evaluated British assistance solely in terms of the number of British troops on French soil, and added that, in his view, it was ridiculous even to think of limiting Britain's role once she was engaged in war.[2] Mr Wise dismissed the argument that Britain's financial contribution should be taken into consideration ('I do not believe that [our money and] our vegetable fats are yet an adequate substitute for British infantry'), and stressed that the Navy and Air Force alone could not defend the French frontiers.[3] The attack on the theory of limited liability developed into criticism of those who proposed the mechanization of the forces Britain would send to the Continent. Lord Apsley set the tone of the arguments of the traditionalists:[4]

> As a rule the Royal Tank Corps units career around country which they [know] pretty well . . . and during the night they move up to a strategic position in time to take off for the grand finale . . . two pounders banging, machine guns chattering and lots of noise and smoke and all done in very much the same manner as the Kaiser's cavalry charges before the war. It is magnificent but not war.

The emphasis was on the value of numbers rather than on strength of fire-power and mobility. With this criterion in mind, many speakers urged the Government to introduce conscription at once,[5] for, as Mr Wise said:[6]

> We have to devise some means for raising an *immediate* expeditionary force, not, I believe, of five divisions, but of at least fifteen divisions, before we can be really reliable as a help to our friends on the Continent of Europe.

The abandonment of limited liability was interpreted as a sign that Britain had to be prepared to commit strong ground forces

[1] 5 *Parl. Debs.* CCCXLIV, 2289–90, 8 March 1939.
[2] *Ibid.*, 2240, 8 March 1939.
[3] *Ibid.*, 2277, 2280, 8 March 1939.
[4] *Ibid.*, 304, 14 March 1939.
[5] E.g. Amery, Viscount Wolmer, Lt.-Col. Macnamara, Sir Alfred Knox, Col. Ponsonby.
[6] 5 *Parl. Debs.* CCCXLIV, 2278, 8 March 1939.

to the Continent. This in turn was taken to mean that Britain would have to build up large numbers of infantry divisions, and the natural corollary to this line of reasoning was that conscription would have to be introduced to ensure that Britain's contribution would be neither half-hearted nor delayed.

The press reactions to Hore-Belisha's speech were varied. The *Daily Telegraph* reported that the unlimited liability announcement was greeted with 'general cheering', and in a leader it wrote that 'it will be a relief to the mass of informed opinion in this country, as well as to our friends in France' to know that Britain was prepared to send '*at least* 19 divisions' to the Continent. The question was: were nineteen divisions sufficient for Britain's purposes? Major-General A. C. Temperley, the *Daily Telegraph*'s Military Correspondent, approved of the no-conscription policy on the grounds that its introduction would overwhelm the Regular Army with 'large numbers of untrained men'. The difficulty was one of timing: how to minimize the disruption that would come from the drafting of civilians, yet avoid 'the tragedy of the last war, when the cream of our young men, who would have been the natural leaders of the nation, took the field as privates'.[1]

The *Birmingham Post* (9 March) held that in trying to explain how Britain would make a significant contribution to the defence of France and Belgium, without abandoning the voluntary system, Hore-Belisha had presented an argument that was 'not only plausible but convincing'. The *News Chronicle* (9 March), however, regretted that the post-Munich situation had compelled Britain to abandon her traditional strategy, whereby she 'won many successes with her own money and with other people's armies'. Similarly the *Evening Standard* (9 March) thought that this departure from long-accepted policy would 'only prescribe our strategy and shackle our finances', while the *Daily Sketch* (10 March) argued that Britain's contribution should be made in the air: 'To undertake this military burden is unnecessary and unwise.' The *Daily Mail* applauded the Government for facing up to the implications of the Munich settlement, and suggested that Hore-Belisha's proposals allowed Britain to retain the necessary degree of flexibility to meet a changing political situation. Only in this way could Britain be prepared for a war the precise nature of which could not be predicted. For this reason it was pointless to press for extreme solutions—either the building of a continental-

[1] *Daily Telegraph*, 9 March 1939.

style Army or the abandonment of any plans ever to send land forces to the Continent again—since the development of air-power and the mechanization of branches of the Army had entirely transformed the military scene, such that 'futile demands' of the kind put forward by Liddell Hart would only chain British strategy to a preconceived plan that might not coincide with the reality of the situation when war did break out.[1] The *Daily Mirror* (14 March) saw the Army estimates as inevitably leading to a repetition of 1914–18: 'What would be the good of our sacrificing more splendid armies to the imbecile strategical ideas of such generals who in France drove millions into mud-pits raked by machine guns during the last war to end peace?' It suggested that 'the best Expeditionary Force for another Western front would be a corps of mental experts to examine the brains . . . of the high command'. *The Times* (10 March) expressed its approval in restrained terms as though it were resigned to the need for a land commitment to Europe, without being enthusiastic about the prospect of British troops fighting in France and Belgium.

The French press reacted favourably to Hore-Belisha's announcement. The London correspondent of *Jour-Echo de Paris* wrote that at last the British government was adopting a firm and realistic policy of land rearmament which, taken with Chamberlain's declaration of Anglo-French unity, would 'have a real and incalculable significance in the practical and political spheres'.[2] The *Daily Telegraph*'s Paris correspondent reported that Hore-Belisha's speech had made a 'deep impression in political and military circles' in France, and had forcefully demonstrated Britain's 'manifest determination' not to engage in war on the Continent on the basis of limited liability.[3] *Le Temps* (9 March) said that the British people were now willing 'to bear all the sacrifices, however hard, necessary to enable the United Kingdom . . . to fulfil its own obligations on the continent'. Despite these reports, Sir Edward Grigg insisted that France was anxiously awaiting the introduction of conscription in Britain, which was needed 'to dispel Europe's doubts upon our moral and material preparedness'. Conscription was the 'decisive test', and so long as the Government refused to establish compulsory nation-wide military training, Britain's potential allies would not rest assured,

[1] *Daily Mail*, 10 March 1939.
[2] Quoted in the *Manchester Guardian*, 10 March 1939.
[3] *Daily Telegraph*, 9 March 1939.

confident in the belief that Britain would be willing and able to intervene strongly on the Continent.[1] Likewise, the *Round Table* spoke of France's 'active resentment' over Britain's shirking of her responsibilities, and warned that 'they are not prepared to spill their blood again whilst we are training our army.'[2]

Chamberlain, however, did not seem to realize the importance of bolstering the confidence of Britain's European allies. Within two days of Hore-Belisha's speech, Chamberlain told the Parliamentary correspondents that he did not believe that war was likely or imminent: 'Europe was settling down to a period of tranquillity, and ... the government was therefore contemplating the possibility of a general limitation of armament.'[3] This statement was made without the knowledge of the Foreign Office, and Halifax immediately wrote a letter of protest to Chamberlain. Although it was couched in mild terms, it showed Halifax's increasing concern over the lack of co-ordination between Chamberlain and his Ministers, especially Halifax himself, who was being bypassed more and more in favour of Sir Horace Wilson, the Prime Minister's personal adviser. Chamberlain had come to rely on the advice of those whose views agreed with his own, and many of the suggestions put forward by Halifax since the September crisis had been ignored by Chamberlain. Halifax was completely loyal to Chamberlain, but he was aware of the bad effect in Britain and especially in Europe that some of Chamberlain's remarks might have. He wrote to him:

> You know that I never wish to be tiresome or take departmental views. . . . But none the less I think that when you are going to make such a general review about Foreign Affairs it might be helpful and well to let me know in advance that you were going to do it, and give me some idea of what you had in mind to say. That would give me the opportunity of saying anything I had to say, which you might or might not think wise.

In particular, Halifax was worried that Chamberlain's statement might encourage Germany to think that Britain was already feeling the strain of rearmament, and might give the French—

---

[1] Edward Grigg, 'The Importance of the Army', *National Review*, CXII (March 1939), 307–16.

[2] 'Man-Power and the War Peril', *Round Table*, XXIX (March 1939), 227–37.

[3] Quoted in Wheeler-Bennett, *Munich*, p. 329.

'their readiness to suspect is very great'—further cause to doubt Britain's commitment to Europe. If the French developed this suspicion, it would make them 'unnecessarily more difficult about other things'.[1]

Halifax had every reason to reproach Chamberlain for his evaluation of the European situation. From the beginning of March the press carried reports of disturbances in Czechoslovakia, as Hitler capitalized on the unrest of the Slovaks. From Berlin, Henderson warned Halifax that there were rumours, from both official and unofficial sources, of fresh German moves. He pointed out that the most likely form these would take would be against Czechoslovakia, thereby allowing Hitler the full measure of success that had been denied him at Munich.[2] This complete contrast with Henderson's February report was commented upon in a minute by Orme Sargent, dated 16 March 1939.[3]

By then, however, it was too late. German troops occupied Prague on 15 March.

[1] Feiling, *Neville Chamberlain*, pp. 396–7.
[2] *DBFP*, IV, 218. Henderson to Halifax, 10 March 1939.
[3] *Ibid.*, 218. Sargent, minute.

10 Does Britain mean business? March 1939

The prospects of Sir Samuel Hoare's 'golden age', which he had envisaged only five days before the occupation of Prague,[1] were rudely destroyed by the German move, the first departure from Hitler's avowed policy of incorporating only areas inhabited by a majority—or near majority—of Germans. Those who had previously defended the racial, self-determination basis of Hitler's demands, were suddenly faced with a situation that was clearly not in accord with his declaration that no more Czechs were wanted in greater Germany. The Munich agreement was contemptuously cast aside, notwithstanding Chamberlain's reliance on Hitler's good faith and Britain's growing strength—in reality, still very much on paper—to back her diplomacy.

The press reports from Czechoslovakia provided an outline of events there within hours,[2] but official communiqués were slower in reaching London, and it was on the basis of the latter that the Government had to act. Despite the prior warnings from British embassies throughout Europe, the Prime Minister was caught by surprise, and ill prepared to answer Attlee's question on 14 March regarding the Government's attitude to the 'possible breakup of Czechoslovakia, which this country has guaranteed'. Chamberlain replied: 'I am not sure what the right hon. Gentleman thinks that we should do.'[3]

There was little that the Government could do, but the realization of this harsh fact was made all the more galling by the guarantee Britain had given Czechoslovakia after the signing of the Munich agreement. It had been apparent in September that the western allies, Britain and France, could not directly assist Czechoslovakia. Poland was at odds with Czechoslovakia over territorial disputes, and the only other country thought to be of

[1] Speech at Chelsea. *The Times*, 11 March 1939.
[2] The *Daily Mail* had advised its readers (14 March) that the unrest in 'Slovakia' 'should not disturb the sleep of the British people'. It was 'probably another bloodless change in the map of Europe'.
[3] 5 *Parl. Debs*. CCCXLV, 223.

any military value was Russia. If the Russians were to go to the aid of the Czechs against Germany, they would have to be granted transit rights across Poland or Rumania. The British Ambassador in Warsaw, Sir Howard Kennard, advised the Foreign Office that the Poles would prove intractable in refusing such permission, and that 'the mere suggestion is calculated to thrust them back into the German fold'.[1] Writing to Phipps, Halifax emphasized that it should be made clear to the French that the British government was of the opinion that 'they cannot undertake a guarantee which obliges them to go to the assistance of Czechoslovakia in circumstances in which effective help could not be rendered'.[2] Yet if in private the Government was reluctant to commit itself to an obligation which it could not honour, it showed no such hesitation in public. In the debate shortly after the signing of the Munich agreement, Sir Thomas Inskip announced that, to all intents and purposes, Britain considered that a British guarantee to Czechoslovakia existed.[3]

> The House will realise that the formal treaty of guarantee has yet to be drawn up and completed in the normal way. . . . Until that has been done, technically the guarantee cannot be said to be in force. His Majesty's Government, however, feel under a moral obligation to Czechoslovakia to treat the guarantee as being now in force. In the event, therefore, of an act of unprovoked aggression against Czechoslovakia, His Majesty's Government would feel bound to take all steps in their power to see that the integrity of Czechoslovakia is preserved.

From the beginning, the Government publicly committed itself to a policy it privately knew could not be carried out. But this was in the glow of the aftermath of Munich, when Hitler was still an 'honourable man'. Six months later, 16 March, there could be no pretence or delusion about his real character.

The day after Attlee's question, Chamberlain was a little more specific. The German action, he said, was not in accord with the spirit of the Munich agreement, and it had violated the racial principle which Hitler had said was the basis of his policy. The

[1] *DBFP*, III, 373–5. Kennard to Sargent, 30 Nov. 1938.
[2] *Ibid.*, 440–1. 21 Dec. 1938.
[3] 5 *Parl. Debs.* CCCXXXIX, 303, 4 Oct. 1938.

confidence of Europe, which 'was beginning to revive', was shattered. In these circumstances, he thought it would be inappropriate for the President of the Board of Trade and the Secretary of the Department of Overseas Trade to visit Berlin for talks, as had been planned. With this minimal gesture of displeasure, he turned to the question of Czechoslovakia itself. Inskip's guarantee of the previous October was given to Czechoslovakia as reconstituted by the Munich agreement. Since, with the Slovakian declaration of independence, Czechoslovakia had ceased to exist, the Government could not 'hold themselves any longer bound by this obligation'. So much for the Czechs. With this cynical justification for the abandonment of a country Britain had guaranteed, Chamberlain went on to reaffirm his policy of appeasement:[1]

> Do not let us . . . be deflected from our course. Let us remember that the desire of all peoples of the world still remains concentrated on the hopes of peace and a return to the atmosphere of understanding and good will . . . .
> The aim of this Government is . . . to promote that desire and to substitute the method of discussion for the method of force in the settlement of differences. Though we may have to suffer checks and disappointments . . . the object that we have in mind is of too great significance . . . for us lightly to give it up.

The mood of the House clearly indicated that a large number of Members thought that it was time the Government saw the realities of the situation, and that, if appeasement was abandoned, there was adequate cause to show that the Government had not done it 'lightly'. Anthony Eden called for national unity under a truly national government,[2] and he was supported by Viscount Wolmer, who added an appeal for national service (i.e. compulsory training, especially in the military), since 'there is one argument . . . alone that the dictator States respect, and that is the argument of force'.[3] (The assumption behind this line of reasoning was that the mass training of the nation's youth would be the best method of 'standing up to Hitler'.) The Labour party was predictably infuriated and shocked. It was, as David Grenfell said, 'a day of

[1] 5 *Parl. Debs.* CCCXLV, 437–40.
[2] *Ibid.*, 461–62.
[3] *Ibid.*, 446–7.

humiliation and shame'.[1] Hugh Dalton firmly rejected the possibility of a national government until there was 'the prospect of a different Prime Minister and a different foreign policy'.[2]

Sir John Simon tried to justify the Government's failure to aid the Czechs by emphasizing that it was a cardinal principle of British foreign policy that the Government should not surrender its freedom of action by entering into 'extensive, indefinite commitments' with other countries, which would thus have a large measure of control over British policy.[3] This 'really necessary' principle, so forthrightly stated—as with the guarantee to Czechoslovakia, was soon to be similarly sacrificed to expediency.

Press reports on 17 March varied, although in general they did not reflect any strong reaction to the occupation of Prague. The *Daily Mail* suggested (15 March) that 'Europe should rejoice that more frontiers have been changed without resort to a big conflict', and the following day endorsed Chamberlain's explanation of the Government's response. It rejected proposals to form an alliance between the democratic nations—'collective security', it thought, under another name—and warned instead: 'One thing, and one thing only, will serve Britain—her own armed might.'[4] The *Daily Mirror* and the *News Chronicle* took a firm stand, the former incredulous that 'our government still retains its amazing capacity for being astonished by Hitler'. The only course open to it now was to begin immediate attempts to enlist the military support of the Soviet Union, the United States, and the Scandinavian nations, and to abandon 'the policy of trying to disarm Dictators by being nice to them and believing their promises or their lies'.[5] The *News Chronicle* described the Government's policy as 'utter futility', which had proved a 'disastrous and expensive failure'. If, in view of Chamberlain's apparent determination not to discard appeasement as the guiding principle of his foreign policy, there could be no change in the management of foreign affairs, the *News Chronicle* called for a change of leadership.[6] The *Daily Mirror*, the *Manchester Guardian*, and the *Birmingham Post* reported that on the evening of 16 March, there had been considerable discussion between Members on the subject of

[1] 5 *Parl. Debs.* CCCXLV, 445.
[2] *Ibid.*, 535.
[3] *Ibid.*, 554.
[4] *Daily Mail*, 16 March, 1939.
[5] *Daily Mirror*, 17 March 1939.
[6] *News Chronicle*, 16 March 1939.

conscription, especially in a meeting of the Conservative Foreign Affairs Committee, where speakers had variously called for the introduction of compulsory national service, the formation of a national (i.e. all-party) government, and the establishment of close ties with Russia.[1]

Halifax realized that the Government's statements in the House of Commons had failed completely to satisfy the country's sense of outrage, and he told Chamberlain that it was necessary to take a firm stand against further German aggression, and that 'the Party, the House of Commons, and above all the British people demanded that this should be done.'[2] Even when it did come, then, Chamberlain's change of heart was, initially at least, dictated to him by another Minister, Halifax, rather than by his own inclinations.

The following day, 17 March, on the eve of his seventieth birthday, Chamberlain spoke at the annual meeting of the Birmingham Unionist Association, and delivered his answer to the German action. Noting that many had been disappointed by his 'somewhat cool and objective statement', thinking that it signified a lack of concern on the part of the Government, he explained that it was made at a time when the official information available to him was incomplete. Any impression that the Government did not feel deeply shocked over the issue would soon be dispelled. In a speech marked by indignation and, at times, petulance, he went on to give notice that, much as he cherished peace, he would not sacrifice it for liberty. Although he was not prepared to 'engage this country by new unspecified commitments operating under conditions which cannot now be foreseen', it would be

[1] The *Birmingham Post* (18 March) suggested that rumours of conscription were 'signs of nervousness' which could be dismissed as 'sheer nonsense', since it was clear that any move to introduce conscription 'would be futile unless the necessary equipment and accommodation were first available.' Yet on 16 March it had called for support of Chamberlain 'even if—as things have turned out—our foreign policy has made necessary a national system of military service which no Minister has yet cared to contemplate.'

[2] Birkenhead, *Halifax*, p. 432. Wilson Broadbent, the *Daily Mail*'s political correspondent, reported (17 March) that Halifax was in favour of 'some form of Military conscription', and had discussed with Chamberlain the formation of a 'more broadly based National Government' to demonstrate national unity. The political correspondent of the *Manchester Guardian* wrote on 18 March that Halifax, 'though he has carried loyalty to his chief to extreme lengths, has had reservations about Mr. Chamberlain's "personal" policy and regretted some of its features'.

wrong, he said, to imagine that Britain would not take all necessary steps to resist challenges to her freedom and to the peace of Europe. This meant that the Government and the British people would have to examine 'every aspect of their national life' and distribute fairly the collective responsibility for national security.[1] *The Times* (18 March) reported that he was greeted with a 'remarkable ovation'. It was as if he had finally signalled the end of a policy of retreat before the demands of the dictators.

The Cabinet met the following day to discuss the implications of Chamberlain's speech. The Prime Minister suggested that, in view of his reference to an examination of every aspect of national life, the Cabinet would have to consider various possible courses of action. The two obvious ones were the establishment of a Ministry of Supply (which would, in fact, have been the logical step following the announcement of a nineteen-division expeditionary force), and the introduction of conscription. Halifax stated bluntly that the mood of the country demanded some concrete action on the part of the Government. A national register was not enough in the present circumstances: something had to be done to give Britain's allies, actual or potential, unmistakable proof that Britain was determined to resist further ventures by Germany. Kingsley Wood, Secretary of State for Air, agreed, saying that there was a large body of opinion which held that the introduction of some form of compulsion would be the 'most striking evidence of the determination of the people of this country, and would have considerable psychological effect'. The timing of such a measure, however, was of crucial importance. Ernest Brown, Minister for Labour, warned that if compulsion was even suggested, the trade-union representatives on the voluntary National Service Committees would resign at once. The entire Labour movement was strongly opposed to any form of compulsion, and Chamberlain agreed that it was extremely doubtful whether Labour would co-operate in any compulsory scheme when it had so strongly supported the existing National Service Appeal precisely because it was voluntary. Brown did suggest, however, that Labour might be able to see its way open to some form of co-operation if, in turn, the Government took more positive steps to enlist the support of Russia: such developments might 'modify the position materially'. These proposals were far-reaching ones that entailed a radical departure

[1] *The Times*, 18 March 1939.

from declared policy, and the Cabinet did not come to any final conclusions.[1]

The public response to Chamberlain's Birmingham speech was immediate. The following day (18 March) was reported to have been one of the busiest ever at the National Service recruiting centres in London, Manchester, Leeds, Birmingham, and Glasgow.[2] The *Daily Herald* (18 March) admitted that Chamberlain had gone some way towards correcting the 'shocking impression' created by his initial reaction to the occupation of Prague, but this did not alter the fact that 'the one service he can now render to the State is to resign'. Several days later it called on the Government to adopt a new foreign policy relying on the formation of close alliances with France and Russia, backed by the strongest ties with the United States, and the endorsement of the voluntary principle of national service: 'The British people can do voluntarily all that is required of them. They will accept their responsibilities without stint if there is a foreign policy in which they can have confidence'.[3] The *Daily Mail* entitled its leader (18 March) 'Words Don't Count Any More', and suggested that there were great advantages in the introduction of conscription before the outbreak of war. It was not yet prepared to call openly for conscription, but limited itself to insisting that if conscription was to be introduced, it should be introduced immediately. Two days later it came out much more positively for conscription: 'It is folly to utter threats or to enter into limitless undertakings if we are not possessed of the force to make them good.' Britain's present military capability enabled her to defend her imperial possessions, but if it became necessary to enter into agreements with countries of eastern Europe, her military plans 'must be based on conscription.' The limiting factor in building up a large expeditionary force was time, and only the immediate introduction of conscription would minimize the dangerous 'limbo' period facing Britain.[4] Similarly the *Daily Mirror* (18 March) endorsed conscription, but added that its introduction could only be justified if the Government abandoned its weak foreign policy and stood up to

[1] Cab. 23/98, Minutes 12(39)3, 18 March, 1939.
[2] *The Times*, 20 March, 1939. On 2 March, the *Manchester Guardian* had deplored 'the extremely poor' recruiting figures for Manchester, which indicated that the public were not fully aware of the dangers facing the country.
[3] *Daily Herald*, 20 March 1939.
[4] *Daily Mail*, 20 March 1939.

Germany: 'Suddenly to demand conscription to back the policy of callous surrender is an insult to the youth that will be conscripted.' Then, echoing the *Daily Mail*, it cried: 'Enough of Words—Prepare!'[1]

> *Action is Imperative.* . . . The Government must move at once. *The first need is universal conscription.* This will convince Hitler that Britain means business. . . . *Away with slackness.* Our slack methods, our lack of discipline, are partly to blame [for Europe thinking that] Britain is decadent and has lost her national spirit. Conscription will alter this false opinion. It will hearten our French ally.

Increasingly in the weeks following the occupation of Prague, conscription was justified on the grounds that it would show Europe, particularly France and Germany, that 'Britain means business'.

In considering the press cries for conscription, Chamberlain had to weigh possible advantages with the certain disadvantages. The introduction of conscription would meet with strong approval from the French, whose pressure on this point had grown even stronger. When Bonnet visited London, he approached Halifax and again sought an assurance that Britain would match the French efforts. In the days following the German action, it had been left to the French government to take concrete steps to strengthen their defences. On 21 March, it announced that certain reservists would be recalled into service, that the number of officers and N.C.O.s would be increased, and that additional native troops would be raised in North Africa. A Committee of Production under the Minister of National Defence was set up with full powers to co-ordinate all phases of production and to enforce absolute priority for government orders over private contracts, even those already in hand. Production in defence factories was boosted by increasing working hours to sixty per week, and the Minister was authorized to make them longer if necessary.[2] On the day that these steps were announced, *Le Temps* wrote that the introduction of conscription was the only way in which Britain could fulfil its proper role in the new loose alliance

[1] *Daily Mirror*, 20 March 1939.
[2] *The Times*, 22 March 1939.

of states that was being formed to resist further aggression. Chamberlain was seen as the stumbling block, considering himself still bound by his pledge not to introduce conscription in peacetime, whereas Halifax was thought to favour its immediate introduction.[1]

When he saw Halifax, Bonnet pressed for an increase in the British land forces. France, he said, with a population of 40 million, could not face the threat posed by Germany and Italy, who had a total of 120 million, without substantial military assistance from Britain. Halifax recounted the interview to Campbell in the British Embassy in Paris:

> M. Bonnet developed the argument, which is familiar enough, from the angles both of the influence of this situation on French opinion and on opinion in Germany and Italy. If the people of France thought that it was impossible to look to Great Britain for any really substantial measure of military help for, say, eighteen months, the consequences might be profound and irretrievable.

Bonnet urged the British government to introduce some form of compulsory service, despite the difficulties that would have to be faced in overcoming trade-union opposition. Halifax was unable to give a reply that would satisfy the French demand.[2] The following day it was noted in the Foreign Office that 'it is now clear that nothing but some form of conscription will really allay French anxiety'.[3] The British government had therefore to cast around for alternative courses of action that would demonstrate to the French that Britain 'meant business' without drawing upon the country the disadvantages that (Chamberlain at least thought) would attend the introduction of conscription.

Chamberlain's opposition was not based on his unwillingness to break the pledges he had given not to introduce conscription in peacetime, but on very practical difficulties. He feared that any move towards a compulsory scheme would alienate the Trades Union Congress: the resultant industrial strife would 'inflict a serious check on aeroplane production'. Far from 'showing the Germans', as was often suggested, it might well demonstrate the

[1] *Le Temps*, 21 March 1939.
[2] *DBFP*, IV, 487–90, 23 March 1939.
[3] Barclay, minute, 24 March, 1939. F.O. 371/22932. C 3874/682/17.

disunity of Britain, to the benefit of any further designs Hitler might have and to the detriment of the efforts of the western allies to resist future aggression. Chamberlain thought he would eventually be able to 'approach' the T.U.C., but he was not going to be pushed into conscription or into any 'rash or foolish commitments which might do us infinite harm'.[1] On 23 and 26 March he met with Lord Chatfield and representatives of the T.U.C. to discuss proposals for accelerating rearmament production in the factories, but his suggestions were rejected by the industrial leaders.[2] With this avenue of action apparently closed, he was forced to consider other possibilities. The French were pressing him for conscription,[3] and Hitler was clearly not deterred by the prospect of a Britain whose determination still rested mainly in words. Within a week of Chamberlain's Birmingham speech, Hitler took over Memel.

During the third week of March, the press reported extensively on conscription. In general there was a demand for action on the part of the Government, and this was usually cast in the form of the introduction of some scheme of compulsory military service. The basic question was whether the Government was, in fact, aware of the mood of the country, and whether its current membership was capable of making the necessary changes in policy. Certainly there was reason to doubt this when Sir Samuel Hoare denied, on 22 March, that the establishment of a complete (i.e. compulsory) national register would add anything to the defence measures the Government was already taking.[4] The *Daily Mirror* reported that M.P.s had found strong support in their constituencies for conscription and the immediate formation of an alliance with Russia, but added that rumour had it that neither Simon nor Hoare favoured these steps. If that was their position, said the *Daily Mirror*, 'Conservatives will demand their resignation and reorganisation of the Cabinet'.[5] The *Daily Herald*

---

[1] Chamberlain to Miss C. Chamberlain, 26 March, 1939. Copy in Templewood Papers, IX(II)C.

[2] Templewood, *Nine Troubled Years*, p. 337.

[3] Phipps reported on 27 March that feeling was increasing in France that the introduction of some form of national service in Britain was the 'touchstone' of British policy towards Germany. On 28 March, Roberts in the Foreign Office noted that 'All our telegrams from Paris tell the same story'. F.O. 371/22932. C 4186/682/17.

[4] 5 *Parl. Debs.* CCCXLV, 1281, 22 March 1939.

[5] *Daily Mirror*, 25, 27 March 1939.

(27 March) suggested that the Government 'is finding it impossible to convince the country whose aid it seeks that the change [in foreign policy] is genuine and permanent'. It was this basic distrust of the Government's intentions, rather than the strengths or weaknesses of Britain's defences, that was the major problem facing the country. The *Daily Telegraph* deplored that 'at such a juncture differences and hesitations should manifest themselves in the counsels of the Government',[1] and the *Daily Mail* (21 March) regretted that there was no indication that the Government was yet prepared to take the necessary steps to put Britain's defences in order.

The 'hesitations' thought to be holding back a change in policy were over the questions of conscription and the formation of an alliance of powers to resist further attempts at expansion by Germany. The *Daily Mail* (22 March) was the loudest supporter of conscription, which, it said, was necessary if the British Army was to operate on a continental scale, as Hore-Belisha had announced in the Army estimates on 8 March. 'Total British rearmament' would encourage other countries to join Britain in her efforts to secure peace: only with conscription 'will others be sure that Britain means business'. By 28 March, the *Daily Mail* was convinced that talks with Poland would fail unless Britain was able to show that her diplomacy was, in fact, backed by armed strength, 'and that, in the Continental view, involves conscription'. The paper's correspondence column was frequently filled with letters on conscription, which increasingly produced the same arguments on the advantages and disadvantages of compulsion. Those published on 25 March, for example, in the 'Letter Writers' Parliament', variously suggested that 'Europe would take us seriously'; conscription would impose an equal obligation on the nation that was lacking under a voluntary system; that it would produce trained men; that it would be introduced in war-time, and it was 'therefore better to have ahead of time'; and that it both was and was not incompatible with individual liberty.

The Times daily featured reports and letters on conscription, ranging from extracts of speeches by Amery urging its introduction,[2] to letters from such Conservative M.P.s as the recently converted Harold Macmillan, Patrick Hanson, and George

---

[1] *Daily Telegraph*, 27 March 1939 ('Ministers and the Nation: Need for a Decision').

[2] *The Times*, 23 March 1939. Speech at Newcastle.

Mitchenson.[1] A *Times* leader (24 March) came out in favour of the immediate attainment of the full Army establishment, and then an increase in the Territorial establishment: 'complete duplication would be no unreasonable aim'. It also endorsed compulsory military training as a means of creating 'healthy citizens and effective soldiers'.

When Liddell Hart wrote to *The Times* objecting to any proposals to introduce conscription, he was answered directly in a number of letters and indirectly attacked in speeches throughout the country. His opposition to the measure was twofold. On practical grounds, he argued that conscription would divert Britain's limited industrial output away from the necessary task of mechanizing the Army, and would force it to be channelled to supply the needs of a large infantry force. The Territorial Army still suffered from a shortage of equipment and instructors, yet it was precisely these troops that would make up the bulk of the proposed nineteen-division expeditionary force that government critics now found inadequate in the light of the latest German moves. This situation, Liddell Hart wrote, would only be worsened by a mass influx of conscripts. Morally, compulsory military service in a democracy could not be justified, and was positively dangerous: 'We ought . . . to think carefully . . . before taking a decisive step towards totalitarianism'.[2] He was supported by Sir Auckland Geddes, now Sir John Anderson's chief adviser on national service, who said: 'So far as any Government can pledge itself, I think you can say there will be no military conscription, because it will not add to fighting strength';[3] in fact, 'our adoption of conscription would inevitably diminish our naval and air preparations . . . . Any war of the future is likely to be won, or lost, in the workshops and factories.'[4]

The practical objections that Liddell Hart raised were all but ignored by his critics, or else answered on the level of Lord Hinchinbrooke, a Territorial officer, who denied that the lack of equipment was an insuperable obstacle to an increase in the size of the Army. Interest in the ranks could still be maintained, he

---

[1] *The Times*, 21, 23 March 1939. Editorial comment: 'The following is a typical selection of the letters which are reaching *The Times* from Members of Parliament and others, on the urgent case for universal national service.'
[2] *Ibid.*, 24 March 1939.
[3] *Daily Mirror*, 29 March 1939.
[4] *The Times*, 26 March 1939.

said, even though individual soldiers might handle the weapons 'for perhaps only three minutes in every hour'. In any case, some training was better than no training at all.[1] As for the moral objections to conscription, Amery asked Liddell Hart if, since he defended individual freedom so vigorously, he supported the use of arms bought with money raised through compulsory taxation.[2]

In general, proponents of conscription ignored the military realities of Britain's situation and the tangible military results that would accrue from such a measure. It was often argued that the Army would somehow 'be good' for Britain's youth, and that from the introduction of some degree of obligatory service miraculous results would flow, overnight producing an immensely powerful Army. This, it was thought, would have an invaluable effect in Europe, where it would strengthen French morale, and act as a deterrent to Germany and Italy, who would interpret it as a sign of Britain's determination to draw the line on further expansion.[3]

By 28 March Chamberlain could not hold off making some sort of announcement. The meeting with Bonnet had convinced Halifax that it was vital that Britain should introduce measures sufficiently important and dramatic to underline its firm stand against Hitler.[4] In the House of Commons back-benchers were openly asserting their discontent, to the alarm of the government whips, and the press was in full cry. Hore-Belisha was already convinced that conscription was necessary, but his professional Army advisers were of two minds. The Adjutant-General's nephew told Liddell Hart shortly after a meeting in the War Office on 25 March that the senior Army advisers were 'on the horns of a dilemma; they are anxious for conscription on principle, but they cannot see what they would do with it if they had it.' The nub of the problem was that 'the number of instructors available made it almost impossible'; without adequate training facilities, a mass of conscripts would be useless in themselves, and only hamper the training and equipping of the Regular Army.[5]

Sir Horace Wilson wrote to Hore-Belisha on 28 March asking

[1] *The Times*, 27 March 1939.
[2] *Ibid*.
[3] See *The Times*, 28 March 1939, editorial and report of a speech by Duff Cooper; and *Spectator*, 24 March 1939, p. 472.
[4] Minney, *Hore-Belisha*, p. 187. Diary entry, 28 March 1939.
[5] Liddell Hart, *Memoirs*, II, 230.

for suggestions on ways to reassure public opinion. That night Chamberlain was to speak to the 1922 Committee (the Conservative Private Members' Committee), and he understood that many of those who would be present wanted him to indicate that the Government intended to make greater use of the recent influx of recruits into the Territorial Army, whose establishment had already been reached, with the result that applicants were being turned away. Wilson thought that it might be possible to form new units and give the volunteers some very basic training, 'even if, for the time being, equipment is not available for them'. Hore-Belisha was asked to have his proposals ready within several hours.[1]

When he lunched with Wilson that afternoon, Hore-Belisha advised him that the turn of events made conscription absolutely necessary. Wilson replied that it was impossible because of the internal political repercussions—the reaction of the Labour party and the T.U.C. Hore-Belisha then went to see Chamberlain in his room at the Palace of Westminster, where he tried to convince him that conscription would have to be introduced. Chamberlain flatly refused to consider it, and went on to discuss the Territorial Army, and how it could be strengthened. Hore-Belisha suggested doubling it, and Chamberlain immediately seized on this idea, which apparently was only put forward casually. When Hore-Belisha explained that there were serious practical difficulties associated with such an undertaking and that existing facilities would be severely strained, Chamberlain brushed his objections aside and said he would like to have the announcement made within twenty-four hours.[2] Thus was military policy formulated.

What was the origin of this proposal? Liddell Hart talked at length with Hore-Belisha on 27 March, and his record of their conversation made no mention of the latter's intention to propose a doubling of the Territorial establishment. Had Hore-Belisha been seriously considering it, it seems strange that he should not have discussed it with one who had formerly been his close personal adviser. Their talk on 27 March covered many subjects relating to defence and political organization, yet Liddell Hart had no inkling that a major step in the building up of the numerical strength of the Army was being discussed.[3] During the preceding week there had been some indications that the War Office was

[1] Premier 1/296; Minney, *Hore-Belisha*, p. 186.
[2] Minney, *Hore-Belisha*, p. 187.
[3] Liddell Hart, *Memoirs*, II, 226–8.

studying plans for enlarging the Territorial Army. The Financial Secretary to the War Office, Sir Victor Warrender, stated on 23 March that 'proposals for effecting increases are under consideration'.[1] On 28 March Hore-Belisha explained that it was impossible to set the Territorial establishment at two million, as one Member had suggested. He advised, however, that the Government was studying certain possibilities.[2] The *Daily Telegraph* (29 March) urged him to think about 'doubling or even trebling the Territorial Army'. Whatever the precise state of planning in regard to the Territorial Army was during the third week of March, Hore-Belisha made his suggestion to the Prime Minister without formally consulting the Army Council.[3]

Normally the announcement of Territorial increases would have been made by the Secretary of State for War, but it was decided that the Prime Minister should do it to maximize the effect it was hoped the decision would have. On 29 March Chamberlain announced to the House that

> the Territorial Field Army, which is now on a peace establishment of 130,000 men, will now be raised forthwith to War Establishment, which will involve an addition of about 40,000 men to this figure . . . . The Territorial Field Army so brought up to War Establishment will be doubled and will, therefore, be allotted an establishment of 340,000 men.

The House ought to accept this as evidence, he explained,

> of the Government's opinion that we have not by any means yet exhausted what can be done by voluntary service, and we shall demonstrate the possibilities of voluntary services to meet all our needs.

Again it seemed that he had firmly closed the door to conscription.[4]

The same day, some thirty dissident Conservatives, including Churchill, Eden, Duff Cooper, Amery, and Viscount Wolmer, tabled a motion in the House of Commons calling for the formation of a truly national government and the immediate introduc-

---

[1] 5 *Parl. Debs.* CCCXLV, 1459.
[2] *Ibid.*, 1871.
[3] Minney, *Hore-Belisha*, p. 187.
[4] 5 *Parl. Debs.* CCCXLV, 2048–50.

tion of conscription. In response to this, at the behest of the government whips, 180 government supporters moved an amendment stating their complete confidence in Chamberlain's policies. Neither motion was debated, and both remained on the order paper until conscription was introduced in April.[1]

Reactions to the announcement varied widely. Anglo-French military conversations opened in London on 29 March, and Group Captain John Slessor, the R.A.F. representative, noted 'the expression of almost incredulous bewilderment on the face of the usually cheerful countenance of the D.C.I.G.S., Ronald Adam . . . who had only just heard about it'.[2] Neither the General Staff nor the Committee of Imperial Defence were consulted,[3] and Lord Chatfield, Minister for Co-ordination of Defence, did not hear of the decision until he attended a Cabinet meeting on the afternoon of 29 March.[4]

The Times (30 March) warmly approved the step the Government had taken, but the *Daily Mail*, while reporting that the announcement was 'rapturously cheered', deplored Chamberlain's 'tenacious respect' for the 'sacrosanct voluntary principle': 'By still letting every citizen choose whether or not to help, the Government conveys both to friends and to potential foes that Britain's leaders have still not reached the point of meaning business.'[5] *Le Temps* (31 March) noted tersely that the British government was trying to maintain the voluntary principle while building up its forces as much as possible. The *Daily Herald* (30 March), however, saw the announcement as a sign that the Government had every faith in the voluntary system: 'The Labour view has won.' Far from being a half-hearted measure, as the *Daily Mail* had suggested, this further endorsement of the voluntary principle would 'convey to the rulers of Germany . . . the determination of this country to organize itself to meet any threat to dominate Europe by force'.

The last had not been heard of conscription, however. As a short-term measure, the doubling of the Territorial Army achieved little. French fears were not assuaged, and it failed to

[1] Wheeler-Bennett, *Munich*, p. 380.
[2] Slessor, *The Central Blue*, pp. 183–4.
[3] Lord Ismay, *The Memoirs of General The Lord Ismay, K.G., P.C., G.C.B., C.H., D.S.O.* (London: Heinemann, 1960), p. 93.
[4] Lord Chatfield, *It Might Happen Again*, vol. II, *The Navy and Defence* (London: Heinemann, 1947), p. 171.
[5] *Daily Mirror*, 30 March 1939.

quiet British demands for conscription. Those who called for equality of sacrifice could complain that the Government's adherence to a voluntary system penalized the patriotic and indicated the Government's inability to appreciate the seriousness of the international situation. Speaking to the 6th Battalion, the Queen's Royal Regiment, on 31 March, Hore-Belisha asserted that 'from a purely military standpoint', conscription had 'inestimable advantages'. Training was naturally more effective when done continuously over a period of months, and the skilled instructors and equipment necessary could be more efficiently organized. However, he explained, Britain was a country that was not ruled by logic alone; it was ruled by 'consent'.[1] Although this was meant to answer those who criticized the Government for not introducing conscription—a criticism that Hore-Belisha himself made privately—it was a telling comment on the formulation of policy at that time. The Government chose to react to opinion in Britain and abroad—variously expressed—rather than to make decisions on the basis of sound military and political reasoning. Opinion was shaped by past events, but future events, particularly in Europe, were not bound by the situation which the Government, acting on the basis of expediency, had created for itself. A policy of firm resistance to aggression that was based on day-to-day decisions and stop-gap measures appeared far from determined when the course of events forced its continual modification.

The German occupation of Bohemia and Moravia deeply involved Britain in the affairs of central and eastern Europe. The strategic position of Poland was undermined since Germany now bordered her on three sides, and the occupation of Ruthenia by Hungarian troops blocked important rail links with Rumania, which in turn, with its rich oil fields, seemed a likely target for further German pressure. During the final destruction of Czechoslovakia, Virgil Tilea, the Rumanian Ambassador in London, called at the Foreign Office and begged Halifax to make some gesture of opposition to the German action, for if nothing was done, he said, 'the effect would be disastrous on . . . [British] prestige throughout Central Europe and the Balkans'.[2] Sir Orme Sargent was also approached by Tilea who, emphasizing that he spoke as a private citizen and

---

[1] *The Times*, 1 April 1939.
[2] *DBFP*, IV, 283–4. Halifax to Sir R. Hoare (Bucharest), 16 March 1939.

not in his official capacity, asked how far Rumania could depend upon Britain's help in the event of her having to resist Germany. Would Britain, for example, grant Rumania a £10 million loan to enable her to buy arms?[1] By the time the Rumanian Foreign Minister denied that Rumania was in imminent danger,[2] Britain was already involved in plans to create a system of defensive alliances against further German aggression. It was quickly realized that Poland was the key to the defence of central and eastern Europe, and British diplomatic efforts concentrated on securing Poland as the basis of this alliance system. So began the short train of events that led to the Polish guarantee.

The British and French were convinced that Polish aid was essential to the defence of Rumania, especially since both countries refused to allow Soviet troops to enter their territory and render military assistance. The Cabinet's military advisers thought that the Soviet Army, with its officer corps shattered by recent purges, would be unable to undertake offensive operations, and rated Poland a more valuable ally.[3] Hoare and Chatfield regarded Russia as 'the greatest deterrent in the East against German aggression', but the rest of the Cabinet thought that Poland was a 'sounder, more reliable ally than Russia'.[4] Halifax therefore, did not press the Polish government when the Soviet Foreign Minister agreed to attend defence consultations only if France *and* Poland would also be there.[5]

The German occupation of Memel on 23 March, and increasing German complaints about Polish treatment of German minorities —by now a familiar forerunner to German action—gave rise to fears that Poland herself might be the next target of German expansion. Negotiations between Poland and Germany merely heightened tension, and as the British government sought to construct some sort of front against Germany, it was subjected to mounting criticism within Britain. The decisive jolt came from a British press correspondent, Ian Colvin, Berlin representative of the *News Chronicle*, who presented the Foreign Office on 29 March with evidence that Hitler intended to launch an attack on

[1] *DBFP*, IV, 284–5. Minute by Sargent, 16 March 1939.
[2] *Ibid.*, 369–70. Hoare (Bucharest) to Halifax, 18 March 1939.
[3] See Cab. 53/10, Minutes of 282nd and 283rd meetings of C.O.S., 18 March 1939.
[4] 'Minutes of a meeting of the Cabinet Committee on Foreign Policy, March 27, 1939.' C.P. 74(39), Cab. 24/284.
[5] *DBFP*, IV, 467. Seeds to Halifax, 27 March 1939.

Poland.[1] In light of this warning, which seemed to be substantiated by reports of the standard German preliminaries to the precipitation of a diplomatic-military crisis, fresh proposals were urgently made. On 30 March the British and French governments advised Poland and Rumania that they could rely upon the support of the two western powers in the event of attack. The guarantee to Poland was conditional upon the Polish government making the agreement reciprocal and undertaking a similar obligation to aid Rumania.[2] But even this did not seem to Chamberlain to satisfy the needs of the situation, and later that evening he instructed the British Ambassador in Warsaw, Sir Howard Kennard, to offer the Polish government a temporary unilateral guarantee.[3] Colonel Beck, the Polish Foreign Minister, agreed to accept.[4]

The following day, 31 March, Chamberlain announced in the House of Commons[5] that

> in the event of any action that clearly threatened Polish independence, and which the Polish Government accordingly considered it vital to resist with their national forces, His Majesty's Government would feel themselves bound to lend the Polish Government all support in their power.
>
> I may add that the French Government have authorized me to make it plain they stand in the same position in this matter as do His Majesty's Government.

Without promising anything in return, Poland had won unconditional British support.

The Times (1 April) tried to restrict the scope of the guarantee by arguing that it did not 'bind Great Britain to defend every inch of the present frontiers of Poland. The key word in the declaration is not integrity but "independence"'; and the *Daily Telegraph* (1 April), noting that the announcement was greeted with 'general deep-voiced cheers', reassured its readers that there was no need

---

[1] Ian Colvin, *Vansittart in Office: An historical account of the origins of the Second World War based on the papers of Sir Robert Vansittart, Permanent Under-Secretary of State for Foreign Affairs. 1930–38* (London: Gollancz, 1965), pp. 303–10; *DBFP*, IV, 545, n. 1; Cadogan told Hoare that 'our Polish guarantee was given at a moment's notice after Neville Chamberlain's talk with Ian Colvin.' 'Notes of a talk with Cadogan, November 14, 1951.' Templewood Papers, IX(B)5.

[2] *DBFP*, IV, 515–17. Halifax to Kennard and Hoare, 27 March 1939.

[3] *Ibid.*, 546. Halifax to Kennard, 30 March 1939.

[4] *Ibid.*, Kennard to Halifax, 30 March 1939.

[5] 5 *Parl. Debs.* CCCXLV, 2415.

to fear that Britain had given Poland control of its foreign policy: 'the guarantee is quite definite about the circumstances.' The *Daily Mail*, however, realized that no literary sleight of hand could conceal the fact that Chamberlain had given Poland a 'blank cheque'.[1] Never before had a British government unilaterally pledged its unconditional support to the foreign policy of another country. Little more than two weeks previously, both Chamberlain and Simon had warned that although the Government's aim was to resist aggression, they were not prepared to enter into 'extensive, indefinite commitments' with other countries. Now Poland could draw its blank cheque on Britain at will.

The Polish guarantee was a gesture of support; it contributed nothing to the improvement of Poland's immediate position. Yet even as a gesture it had little impact. It should have been obvious to the most amateur strategist that Britain and France could not aid Poland directly and that, as Chamberlain pointed out at the Anglo-French talks on 22 March, 'their assistance would have to take the form of pressure on Germany's western front',[2] that is, an offensive against the Siegfried Line, an operation that clearly demanded a much greater military contribution than that upon which Britain's plans were based. Direct military assistance to Poland could be provided only by Russia, but the Polish government was implacably opposed to any form of association with Russia, and the British—being advised that the Soviet Army had no significant striking power—did not push the point. Irrespective of the military reports it received, the British government expressed little enthusiasm for ties with Russia. Although in the House of Commons Chamberlain readily gave an assurance that 'no ideological impediments' existed between Britain and the Soviet Union that would stand in the way of an alliance,[3] he wrote in his diary:[4]

> I must confess to the most profound distrust of Russia. I have no belief whatever in her ability to maintain an effective offensive, even if she wanted to. And I distrust her motives, which seem to me to have little connection with our ideas of liberty, and to be concerned only with getting everyone else by the ears.

[1] *Daily Mail*, 3 April 1939.
[2] *DBFP*, IV, 457–63.
[3] 5 *Parl. Debs.* CCCXLV, 2417, 31 March 1939.
[4] Feiling, *Neville Chamberlain*, p. 403. Diary entry, 26 March 1939.

At the Moscow end of Britain's diplomatic contact with the Soviet Union was Sir William Seeds, whose ideal of Anglo-Soviet relations was 'friendliness and contacts but no obligations'.[1] Even when allowance is made for the Polish intransigence, the British efforts to enlist Soviet aid were half-hearted at best.

As with the doubling of the Territorial Army, Chamberlain made a decision without proper consultation with his professional advisers. Lord Beaverbrook told Liddell Hart that the General Staff had specifically warned against giving a guarantee to Poland because, on the basis of her military strength and resources, Britain was incapable of fulfilling the obligations involved. Chamberlain had refused to accept this view, and would not allow Hore-Belisha to circulate to the Cabinet a paper detailing the General Staff's appreciation, 'saying that this would be tantamount "to criticism of his policy!" '[2]

The Polish guarantee was acclaimed in Parliament as a sign of the determination of Britain and France to go to any lengths to protect Europe against further encroachments by Germany and, to a lesser extent, Italy. The Opposition parties supported the Government's action, but strongly urged that the Soviet Union be brought into the alliance forthwith.[3] Churchill typified the feeling of the House when, in speaking of a sudden and 'surprising transformation' in British policy, he said: 'It is indeed wonderful that our country had been led by the Prime Minister to declare ... that the defence of European freedom and the reign of law constitute causes in which this country will dare all and do all.'[4] It was left to Lloyd George, on the basis of a strategic appreciation given him by Liddell Hart,[5] to point out the realities of the situation: that neither Britain nor France could send any troops to Poland, and that, in such circumstances, 'if we are going in without the help of Russia we are walking into a trap'.[6] His warnings were ignored by the Government and its supporters alike. The fact that Britain had finally taken a stand obscured the shakiness of the ground on which that stand was made.

[1] *DBFP*, IV, 523–4. Seeds to Halifax, 28 March 1939.
[2] Liddell Hart, *Memoirs*, II, 221; Lord Strang, *Home and Abroad* (London: Deutsch, 1956), p. 161.
[3] 5 *Parl. Debs.* CCCXLV, 2569–73, Hugh Dalton, 3 April, 1939.
[4] *Ibid.*, 2499, 3 April 1939.
[5] Liddell Hart, *Memoirs*, II, 218.
[6] 5 *Parl. Debs.* CCCXLV, 2509. 3 April 1939.

The two weeks following the German occupation of Bohemia and Moravia marked the turning point in British policy. From a refusal to commit Britain (and, indirectly, France) to the defence of Czechoslovakia, Chamberlain was propelled by the German initiative, and by the pressures of public opinion in Britain and France, to draw the line on further gains by Hitler, and to issue an unequivocal and unilateral guarantee to Poland. This change of policy, however, was not accepted at face value either in Britain or in France, and there were growing demands for evidence that the Government was convinced of the need for drastic action. Chamberlain himself had said on his return from Munich that British diplomacy had to have an effective backing of armed strength. A diplomacy of symbolism now demanded symbolic action. The doubling of the Territorial Army establishment was thought to be useful, but of secondary importance. What was needed was a dramatic gesture to set the seal on Britain's determination. There was widening support for the view that conscription alone would show that Britain 'meant business'.

11 The introduction of conscription April 1939

Under pressure from events in Europe and opinion in France and Britain—within his Cabinet, the press, and Parliament—Chamberlain had abandoned his policy of optimism and appeasement, begun to establish a system of defensive alliances in Europe to guard against further German expansion, and delivered British foreign policy into the hands of a 'far away country', 'people of whom we know nothing'. Chamberlain recognized that these were revolutionary departures from previous policy:[1]

> It really does constitute a new point—I would say a new epoch—in the course of our foreign policy. . . . It constitutes a portent in British policy so momentous that I think it safe to say it will have a chapter to itself when the history books come to be written.

But these changes had only encouraged his critics to press for stronger measures, especially the introduction of conscription, which they saw both as the crowning symbol and the practical basis of a new, determined British foreign policy. For several weeks after giving the guarantee to Poland, Chamberlain tried to resist the mounting criticism, until senior Cabinet Ministers convinced him that conscription was politically desirable, necessary, and possible. Finally, on 26 April, he caught up with prevailing opinion and, despite his pledges to the contrary, became the first Prime Minister to introduce conscription in peacetime.

During the last week in March, when the Government extended the guarantee to Poland and doubled the establishment of the Territorial Army, the Cabinet discussed a number of the proposals that were being aired in the press and in Parliament. At a meeting of the Cabinet on 29 March, the subject of conscription came under review. This was the first time that Chamberlain had made his opinions known to the Cabinet as a whole. He

[1] 5 *Parl. Debs.* CCCXLV, 2482, 3 April 1939.

admitted the strength of the argument that the introduction of conscription, more than any other measure, would impress foreign opinion, and said that he agreed the effect would be good 'if such a step were carried through successfully'. The point at issue, however, was whether it could, in fact, be done. Although he had endorsed Baldwin's pledge not to introduce conscription in peacetime, that pledge was hardly binding in the present circumstances. Much more important—indeed, decisive in his view—was the attitude of the Labour party and the trades unions. Their co-operation in the industrial sphere had been partially responsible for a marked increase in armament production. The introduction of conscription, or even its proposal, might threaten that co-operation to the grave detriment of the munitions industry. If, as a result, the unions called a strike, nations abroad could not fail to notice the lack of national unity in Britain, which the introduction of conscription was designed to promote and demonstrate. For this reason Chamberlain had chosen to increase the strength of the Territorial Army as a sign that Britain was prepared to play its part in the defence of European security, and the Labour party had indicated its approval.[1]

Halifax admitted that he would have preferred 'a measure on somewhat wider lines', but he agreed that the Government could not risk alienating the Labour movement. There was 'abundant evidence' of the need to give foreign countries unmistakable proof —in practical terms—of Britain's determination. In view of the internal political difficulties, the doubling of the Territorial Army would best serve this purpose.[2]

This had long been advocated in the press and in Parliament: on 5 April, the *Daily Telegraph* wrote approvingly of the doubling of the Territorial Army and the favourable impression it had created in Europe, and suggested that the establishment of a Ministry of Supply would 'certainly serve to strengthen that impression'. *The Times* warned against under-estimating the difficulties associated with the expansion of the Territorials, but added that conscription would have presented even greater ones.[3] Chamberlain, however, realized that a Ministry of Supply would have to be given some compulsory powers over industry if it was to be effective in supervising the production and distribution of

[1] Cab. 23/98, Minutes 15(39)5.
[2] *Ibid.*
[3] *The Times*, 3 April 1939.

material for the Army. He was convinced that any move to introduce compulsory powers would immediately arouse Labour and T.U.C. hostility. For this reason he opposed the establishment of a compulsory national register which, he said, would unnecessarily hinder the workings of the voluntary system.[1] Indeed he could claim that the response to his appeal had justified his faith in the voluntary system, for by 17 April, over half the Territorial infantry battalions had reached war establishment and were beginning to complete their second line.[2]

At the Cabinet meeting on 29 March, Hore-Belisha pressed for an increase of 50,000 in the size of the Regular Army, and suggested that, if approved, the increase should be announced simultaneously with the doubling of the Territorial Army. Simon thought that such an increase would impose severe financial burdens on the country, and concluded that, although in the present circumstances the question could not be considered in the light of financial factors, alone he could not agree to the proposals. In any case, he did not think that increasing the Regular Army would have the same impact as the Territorial decision.[3] Hore-Belisha tried again on 5 April. Despite the fact that the Polish guarantee had contractually engaged Britain in the defence of eastern Europe in alliance with France, which was pushing for an increase in Britain's land commitment to western Europe, Simon still rejected his proposal.[4]

Meanwhile, proponents of conscription continued to urge its introduction. Sir Edward Grigg argued that the immediate establishment of a compulsory national register and the passing of a Bill to enable the Government to introduce conscription on the outbreak of war (a significant departure from his earlier demands for its introduction at once) would prove to be a decisive demonstration to Germany and Italy.[5] Amery was now talking in terms of Britain needing an Army of between 1,700,000 and 2,500,000, and numbers of this magnitude, he stressed, could only be obtained through conscription.[6] Vernon Bartlett, an Independent Progressive M.P., reluctantly decided that conscription would be a 'great deterrent' to the Fascist powers, but added—clearly as an

[1] 5 *Parl. Debs.* CCCXLV, 2443, 3 April 1939.
[2] *The Times*, 17 April 1939.
[3] Cab. 23/98, Minutes 15(39)5.
[4] Cab. 23/98, Minutes 18(39)9.
[5] *The Times*, 1 April 1939.
[6] 5 *Parl. Debs.* CCCXLV, 3118–20, 6 April 1939.

appeal to Labour sentiment—that its introduction should be accompanied by a rigorous policing of war profiteering: 'conscription of manpower' should be matched by 'conscription of wealth'.[1]

The *Daily Mail* (5 April) decried the Government's reluctance to face the fact that Britain was in a precarious situation, and to take the appropriate steps. Weak leadership was the reason why the Government had not established a Ministry of Supply or introduced conscription. A week later (11 April), it warned that part-time Territorial soldiers could not hope to fight on equal terms against the 'highly-trained, well-equipped troops of Germany and Italy'. The implication was that only a Ministry of Supply and the introduction of conscription would ensure that continuous, intensive training and the necessary equipment would back British forces employed on the Continent. Meanwhile a 'Youth Parliament' poll conducted by the *Daily Mirror* reported a large majority of replies in favour of conscription ('Yes': 12,662; 'No': 6,569).[2]

International developments afforded Chamberlain no respite. Mussolini, peeved by Hitler's failure to give him advance notice of the occupation of Bohemia and Moravia, demonstrated his own abilities and invaded Albania on 7 April. The following day the Greek Premier told the British Ambassador in Athens that he had reliable information of an Italian plan to attack Corfu.[3] On 10 April the Secretary-General of the Rumanian Ministry for Foreign Affairs arrived in London to seek assurances of British support if Rumania was attacked, as seemed increasingly likely. Halifax gave a vague reply, for at the time the security of Greece was his immediate prime concern.[4] The French had already agreed to join in giving a guarantee to Greece,[5] but when Halifax received the text of the declaration which Daladier proposed to make, he found it also contained a guarantee to Rumania.[6] Protest was to no avail, and 'in the interests of solidarity', Chamberlain announced in the House of Commons on 13 April that Britain had extended to Greece and Rumania guarantees similar to that given to Poland.[7]

[1] 5 *Parl. Debs*. CCCXLV, 3124, 6 April 1939.
[2] *Daily Mirror*, 8 April 1939.
[3] *DBFP*, V, 145. Sir S. Waterlow (Athens) to Halifax, 9 April 1939.
[4] *DBFP*, V, 74–7. Halifax to Hoare (Bucharest), 10 April 1939.
[5] *Ibid.*, 96–7. *Aide-mémoire* from French Ambassador (London), 12 April 1939.
[6] *Ibid.*, 183–4. Halifax to Phipps, 12 April 1939.
[7] 5 *Parl. Debs*. CCCXLVI, 13.

The press campaign for greater efforts in defence was given added strength by these events. The *Daily Telegraph* (10 April) urged the Government to 'accelerate ... the fulfilment of the nation's defensive organization', and to abandon its half-hearted approach to the problems of building up the Territorials. Secondly, it pressed for the extension of the defensive alliances between Britain, France, and the countries of eastern and south-eastern Europe. The *Daily Mirror* pointedly asked how Britain could aid Rumania without the support of Russia. The Government's 'yes men' had lost sight of all strategic realities:[1]

> To hear the howls of disapproval in the House yesterday
> when back-bench Tory noodles hear the Opposition ask
> about Russia! These imbeciles have helped us to lose
> Spain; to get France partly encircled; they now want to
> deprive us of our one powerful ally in the East.

The *Daily Mail* warned against further continental commitments on Britain's part:[2]

> High military authorities on the Continent look with
> scorn on our puerile attempts to train a Territorial Army
> in the use of mechanised apparatus by means of weekly
> drills and an annual fortnight in camp. .... Where are our
> resources for a war of 'unlimited liability'? Are we using
> every endeavour to fulfil our obligations?

Conscription was the only answer, but since the Government— for reasons of expediency, the *Daily Mail* noted—had decided against it, the least the Treasury, headed by Simon, could do would be 'to spare no effort to get the Territorial recruits and not allow ... parsimony ... to stand in the way.'[3] It was no use calling, as the Labour party continually did, for Britain to enlist the military support of Russia: 'We cannot expect others to fight our battles for us.' Far from an alliance with Russia being the best way to promote national 'freedom and unity', Labour's acceptance of conscription—the 'only real, democratic way of raising a truly national Army'—would immeasurably strengthen Britain's security and credibility vis-à-vis Europe.[4]

---

[1] *Daily Mirror*, 14 April 1939.
[2] *Daily Mail*, 10 April 1939.
[3] *Ibid.*, 12 April 1939.
[4] *Ibid.*, 14 April 1939.

The practical objections to conscription, increasingly over-looked in the emotional, full-throated cry for the democratic obligation to defend democracy and show Europe that 'Britain means business', were stressed in a letter to the *Manchester Guardian* by Lt.-Colonel G. J. Scovell, Deputy Director of Recruiting, 1917–18. Conscription, he wrote, could not be introduced without repeating the mistakes of the last war unless there was already in existence a comprehensive national register. Until that was established, the proposals for conscription seemed 'somewhat academic'. Secondly, there was the question of equipment and full training facilities. Previous experience had shown 'what a heartbreaking and time-wasting business it was for the first twelve months or so of the war period until arms and equipment were forthcoming'. The Government's priorities, he implied, should therefore be the compilation of a national register and the establishment of a Ministry of Supply. Without this essential ground-work, the introduction of conscription would be precipitate and counter-productive.[1]

The French press was also uneasy over the British government's failure to introduce conscription. The *Daily Telegraph* reviewed a number of French newspapers, all of them anxious that Britain as yet showed no signs of being willing to accept its responsibilities. The mood of the French press, according to the *Daily Telegraph*, was summed up by *Liberté*, which wrote:[2]

> In the trenches of tomorrow there must be by the side of every 'poilu' a British 'Tommy', for nobody in France wishes to be the soldier of a country desirous of defending its own interests at the expense of Frenchmen's lives.

France, the *Daily Mail* and *Daily Telegraph* stressed, was not about to let Britain fight to the last French soldier.

Chamberlain was well aware that the decision to double the Territorial Army posed serious problems and, on 11 April, he wrote to Hore-Belisha to tell him that he had asked Chatfield and Morrison to prepare a paper on the question of a Ministry of Supply for consideration by the Cabinet. Hore-Belisha expressed his warm approval to Chamberlain and used this opportunity to raise the question of conscription:[3]

[1] *Manchester Guardian*, 14 April 1939.
[2] Quoted in *Daily Telegraph*, 12 April 1939.
[3] Minney, *Hore-Belisha*, pp. 190–1.

> Our new foreign policy carries the inevitable implication
> that, should war break out, the land forces will have to
> bear a heavy part. . . . I fervently hope that we may be
> able to overcome any opposition to compulsion at this time.

Chamberlain, however, was intent on preserving industrial harmony by maintaining the voluntary system. He proposed, for example, that the Territorials keep their regular working hours and man the anti-aircraft defences at night for periods of three to six months. Hore-Belisha told him that the General Staff had advised that the suggestion was 'absolutely impracticable . . . [and] would completely dislocate the Territorial Army', but he continued, through Horace Wilson, to press Hore-Belisha to consider the proposal.[1] The General Staff had come to the conclusion that the only way to man effectively Britain's anti-aircraft defences was to declare an emergency and call up the Territorial A.A. forces. While they were on active duty, conscripts should be trained as permanent A.A. troops. Hore-Belisha forwarded their recommendations to Chamberlain, and added another plea for conscription as the only means by which the existing deficiencies in A.A. defence could be overcome.[2]

Chamberlain asked Hore-Belisha to send copies of these papers to Chatfield and the Treasury, but refused his request to be allowed to circulate them to all members of the Cabinet. Hore-Belisha disregarded this to the extent of giving a copy to Halifax, who told him later that afternoon (17 April) 'he had good reason to believe that conscription was the only course that would have any effect on Germany', and that anxiety was mounting in France over Britain's failure to go beyond the voluntary system. He proposed to speak to Chamberlain about the War Office papers, but would not tell him that Hore-Belisha had shown them to him. Hore-Belisha, however, preferred that Chamberlain know who Halifax's source was.[3] He was at the point of resignation,[4] and no doubt hoped that knowledge of his dealings with Halifax might sway Chamberlain's opinion.

The following day Hore-Belisha had a stormy interview with Chamberlain, who accused him of mounting a campaign to force the Government to introduce conscription. Chamberlain referred

---

[1] Minney, *Hore-Belisha*, p. 192.
[2] Hore-Belisha to Chamberlain, 15 April 1939. Premier 1/296.
[3] Minney, *Hore-Belisha*, p. 195.
[4] As he told Warren Fisher, 17 April 1939. *Ibid.*

to the Government's repeated pledges not to introduce conscription in peacetime, but Hore-Belisha thought that the deciding factor in setting Chamberlain against it was the opposition of the Labour party and the T.U.C. Chamberlain refused to believe that the Territorials could not be employed on a nightly basis for A.A. work, even though Hore-Belisha had submitted papers to him detailing the considered opinions of the War Office, the Chairman and Council of the Territorial Association, and various employers. Hore-Belisha argued that there had to be a co-ordinated and integrated approach to the study of defence problems and, on this basis, he had come to the conclusion that conscription was necessary. Chamberlain's answer to was tell Hore-Belisha to reconsider his [the Prime Minister's] proposals![1]

Chamberlain's refusal to consider the War Office plans could not stand up to the pressures that were mounting on all sides. Halifax was already in favour of conscription, and shortly after his meeting with Chamberlain, Hore-Belisha met Simon, who told him that when he had read the War Office papers with the intention of finding fault with their arguments, he had been convinced that the Government would have to introduce conscription.[2] This support was invaluable, coming as it did from one who in 1916 had resigned and almost wrecked his political career in protest against conscription.

The press kept up its campaign. The *Manchester Guardian* (18 April) hoped that some mention would soon be made of a Ministry of Supply, which was the very minimum the Government could do, 'and Mr. Chamberlain has a long record of doing just the minimum'. Both the *Manchester Guardian* and the *Daily Mail* pointed to a potential rebellion in the House of Commons. On 18 April, forty-six M.P.s, mostly Conservatives, tabled a resolution stating that 'this House is in favour of the compulsory mobilization of the man, munition, and money power of the nation'.[3] As the *Manchester Guardian* wrote:[4]

[1] Minney, *Hore-Belisha*, pp. 196–7.
[2] *Ibid.*, p. 197. On 17 April, Simon had written in alarm to Chamberlain about the 'great change in the role of the Army' which had not been properly discussed. He also wrote to Chatfield to deny that he was not equally concerned about defence: 'One of the things which we have to assure is that our military efforts do not so far impair our economic resources as to render us powerless, through incapacity, to . . . bring a long war or indeed any war to a successful conclusion.' Premier 1/296.
[3] *Daily Mail*, 19 April 1939.
[4] *Manchester Guardian*, 18 April 1939.

P

> Nothing could better show the drastic change of opinion
> on the need for a greater national defence effort than [this]
> resolution. . . . These Tories, it is true, do not belong
> to the plutocratic wing of their party and they may not
> command the support of that wing, but here, nevertheless,
> are Tories demanding something like the conscription of
> wealth, an astonishing advance. Their justification is that
> the time for half-measures is past.

The question was, how long could Chamberlain hold out against growing numbers in his own Cabinet and party in the hope that he might avoid a head-on clash with Labour.

Chatfield and Morrison concluded that increases in the Regular and Territorial Armies made necessary the establishment of a Ministry of Supply, which should be responsible for Army supply and those associated services run by the War Office.[1] Instead of using this opportunity to broaden the base of his government, and thereby satisfy some of the demands of the press and Parliament, Chamberlain made the appointment from within Ministerial ranks. Leslie Burgin, Minister of Transport and a National Liberal, was chosen to head the new Ministry.[2] The *Manchester Guardian* (21 April) reported that the announcement of Burgin as Minister was 'received almost in silence', and the *Daily Herald* deplored the appointment which, it said, 'surely must be the most unsuitable . . . [one] since Mr. Baldwin made Sir Thomas Inskip the Minister for Coordination of Defence'.[3]

On 19 April, the day after Chamberlain had testily rejected Hore-Belisha's appeal for conscription, and the motion calling for its introduction had been tabled in the House of Commons, Chamberlain told Hore-Belisha that he could give the Cabinet a verbal report on his proposals.[4] In the Cabinet meeting, Hore-Belisha outlined the critical state of Britain's defences against air attack. His advisers had unanimously agreed that it was not possible to 'work a voluntary system within a voluntary system'. The War Office therefore proposed a threefold plan: first, to call out A.A. Territorial units under declaration of emergency to

---

[1] Chatfield and Morrison, 'A Ministry of Supply'. C.P. 84 (39), Cab. 24/285.
[2] 5 *Parl. Debs.* CCCXLVI, 496–7, 20 April 1939.
[3] *Daily Herald*, 21 April 1939. A. J. P. Taylor makes the obvious parallel: 'This was not a dynamic appointment, rather another horse from Caligula's well-stocked stable.' *English History*, p. 444.
[4] Minney, *Hore-Belisha*, pp. 197–8.

man the A.A. defences for several months; second, to call out Regular reservists to be trained as a permanent A.A. force; and third, because there were insufficient Regulars available for this work, to introduce a scheme of compulsory service, whereby men would be conscripted for one year, six months of which would be spent in training.[1]

Chatfield had reservations about the War Office proposals. Was it fair to compel those who had volunteered to serve during war to man A.A. defences in time of peace, or was the introduction of compulsion a case of 'employing a sledge-hammer to crack a nut'? Halifax emphasized the strength of foreign opinion, and suggested that if the Government decided to limit compulsory service to A.A. defence units, this would have 'unfortunate' results.[2]

Chamberlain admitted that the situation was serious, but stressed the necessity of not alienating the trades unions leaders, whose co-operation was essential to the smooth running of the rearmament programme. The Cabinet accepted Chamberlain's proposal that it should defer any decision until the next scheduled Cabinet meeting on 22 April.[3]

If further proof of French feeling was needed, it reached Halifax on 20 April. Daladier approached Phipps and asked him to send an 'urgent and pressing' appeal to London. The French realized that the introduction of conscription would only be a gesture initially, but 'it was a vital one for friends and foe alike'. Phipps wrote to Halifax:[4]

> This moving appeal made to me by the President of the Council only bears out what I have recently reported almost *ad nauseam*. I earnestly hope that His Majesty's Government will take it into immediate and most serious consideration. This is the moment when the imponderables count more than mere material considerations. Moreover ... German propaganda is terribly busy in France just now, and only by the adoption of this measure can it be countered.

The same day Wilson told Hore-Belisha that Chamberlain had decided to introduce conscription.[5]

---

[1] Cab. 23/98, Minutes 21(39)7, 19 April 1939.
[2] *Ibid.*
[3] *Ibid.*
[4] *DBFP*, V. 239–40. Phipps to Halifax, 19 April 1939.
[5] Minney, *Hore-Belisha*, p. 199.

On 22 April the Secretary to the Cabinet circulated to all members a memorandum by Chamberlain setting forth his proposals for a scheme of compulsory military service. Chamberlain hoped that his plan would satisfy the main needs and meet the strongest objections. Public opinion in Britain and France demanded conscription as a sign of Britain's determination to stand firm against aggression. Problems of manning Britain's A.A. defences over a long period had led to the conclusion that conscription was the only way of providing the necessary troops for this vital task. There was also, however, the attitude of the Labour movement to consider, for it was apparent that the Government could expect strong opposition from that quarter if it tried to establish conscription as a permanent feature of Britain's defence organization. The Cabinet therefore had to develop a scheme that would fulfil the first two objectives without causing a serious split in national unity that would undermine the effectiveness of the scheme.[1]

With these qualifications in mind, Chamberlain suggested that, in presenting the proposals to Parliament, the Government emphasize that compulsory service should merely supplement and not supplant normal voluntary service, and that it should be linked with special powers that would enable the Government to put the defence organization on any level of readiness it thought fit without having to ask for a Royal Proclamation of an emergency. A declaration of emergency was traditionally made when war appeared imminent, but what was needed was the authority to man the defences of Britain at various levels of preparedness to meet differing degrees of tension. At the moment, the Government lacked any intermediate powers of this sort. Labour opposition might be minimized by reference to the conscription of wealth and the control of excessive armament profits both before and during the war.[2]

Chamberlain's proposals fell into two distinct, but allied, categories. First, Parliament should be asked to pass an Exceptional Powers (Defence) Bill at once, giving the Government special powers that would be exercised only as were needed to meet the exigencies of crises that might arise. Second, a Military Training Bill would enable the Government to call up all men who

[1] Chamberlain, 'Proposals for Compulsory Military Training'. C.P. 91(39), Cab. 24/285.
[2] *Ibid.*

turned twenty in a particular year. The War Office estimated that, after allowance was made for medical exemptions, about 200,000 would be available each year. Of these, 80,000 would be trained and enrolled in A.D.G.B. units so that, once the scheme was properly operating, there would be a permanent nucleus manning A.A. defences. Conscripts would complete six months' training, and then join Territorial units for three and a half years, during which they would have the usual Territorial obligations of about thirty drills and two weeks' camp each year. It would be specified —partly to minimize Labour opposition—that men called up would be eligible solely for home service unless war broke out. Those who were not allotted to A.D.G.B. units would be attached to Regular Army or specially organized units. Once conscription had been adopted, the War Office intended to call up a certain number of reservists to complete the establishment of deficient Regular units, man the A.A. defences after three months, and act as instructors for the new Territorial units and conscripts.[1]

When the Cabinet came to consider these proposals on 24 April, Chamberlain explained that, although he had 'long been in favour' of conscription, he had hesitated to introduce it because of certain Labour opposition. The present scheme, however, should minimize that opposition. So far as his pledges were concerned, he was not unduly worried, since conditions could hardly be described as peacetime in the normal sense of the word. He intended to meet with the General Council of the T.U.C. as a 'matter of courtesy' before he made any public announcement, but, although he hoped he could persuade them that the Government had no ulterior motive, he was not going to seek their specific approval. He would announce the Government's intentions on the same day, since it was desirable that this be done before 28 April, the day on which Hitler was scheduled to make a speech.[2]

The Cabinet was uneasy about the proposed legislation. Halifax stressed that undue emphasis on home defence—which was the essence of the scheme—would not carry the same weight in foreign circles as was necessary to demonstrate Britain's determination. Colville, Secretary of State for Scotland, added that foreign nations, whose greatest interest was in Britain's expeditionary force, would be neither impressed nor heartened if an emergency was declared and only A.A. units were called up,

[1] Chamberlain, C.P. 91(39).
[2] Cab. 23/99, Minutes 22(39)3. 24 April 1939.

but Halifax thought the French could be satisfied if they saw that steps were also being taken to strengthen field units. The main objections, however, centred on the legislation relating to special emergency powers. Some Ministers doubted that Parliament would pass such a Bill quickly, even under a guillotine, as Chamberlain suggested; there was likely to be considerable debate over the extent of the powers given the Government before war actually broke out. In view of these disagreements and hesitations, Chamberlain proposed that an *ad hoc* Cabinet committee, consisting of himself, Simon, Hoare, Halifax, Inskip, Chatfield, and Hore-Belisha, examine the scheme and report to the Cabinet on 25 April.[1]

When the Cabinet next met, Chamberlain reported that the committee had recommended that the Exceptional Powers (Defence) Bill be postponed, and the Government introduce two separate Bills, one setting up a scheme of compulsory military training, and the other authorizing the mobilization of the reserve and auxiliary forces. The difficulty was how to show that circumstances justified the use of special powers to call out the Territorials and Reservists without causing undue alarm. Simon suggested that Territorial objections to mobilization would be minimal in view of the fact that their service would only be temporary, pending the training of conscripts to man the A.A. defences on a full-time basis. After some discussion, the Cabinet accepted Halifax's view that, taken together, the Government's proposals constituted a coherent defence scheme that would meet the needs of the situation. There was no disagreement over conscription as such, the only substantial question being raised in connection with its application to 'persons normally resident in any part of His Majesty's Dominions outside the United Kingdom'. How was it to be applied to a citizen of Eire who worked in England on a long-term basis? Was he to be considered 'ordinarily resident' in England? In agreeing to introduce two Bills on the lines suggested by the Cabinet committee—once the appropriate wording to define the political circumstances could be found—the Cabinet insisted that the question of 'ordinary residence' be applied equally to all the Dominions.[2]

---

[1] Cab. 23/99, Minutes 22(39)3.
[2] Cab. 23/99, Minutes 23(39)1, 25 April 1939. The Military Training Bill provided for conscription to be extended to Northern Ireland and the Isle of Man by Order in Council. There was strong opposition, however, not

That afternoon, Chamberlain had a meeting with leaders of the T.U.C., and explained to them that the Government had decided to introduce conscription immediately. The reasons he gave were that Britain needed round-the-clock protection against a possible lightning air strike, and that the French were pressing for some form of compulsion in Britain. As was to be expected, the T.U.C. representatives were furious, and Walter Citrine, the General Secretary, complained bitterly that 'they now felt that they had been led up the garden path'.[1]

Before a formal announcement was made in Parliament, the Government's decision was relayed to British embassies. In Paris, Phipps exploited the morale value of the news to the full, even to the extent of suggesting that, in return for this significant British contribution to the efforts of the allies, the French should likewise make concessions and give favourable consideration to the British proposals regarding the improvement of Franco-Italian relations.[2] Halifax was contacted to see if the announcement could be moved forward from 26 April to the 25th, because Phipps thought that the French would not take the initiative vis-à-vis Italy until conscription had been announced. If this was not done before 26 April, there would not be time to achieve any results without making the Franco-Italian moves appear a last-minute attempt to embarrass Hitler on the eve of his speech. The Foreign Office was unable to comply.[3]

Halifax instructed Henderson to inform the German government that the

---

only from the Ulster trades unions, but also from the Roman Catholic hierarchy. Ulster Protestants urged the inclusion of Ulster in the Bill, and the Prime Minister, Lord Craigavon, personally made such representations to Chamberlain and Hoare (Home Secretary). Pressure from Eire and fears of a repetition of the conscription problems of the Great War, however, prevailed, and this clause of the Bill was removed during the committee stages in the House of Commons. The Government tried to soften the blow by promising added opportunities for voluntary service in Ulster. Ulster M.P.s showed their dissatisfaction by voting against this alteration to the Bill. See Cab. 23/99, Minutes 25(39)3, 1 May 1939; 5 *Parl. Debs.* CCCXLVI, 2104–5, 4 May 1939; John W. Blake, *Northern Ireland in the Second World War* (*History of the Second World War: United Kingdom Civil Series*, ed. W. K. Hancock) (Belfast: H.M.S.O., 1956), p. 194.

[1] Templewood Papers, X(5), Cabinet file, typed notes, p. 22; also Premier 1/387.

[2] *DBFP*, V, 278. Phipps to Halifax, 22 April 1939.

[3] *Ibid.*, 279. Phipps to Halifax, 22 April 1939. Reply by Cadogan.

decision to introduce . . . [conscription] is due very largely to a change in public opinion which has been developing steadily for some considerable time. There had been a widespread expression of feeling that a more general system of training than is afforded by the Territorial Army is, in itself, desirable.[1]

Halifax's intention was to minimize the provocative effect of the decision, at the same time retaining its value as a response to the publicly voiced determination of Britain to resist further encroachments on European states. Henderson chose to interpret this in a way that deprived the announcement of much of its expected value:[2]

I mentioned casually to the State Secretary that the scheme for partial and temporary introduction of military service in England had been contemplated and was in the course of elaboration long before the last Prague *coup* or President Roosevelt's message [to Hitler seeking assurances of Germany's peaceful intentions].

On 26 April Chamberlain announced the Government's plan in the House of Commons. Referring to the guarantees which Britain had recently given, he said:[3]

We cannot but be impressed by the view, shared by other democratic countries and especially by our friends in Europe, that despite the immense efforts this country has already made by way of rearmament, nothing would so impress the world with the determination of this country to offer a firm resistance to any attempt at general domination as its acceptance of the principle of compulsory military service, which is the universal rule on the Continent.

Later in the debate he was more explicit in detailing the reasons for the Government's decision:

Evidence has been accumulating rapidly in the past week that these doubts [about Britain's determination] were increasing as we were increasing our engagements. That gibe that Britain was 'ready to fight to the last French

[1] *DBFP*, V, 320–1. Halifax to Henderson and Sir N. Charles (Rome), 25 April 1939.
[2] *Ibid.*, 289–90. Henderson to Halifax, 26 April 1939.
[3] 5 *Parl. Debs.* CCCXLVI, 1151.

soldier' is one that has been bandied about from capital to capital.[1]

The second factor to be considered was the need to provide troops to man A.A. defences, a duty which the Territorials, holding full-time jobs, could not undertake.[2]

Chamberlain realized that he would be attacked for breaking his pledges, the last one given as recently as 29 March. He therefore explained that although Britain was not in a state of war, neither was it peacetime in the normal sense of the word, since all Europe was straining under the pressure of rearmament programmes and international tension. To take the sting out of the tail for the Opposition, especially Labour, generous provision was made for conscientious objectors, and measures were to be taken for the conscription of wealth, in the form of legislation against war profiteering and excessive profits from rearmament.[3]

These concessions had no effect on the Liberal and Labour parties, but the outcome of the debate was never in doubt.[4] The Opposition complained about Chamberlain's failure to consult them beforehand,[5] and the Liberals rightly pointed out the inconsistency of Chamberlain's argument that the voluntary system was unfair in that it allowed the shirker to avoid the burdens and risks of military duty:[6] a few weeks before, in announcing the expansion of the Territorial Army, he had loudly extolled the virtues of the system he now said was inequitable. Similarly they were on firm ground in attacking Chamberlain for breaking his repeated pledges. Their objection was not over the definition of 'peacetime', but the fact that little more than three weeks before, Chamberlain had again promised not to introduce conscription in peacetime. This was two weeks after the occupation of Bohemia and Moravia, and Chamberlain's Birmingham speech, and a week after the

---

[1] 5 *Parl. Debs.* CCCXLVI, 1347. A good example of this attitude appeared in the *Manchester Guardian* (26 April) in the form of a cartoon originally published in the Florence newspaper, *Il 420*. It depicted a bragging France humbled by the realization of its one weak spot: 'France: "I have the Maginot Line. I have the Alps fortified. I have the Senegalese. I have the Bank of France stuffed with gold. [To England] But if you don't send me a hundred divisions I am ruined." '

[2] *Ibid.*, 1153.

[3] *Ibid.*, 1153–4.

[4] The Military Training Bill passed the House of Commons, 18 May, on a 337–140 vote. Royal Assent was received on 26 May. *Ibid.*, CCCXLVII, 1777–82, 2703.

[5] *Ibid.*, CCCXLVI, 1353–4 (Attlee), 1369 (Sinclair).   [6] *Ibid.*

occupation of Memel. There was also increasing tension between Germany and Poland and Rumania, and negotiations were already in progress to give some sort of guarantee to Poland. If those conditions could qualify as 'peacetime', what had changed since then—surely not the Italian takeover of Albania—to release the Government from its pledges, which had been the basis of Labour's co-operation in the National Service and Territorial appeals.

Labour's opposition was based on the argument that the need was for more arms and equipment, and that if more men were required, the Territorials could be called out. In themselves, these criticisms were well-founded, but they skirted the central issue— the need to provide a tangible and unmistakable sign that Britain took its guarantees seriously. Hugh Dalton recorded later that the Labour party was embarrassed by the Government's action which, on the evidence available, was necessary and in keeping with Labour's demand that the Government take a firm stand against the dictators. Labour's arguments, he admitted, were 'not nonsense, but not, in present circumstances, very convincing'.[1]

For their part, the Government's supporters repeated the assertions that the introduction of conscription would strengthen the morale of the states to which Britain had given guarantees, and in some way deter Hitler.[2] The gesture seemed more important to many of them than the substance, for it was left to Aneurin Bevan (Labour) to ask if it was being seriously suggested that the training, some months hence, of about 200,000 men between the ages of 20 and 21 would 'deter' Hitler.[3] The deterrence theory rested on the assumption that Hitler would see that in six to nine months' time Britain would have an army which, in alliance with other European forces, would be too strong for him to challenge, and that he would not therefore bring on another crisis that would lead Britain to implement its guarantees. There was, however, another possibility: that the introduction of conscription, with a six to nine months' lapse before its results—trained manpower— became available, would provoke Hitler into advancing his aggressive designs into the period when the British Army would be struggling with the influx of conscripts, and would temporarily suffer a degree of dislocation and consequently a loss of efficiency.

---

[1] Hugh Dalton, *The Fateful Years 1931–1945* (London: Muller, 1957), p. 250.
[2] 5 *Parl. Debs.* CCCXLVI, 1370–1 (Churchill), 1406 (Duff Cooper), 1432–4, (Brig.-Gen. Sir Henry Croft), 2144 (Eden).
[3] *Ibid.*, 2136, 4 May 1939.

Whatever the long-range effects of the Government's decision, it appeared to offer no immediate deterrent to Hitler. In his speech to the Reichstag on 28 April, he denounced the German-Polish Treaty and the Anglo-German Naval Agreement.[1]

The British press by no means unanimously approved of the conscription decision. The arguments which Chamberlain put forward were convincing only to those newspapers which had already committed themselves to supporting compulsory service. *The Times,* the *Daily Telegraph,* and the *Birmingham Post* were relieved that at last the Government had taken an essential step, and the *Daily Mail* warned that 'there will be no division of opinion unless the Socialists and other Leftists try to wreck this democratic measure'.[2] The *Daily Herald* (27 April) was predictably outraged that 'solemnly, plainly, and repeatedly the pledges were given . . . [and] shamelessly they have been broken'. The *News Chronicle* (27 April) predicted that the abandonment of the principle of voluntary service and one of Britain's 'fundamental traditions' would do nothing more than cause dissension within the country. The *Manchester Guardian* (27 April) saw the conscription decision as another sorry episode in the record of the Chamberlain government which, in trying to establish a credible image of national determination, had sacrificed any chance it ever had of associating the Opposition with government policy. The solution to the problems facing Britain was clear:[3]

> Because of the natural suspicions of Mr. Chamberlain's 'determination' Britain has to make a big 'gesture' in a hurry. The obvious course does not occur to him or to the 'Yes men' of his Cabinet. What would really remove all doubts would be Mr. Chamberlain's resignation, or, if that is more than human vanity could bear, the reconstruction of his Government on a really 'National' basis. . . . Our allies in the peace front will never feel secure so long as Mr. Chamberlain is permitted unchecked to exercise his autocratic personal diplomacy.

These criticisms, well-founded as they were, underrated the psychological value of the introduction of conscription, a value which had to be appreciated in the context of recent events.

---

[1] Norman H. Baynes (ed.), *The Speeches of Adolf Hitler: April 1922–August 1939* (2 vols. London: Oxford University Press, 1942), II, 1626, 1633.
[2] See editions of 27 April 1939.
[3] *Manchester Guardian*, 28 April 1939.

The French press had no doubts about the importance of the conscription decision. *Le Temps* (27 April) hailed it as a strong and courageous step that would make an important contribution to the maintenance of peace; courageous in view of the heavy financial sacrifices Britain was already making, and the traditional British aversion to compulsion. Not content with a financial contribution alone, Britain now showed that she was willing to share the moral burdens. *Paris Soir* noted with satisfaction that 'Germany will no longer be able to say "England makes war with other countries' soldiers"'.[1] This was also the line followed by *Intransigeant*, which wrote: 'France will know that her soldiers will not be alone if obliged to shed their blood to defend the common cause.'[2] Writing in *Le Populaire*, Léon Blum chided the Labour party for their opposition to conscription: 'I do not hesitate to state to my Labour comrades my deepest conviction that at the very moment at which I write, conscription in England is one of the capital acts upon which the peace of the world hangs.'[3] The French Socialists had tried to persuade the Labour party to support conscription and, on 10 May, Blum went to London to get the Labour leaders to withdraw their opposition, but to no avail.[4]

The *Daily Telegraph* (27 April) reported that the announcement was 'hailed as the greatest contribution Britain could make towards ensuring the peace of Europe and reviving confidence in the Western democracies'. Bonnet told Phipps that he was 'deeply grateful' for the British decision, which would have 'far-reaching and most healthy results everywhere'.[5] Phipps later said that French opinion was unanimously favourable, and everyone, including the left, 'deplore[s] the inconceivably foolish and unpatriotic attitude' of the British Labour movement.[6]

In Poland, the official *Gazeta Polska* stated that the decision would 'reinforce the confidence of those states which had received guarantees from Britain'.[7] *The Times* reported that there had been

---

[1] Quoted in *Daily Mail*, 27 April 1939.
[2] Quoted in *Daily Telegraph*, 27 April 1939.
[3] *Le Populaire*, 27 April 1939.
[4] Joel Colton, *Léon Blum: Humanist in Politics* (New York: Knopf, 1966), p. 321. Blum had been persuaded to go to London by Mandel, French Minister for the Colonies. Phipps to Halifax, 26 April 1939. F.O. 371/22971. C 6039/15/18.
[5] *DBFP*, V, 342. Phipps to Halifax, 27 April 1939.
[6] *Ibid.*, 356. Phipps to Halifax, 28 April 1939.
[7] Quoted in *Le Temps*, 28 April 1939.

a favourable reaction in Rumania, where conscription was seen as 'a necessary corollary to the British Continental guarantees'. No one now doubted that Britain could fulfil its guarantees.[1] The Italian press suggested that French pressure had been the deciding factor, and that the decision had been taken in the face of strong Labour opposition. Conscription was intended to reassure the countries which had been given guarantees by Britain, but above all it was meant to impress Hitler.[2] The German press, under government control, published the news under headlines such as: 'Excitement about Britain's compulsory service—a sensation that isn't'; 'Britain's new political bluff'; and 'Chamberlain's Laughable Threat'.[3] Daladier, however, told Phipps that he thought Hitler had been 'greatly impressed' by the introduction of conscription and, as a result, had toned down his speech on 28 April.[4]

Whatever the feelings of the Liberal and Labour parties, Chamberlain's decision to introduce conscription temporarily, at least, united his own party and the western allies and appeared to give them, for the first time since Munich, the initiative in international affairs. Its military value may have been slight, but psychologically conscription boosted morale and gave a new feeling of confidence. The military limitations of the measure became apparent in the months that followed, as thousands of conscripts began training in an Army that was painfully short of equipment and facilities for handling the influx. But then, conscription had not been introduced as the answer to a military problem, but as a symbolic commitment of Britain's manhood to the Continent, and to that extent the gesture was more important than the substance.

[1] *The Times*, 27 April 1939.
[2] *Ibid.*
[3] See *Daily Telegraph*, 27 April 1939.
[4] *DBFP*, V, 356. Phipps to Halifax, 28 April 1939.

Select bibliography

I *Archives*
Great Britain, Public Record Office
    Air Ministry Papers
    Cabinet Office Papers
    Foreign Office Papers
    Treasury Papers
    War Office Papers

II *Private Papers*
Ismay Papers: King's College, London
Liddell Hart Papers: States House, Medmenham, Marlow, Bucks.
Templewood Papers: Cambridge University Library

III *Published Documents*
Baynes, Norman H. *The Speeches of Adolf Hitler: April 1922–August 1939.* 2 vols. London: Oxford University Press, 1942.
France, Ministère des Affaires Étrangères. *Documents diplomatiques français, 1932–1939.* 2e serie (1936–9). 3 tomes. Paris: Imprimerie nationale, 1963–6.
German Foreign Ministry. *Documents on German Foreign Policy, 1918–1945.* Series D. 12 vols. Washington: Government Printing Office, 1949–54.
Great Britain. *Documents on British Foreign Policy, 1919–1945.* Third Series (1938–9). 12 vols. Edited by E. L. Woodward and Rohan Butler. London: H.M.S.O., 1949–55.
—— *Parliamentary Debates (House of Commons).* Fifth Series. 1934–9.
—— *Parliamentary Papers.* 1922–39.
United States. *Foreign Relations of the United States, 1938,* vol. I. *1939,* vol. I. Washington: Government Printing Office, 1955–6.

IV *Memoirs and Biographies*
Amery, Leo S. *My Political Life.* vol. III. *The Unforgiving Years, 1929–1940.* London: Hutchinson, 1955.
Attlee, Clement R. *As It Happened.* London: Heinemann, 1954.
Avon, Earl of (Rt Hon. Sir Anthony Eden). *Facing the Dictators.* London: Cassell, 1962.

—— *The Reckoning*. London: Cassell, 1965.

Baldwin, A. W. *Baldwin My Father: The True Story*. London: Allen and Unwin, 1955.

Birkenhead, Earl of. *Halifax: The Life of Lord Halifax*. London: Hamish Hamilton, 1965.

Bonnet, Georges E. *La Défense de la paix*. 2 vols. Geneva: Éditions du Cheval ailé, 1946–8.

Boothby, Robert. *I Fight to Live*. London: Gollancz, 1947.

Bullock, Alan. *Hitler: A Study in Tyranny*. London: Odham's, new ed., 1964.

Campbell Johnson, Alan. *Viscount Halifax*. London: Robert Hale, 1941.

Chatfield, Lord. *It Might Happen Again*. Vol. II. *The Navy and Defence*. London: Heinemann, 1947.

Colton, Joel. *Léon Blum: Humanist in Politics*. New York: Knopf, 1966.

Colvin, Ian. *Vansittart in Office: An historical account of the origins of the Second World War based on the papers of Sir Robert Vansittart, Permanent Under-Secretary of State for Foreign Affairs, 1930–38*. London: Gollancz, 1965.

Cooper, A. Duff. *Old Men Forget: The Autobiography of Duff Cooper (Viscount Norwich)*. London: Rupert Hart-Davis, 1954.

Dalton, Hugh. *The Fateful Years, 1931–1945*. London: Muller, 1957.

von Dirksen, Herbert. *Moscow, Tokyo, London: Twenty Years of German Foreign Policy*. Norman: University of Oklahoma Press, 1952.

Feiling, Keith. *The Life of Neville Chamberlain*. London: Macmillan, 1946.

Fergusson, Bernard (ed.). *The Business of War: The War Narrative of Major-General Sir John Kennedy G.C.M.G., K.C.V.O., K.B.E., C.B., M.C.*, London: Hutchinson, 1957.

Gale, Richard. *Call to Arms*. Hutchinson: 1968.

Gamelin, Maurice *Servir: Le Prologue du Drame (1930-Août 1939)*. Paris: Librairie Plon, 1946.

de Guingand, Francis. *Operation Victory*. London: Hodder and Stoughton, 1947.

Halifax, Lord. *Fullness of Days*. London: Collins, 1957.

Harvey, John (ed.). *The Diplomatic Diaries of Oliver Harvey, 1937–1940*. London: Collins, 1970.

Henderson, Nevile. *Failure of a Mission: Berlin 1937–1939*. London: Hodder and Stoughton, 1940.

Ismay, Lord. *The Memoirs of General the Lord Ismay K.G., P.C., G.C.B., C.H., D.S.O.* London: Heinemann, 1960.

James, Robert Rhodes (ed.). *Chips: The Diaries of Sir Henry Channon*. London: Weidenfeld and Nicolson, 1967.

Jones, Thomas. *A Diary with Letters, 1931–1950*. London: Oxford University Press, 1954.

Kirkpatrick, Ivone. *The Inner Circle*. London: Macmillan, 1959.

Liddell Hart, Basil H. *The Memoirs of Captain Liddell Hart*. 2 vols. London: Cassell, 1965–6.

Macksey, Kenneth. *Armoured Crusader: A Biography of Major-General Sir Percy Hobart*. London: Hutchinson, 1967.

Macleod, Iain. *Neville Chamberlain*. London: Muller, 1961.

Macleod, Roderick, and Kelly, Denis (eds). *Time Unguarded: The Ironside Diaries 1937–1940*. New York: McKay, 1962.

Macmillan, Harold. *Winds of Change, 1914–1939*. London: Macmillan, 1966.

Middlemas, Keith, and Barnes, John. *Baldwin: A Biography*. London: Weidenfeld and Nicolson, 1969.

Minney, R. J. *The Private Papers of Hore-Belisha*. London: Collins, 1960.

Nicolson, Harold G. *Diaries and Letters, 1930–1939*, edited by Nigel Nicolson. London: Collins, 1966.

Pile, Frederick. *Ack-Ack: Britain's Defence against Attack During the Second World War*. London: Harrap, 1949.

Simon, Viscount, *Retrospect: The Memoirs of the Rt. Hon. Viscount Simon, G.C.S.I., G.C.V.O.* London: Hutchinson, 1952.

Slessor, John. *The Central Blue: The Autobiography of Sir John Slessor, Marshal of the R.A.F.* London: Cassell, 1956.

Strang, Lord. *Home and Abroad*. London: Deutsch, 1956.

Templewood, Viscount (Rt Hon. Sir Samuel Hoare). *Nine Troubled Years*. London: Collins, 1954.

Vansittart, Lord. *The Mist Procession*. London: Hutchinson, 1958.

Wheeler-Bennett, John W. *John Anderson: Viscount Waverley*. London: Macmillan, 1962.

Williams, Francis. *A Prime Minister Remembers: The War and Post-War Memories of the Rt. Hon. Earl Attlee K.G., P.C., O.M., C.H., Based on his Private Papers and on a Series of Recorded Conversations*. London: Heinemann, 1961.

Wrench, John Evelyn. *Geoffrey Dawson and Our Times*. London: Hutchinson, 1955.

Young, G. M. *Stanley Baldwin*. London: Hart-Davis, 1952.

V Secondary Works

Albrecht-Carrié, René. *A Diplomatic History of Europe since the Congress of Vienna*. New York and Evanston: Harper and Row, 1958.

Ashton-Gwatkin, F. T. A. *The British Foreign Office*. Syracuse: Syracuse University Press, 1949.

Carr, E. H. *International Relations Between the Two World Wars (1919–1939)*. London: Macmillan, 1947.

'Cato'. *Guilty Men*. London: Gollancz, 1940.

Churchill, Winston S. *The Gathering Storm. (The Second World War*, vol. I). London: Cassell, 1948.

Cienciala, Anna M. *Poland and the Western Powers, 1938–1949*. London: Routledge and Kegan Paul, 1968.

Collier, Basil. *The Defence of the United Kingsom. (History of the Second World War. United Kingdom Military Series*. Edited by J. R. M. Butler). London: H.M.S.O., 1957.

Connell, John. *The 'Office': A Study of British Foreign Policy and its Makers, 1919–1951*. London: Wingate, 1958.

Craig, Gordon A., and Gilbert, Felix. *The Diplomats 1919–1939*. Princeton: Princeton University Press, 1953.

Eubank, Keith. *Munich*. Norman: University of Oklahoma Press, 1963.

George, Margaret. *The Warped Vision: British Foreign Policy 1933–1939*. Pittsburgh: University of Pittsburgh Press, 1965.

Gibbs, Norman. 'British Strategic Doctrine, 1918–1939', in Howard, Michael (ed.). *The Theory and Practice of War: Essays presented to Captain B. H. Liddell Hart on his seventieth birthday*. London: Cassell, 1965.

Gilbert, Martin. *The Roots of Appeasement*. New York: New American Library, 1966.

Gilbert, Martin, and Gott, Richard. *The Appeasers*. London: Weidenfeld and Nicolson, 1963.

Hancock, W. K., and Gowing, M. M. *British War Economy (History of the Second World War. United Kingdom Civil Series*. Edited by W. K. Hancock). London: H.M.S.O., 1949.

Higham, Robin. *Armed Forces in Peacetime: Britain, 1918–1940, a case study*. Hamden, Conn: Archon Books, 1962.

Kennedy, John F. *Why England Slept*. New York: Wilfred Funk, Inc., 1940

Liddell Hart, Basil H. *The British Way in Warfare*. London: Faber, 1932.

—— *When Britain Goes to War: Adaptability and Mobility*. London: Faber, rev. and enlarged ed., 1935.

—— *Europe in Arms*. London: Faber, 1937.

—— *The Defence of Britain*. London: Faber, 1939.

Luvaas, Jay. *The Education of an Army: British Military Thought, 1815–1940*. Chicago: University of Chicago Press, 1964.

Medlicott, W. N. *British Foreign Policy Since Versailles, 1919–1963*. London: Methuen, 2nd rev. ed., 1968.

—— The Coming of War in 1939 (The Historical Association General Series G.52). London: Routledge and Kegan Paul, 1963.

Monger, George W. The End of Isolation: British Foreign Policy 1900–1907. London: Nelson, 1963.

Mowat, Charles Loch. Britain between the Wars, 1918–1940. London: Methuen, 1955.

Namier, L. B. Diplomatic Prelude 1938–39. London: Macillan, 1948.

—— Europe in Decay, 1936–40. London: Macmillan, 1950.

Northedge, F. S. The Troubled Giant: Britain among the Great Powers, 1916–1939. London: London School of Economics and Political Science; Bell, 1966.

Postan, M. M. British War Production. (History of the Second World War. United Kingdom Civil Series. Edited by W. K. Hancock). London: H.M.S.O., 1952.

Robbins, Keith. Munich 1938. London: Cassell, 1968.

Rock, William R. Appeasement on Trial: British Foreign Policy and its Critics, 1938–1939. Hamden, Conn.: Archon Books, 1966.

Rowse, A. L. All Souls and Appeasement: A Contribution to Contemporary History. London: Macmillan, 1961.

Salter, Arthur. Personality in Politics: Studies of Contemporary Statesmen. London: Faber, 1942.

Scott, William E. 'Neville Chamberlain and Munich: Two Aspects of Power', in Krieger, Leonard and Stern, Fritz, The Responsibility of Power: Historical Essays in Honor of Hajo Holborn. New York: Doubleday, 1967.

Seton-Watson, R. W. From Munich to Danzig. London: Methuen, 1939.

Spier, Eugen. Focus: A Footnote to the History of the Thirties. London: Oswald Wolff, 1963.

Strang, Lord. Britain in World Affairs: A Survey of the Fluctuations in British Power and Influence. Henry VIII to Elizabeth II. London: Faber, Deutsch, 1961.

Taylor, A. J. P. English History 1914–1945. Oxford: Clarendon Press, 1965.

Thorne, Christopher. The Approach of War, 1938–1939. London: Macmillan, 1967.

Toynbee, Arnold J., and Ashton-Gwatkin, F. T. A. (eds). The World in March 1939. (Survey of International Affairs, vol. XI.) London: Oxford University Press, 1952.

Watt, D. C. Personalities and Policies: Studies in the Formulation of British Foreign Policy in the Twentieth Century. Notre Dame, Ind.: University of Notre Dame Press, 1965.

Wheeler-Bennett, John W. Munich: Prologue to Tragedy. New York: Viking Press, 1964.

VI *Articles*

In addition to the articles listed below, the journals from which they are drawn contain much valuable information in the form of weekly or monthly editorial comments, regular columns, and correspondence. See particularly the following journals:

Army Quarterly
Fortnightly Review
Journal of the Royal United Service Institution (JRUSI)
National Review
New Statesman and Nation
Nineteenth Century and After
Round Table
Spectator

Amery, L. S., 'National Service', *National Review*, CXI (December 1938), 725–35.

Barker, M. G. H., 'Army Recruiting', *JRUSI*, LXXXIII (February 1938, no. 529), 69–83.

Beadon, R. H., 'Defence and Defeat', *JRUSI*, LXXXIII (February 1938, no. 529), 58–68.

Bryan, H., 'Who keepeth his goods in peace?', *National Review*, CX (May 1938), 585–92.

Carlton Hall, W. G., 'British Rearmament', *JRUSI*, LXXX (August 1934, no. 515), 595–9.

Collins, R. J., 'The Influence of Aircraft on Land Operations', *JRUSI*, LXXXIV (February 1939, no. 533), 57–71.

Dunlop, J. K., 'The Territorial Army', *JRUSI*, LXXX (May 1935, no. 518), 308–27.

Eady, C. W. G., 'The Progress of Air Raid Precautions', *JRUSI*, LXXXIV (February 1939, no. 533), 1–23.

Fawkes, G. B. H., 'British Strategy', *JRUSI*, LXXX (August 1934, no. 515), 591–4.

Fuller, J. F. C., 'Conscription pros and cons', *Spectator*, CLX (24 June 1938), 1138–9.

Germains, V. W., 'The Case for Conscription', *National Review*, CIX (October 1937), 474–82.

Grigg, E., 'The Importance of the Army', *National Review*, CXII (March 1939), 307–16.

Gwynn, S., 'Ebb and Flow: An Experiment in Freedom', *Fortnightly Review*, CLI (January 1939), 106–9.

Huizinga, J. H., 'Democracy and Compulsory Service', *Fortnightly Review*, CLI (May 1939), 527–33.

Liddell Hart, Basil H., 'Economic Pressure or Continental Victories', *JRUSI*, LXXVI (August 1931, no. 503), 486–510.

Macready, G. N., 'The Trend of Organization in the Army',
JRUSI, LXXX (February 1935, no. 517), 1–20.
Maitland Dougall, W. E., 'Elijah and the Ravens', *Army Quarterly*,
XXXV (October 1937), 50–6.
Smith, K. P., 'The National Will to War', *JRUSI*, LXXXIII
(February 1938, no. 529), 44–57.
Wells, W. T., 'National Service and a national register',
Fortnightly Review, CL (November 1938), 549–58.

VII *Newspapers*

The following newspapers were consulted for the period March
1938 to May 1939, except for *The Times*, which was consulted from
January 1933 until May 1939.

Birmingham Post
Daily Herald (London)
Daily Mail (London)
Daily Mirror (London)
Daily Telegraph (London)
Le Temps (Paris)
Le Populaire (Paris)
Manchester Guardian
News Chronicle (London)
The New York Times
The Times (London)

Index